Crises in European Integration

New German Historical Perspectives

Series Editors: Jane Caplan (Executive Editor), Timothy Garton Ash, Jürgen Kocka, Gerhard A. Ritter and Margit Szöllösi-Janze

Originally established in 1987 as an English-language forum for the presentation of research by leading German historians and social scientists to readers in English-speaking countries, this series has since become one of the premier vehicles for the dissemination of German research expertise on contemporary academic debate and of broad topical interest to Germans and non-Germans alike. Its coverage is not limited to Germany alone but extends to the history of other countries, as well as general problems of political, economic, social and intellectual history and international relations.

Volume 1
Historical Concepts between Eastern and Western Europe
Edited by Manfred Hildermeier

Volume 2
Crises in European Integration: Challenge and Response, 1945–2005
Edited by Ludger Kühnhardt

Crises in European Integration
Challenge and Response, 1945–2005

Edited by
Ludger Kühnhardt

Berghahn Books
New York • Oxford

First published in 2009 by
Berghahn Books
www.berghahnbooks.com

© 2009, 2011 Ludger Kühnhardt
First paperback edition published in 2011

All rights reserved. Except for the quotation of short passages
for the purposes of criticism and review, no part of this book
may be reproduced in any form or by any means, electronic or
mechanical, including photocopying, recording, or any information
storage and retrieval system now known or to be invented,
without written permission of the publisher.

Library of Congress Cataloging-in-Publication Data

Crises in European integration : challenge and response, 1945-2005 /
edited by Ludger Kühnhardt.
    p. cm. -- (German historical perspectives ; v. 2)
    Includes bibliographical references and index.
    ISBN 978-1-84545-441-8 (hbk) -- ISBN 978-0-85745-163-7 (pbk)
    1. European cooperation--History. I. Kühnhardt, Ludger, 1958-
    D1060.C69 2008
    337.1'409045--dc22

2008031375

British Library Cataloguing in Publication Data

A catalogue record for this book is available from the British Library

Printed in the United States on acid-free paper

ISBN 978-1-84545-441-8 (hardback)
ISBN 978-0-85745-163-7 (paperback)

Contents

Editorial Preface   vii
Jane Caplan (Executive Editor), Timothy Garton Ash, Jürgen Kocka, Gerhard A. Ritter, Nicholas Stargardt, Margit Szöllösi-Janze

Introduction
   European Integration: Success through Crises   1
   Ludger Kühnhardt

1 Sources of European Integration:
   The Meaning of Failed Interwar Politics
   and the Role of World War II   19
   Wilfried Loth

2 The Failure of EDC and European Integration   33
   Manfred Görtemaker

3 The Institutional Paradox:
   How Crises Have Reinforced European Integration   49
   Jürgen Elvert

4 Through Crises to EMU:
   Perspectives for Fiscal Union and Political Union   61
   Jürgen von Hagen

5 Opportunity or Overstretch? The Unexpected Dynamics
   of Deepening and Widening   79
   Wolfgang Wessels and Thomas Traguth

6 Learning from Failure:
The Evolution of the EU's Foreign, Security and Defense
Policy in the Course of the Yugoslav Crisis 95
Mathias Jopp and Udo Diedrichs

7 Challenges and Opportunities:
Surmounting Integration Crises in Historical Context 109
Michael Gehler

8 Frontiers and Chances for the European Union 131
Hans-Gert Pöttering

Select Bibliography 143

Notes on Contributors 157

Index 163

Editorial Preface

The *German Historical Perspectives* series was established in 1987 as an English-language forum for the presentation of research by German historians and social scientists to readers in English-speaking countries. Each of the volumes is devoted to a particular theme that is discussed from different points of view in separate essays by specialists. The series addresses questions that are prominent in contemporary academic debate and of broad topical interest to Germans and non-Germans alike. It is not limited to issues within Germany alone but also includes publications and individual essays covering the history of other countries, as well as general problems of political, economic, social and intellectual history and international relations, and issues in comparative history. The editors hope that the series will help to overcome the language barrier that can obstruct the rapid appreciation of German research in English-speaking countries.

The publication of the series is closely linked with the German Visiting Fellowship at St Antony's College, Oxford. This Fellowship was originally funded by the Volkswagen Stiftung, and later by the British Leverhulme Trust and by the Ministry of Education and Science in the Federal Republic of Germany. From 1990 the Fellowship has been supported by the Stifterverband für die Deutsche Wissenschaft, with special funding since 2000 from the Marga and Kurt Möllgaard-Stiftung. Each volume is based on the seminar series held annually in Oxford which the Visiting Fellow devises from his or her field of interest, in collaboration with the European Studies Centre at St Antony's College.

The editors wish to thank the Stifterverband für die Deutsche Wissenschaft and the Marga and Kurt Möllgaard-Stiftung for meeting the expenses of the original seminar series and for generous assistance with the publication. We hope that this enterprise will help to overcome national introspection and to further international academic discourse and co-operation.

Jane Caplan (Executive Editor)
Timothy Garton Ash
Jürgen Kocka
Gerhard A. Ritter
Nicholas Stargardt
Margit Szöllösi-Janze

Introduction

European Integration: Success through Crises

Ludger Kühnhardt

The European Union discovers its opportunities and encounters its global challenges in a way that recalls the work of Henry the Navigator in the fifteenth century: he sailed around Cape Bojador with hesitancy, limited knowledge and caution, without clear goals and yet with a yearning to learn what might lie behind the Cape. In the fifteenth century, Europe brought about the first wave of globalization. In the early twenty-first century, it seems to be the other way around: globalization seems to slowly bring about a new rationale for European integration as it forces the EU to learn faster, to look further, and to come together more convincingly.[1] Gradually, the EU is discovering its new global role.

Periodically, the discovery of a new global role for the EU seems to happen parallel to the experience of domestic crises, such as the constitutional debacle of 2005. Ironically, it is often accompanied by the rhetoric of internal failure. Not only the EU's foreign policy, as Jan Zielonka has so aptly shown with one of his fine publications, is full of paradoxes.[2] One could raise the question why so much of European integration is seemingly driven by the dialectics of paradox and crisis. This, of course, is no dogmatic assessment that could claim to alter any of the established insights into European integration. To look at crises as engines of integration does not mean to define any new theory of integration. A lot of more empirical work and theoretical study would have to be done in order to create a new theoretical paradigm.

"Crises of" and "Crises in" Integration

It is obvious to analytically distinguish between "crises of integration" and "crises in integration:" the first type of crises is of a principal nature and might challenge the rationale, if not even the existence, of integration; the second type of crises is related to difficulties in implementing certain policy objectives or goals without implying that the failure in achieving these objectives could derail the integration process as such or unravel its rationale and legitimacy.[3] Crises of integration only rarely occur. It is, for example, debatable whether or not the constellation of 1945 or of 1989 could be called a "crisis" at all. For sure, these were momentous years that required courageous decisions in the shadow of thorough and multidimensional challenges. It will require further academic clarification to measure the degree of crisis in European integration. One point of reference is the extent to which substantive outcomes, failures, and deadlocks in European integration can be measured against the declared political aspirations of EU institutions or treaty-based objectives. The European integration treaties, European legislation and its legal review by the European Court of Justice, the declaratory ambitions of EU Summits, and statements by the European Parliament produce the background on which to judge the relationship between integration expectation and implementation failure in European integration. While I do not claim to contribute to any scientific model of how the European Union will react to presumptive future crises, and while I will not deny the regular overstretch of crisis talk in media and academia, I would propose that the meaning of crises as engines of European integration has been under-researched.[4] Of course, not every crisis in European integration turned out to be productive and not every turning point in European integration went through the exercise of a daunting crisis.

This collection of scholarly essays looks at the potential and the limits of discussing crises as an element of some of the main issues and turning points in European integration history. By way of introducing this collection, my essay is divided into five parts. Some of them will hopefully be controversial enough to invite criticism and, wherever need be, correction in order to raise my own level of understanding on the issue. Firstly, I will introduce the idea of crisis as an engine of progress in European integration history and the classical concept of challenge and response as one additional explicatory variable. Secondly, I will ask to what degree the periodization of European integration history may benefit from taking the effect of its most defining adaptation crises into account. Thirdly, I will allude to some examples of formative integration experiences that will be analyzed and discussed in more depth in this book. Some of the authors support the notion of crises as engines while others suggest different approaches to understand the intricacies of integration progress. Fourthly, I will look into the interconnectedness between European adaptation crises and adaptation periods in transatlantic relations. And, finally, I will introduce the authors of this book. This book raises questions without claiming to give ultimate answers to how the EU has been coping with crises and challenges of a defining nature.

The Logic of "Challenge" and "Response"

More than once, and sometimes very surprisingly, new dynamics in European integration has originated in dialectical processes, guided by the powerful and ironic law of unintended consequences.[5] Sometimes progress in European integration was the result of trial and error. One might formulate a cautious hypothesis that, more often, it came about not in spite of, but because of crises. It seems to me that we could make more use of the classical concept of challenge and response—introduced by Arnold J. Toynbee in his seminal work on world history—in order to understand and frame the often unimaginable and irrational, uninspiring or dubious, yet all in all highly successful course of European integration.

One may be inclined to describe European integration as a contingent process of oscillation between failure and success, or between challenge and response. The concept of challenge and response represents what Toynbee called—although in a completely different context—the "alternating rhythm of static and dynamic, of movement and pause and movement fundamental to the nature of the universe."[6] With a view on world history, Toynbee explained with great erudition that challenges instigate responses, which, of course, can be either appropriate or misleading. Depending on the nature of the response, challenges can lead to negative or even catastrophic consequences for the structure they are affecting. If the response to a challenge is appropriate and well focused, it will reinvigorate and strengthen the structure it originates from or affects. Challenge and response are as interwoven as our notions of "to be" and "to become." Toynbee argued about this relationship in the following words: "In the language of science we may say that the function of the intruding factor is to supply that on which it intrudes with a stimulus of the kind best calculated to evoke the most potently creative variations."[7] Is it too far-fetched to relate this scientific insight to the EU's constitutional debacle of 2005? Was the rejection of the European Constitutional Treaty in referendums in France and the Netherlands not the stimulus for the first reasonably serious constitutional debate in the EU? Could one not argue that the failure of ratifying the elite-made European Constitutional Treaty evoked a paradoxical new beginning for European constitution-making through a broadened inclusion of public opinion? During its first fifty years, European integration has been accompanied by many detours, rough roads, and happy endings. In terms of integration theory, the permanent path of challenge and response tends to confirm many constructivist assumptions and the insights of rational institutionalism.[8] This is not the place to engage with the substantial discourse on European integration theory. We do not know what type of crisis could be of such a fundamental nature as to cause a terminal destruction of the European integration project. We only know that so far, such a terminal crisis—some skeptics of the integration process might hope for it occasionally—has not occurred. To the contrary, European integration has not only survived past crises of integration and past crises in integration. One could possibly even argue that in the end crises have strengthened European integration. There are sufficient examples to support this thesis, both in the ability of the EU to incorporate new members and in its capacity to broaden and deepen the policy agenda mandated to the EU and its institutions.

To introduce the concept of challenge and response to our understanding of the paths of European integration does not mean that the rationale of these processes could be simplified and reduced to this single explanatory variable. If this were the case, we would become submissive to deterministic notions of history that surely run counter to social theory and anthropological evidence. Nevertheless, it is not too far-fetched to conceptualize the history of European integration around the assumption that European integration is a series of continuous efforts to conceive appropriate responses in reaction to contingently changing challenges to all EU member states. These responses are usually executed, of course, by a genuine set of political processes with their contingent strategic and tactical logics. Many of these processes have been instrumental and functional reactions to structural challenges for the European integration project. In this essay, I simply raise the question to what degree the logic of "challenge and response" and the idea of crises as catalysts for progress could add value to the intellectual navigation system that can help us to comprehensively conceptualize European integration, why it began, and how it has developed, often against all the odds?[9]

Periodization

I turn to my second point. When reflecting about the defining periods in European integration, one cannot but underline the importance of the formative years before the European Economic Community began. The most serious challenge to initiate European integration stood at the very beginning: the destruction of Europe in two wars, the democratic revitalization of its Western part (West Germany included) with the help of America's policy of enlightened self-interest (Marshall Plan) and continuous strategic presence as a "European power," but also the end of Europe's global colonial power marked the beginning of Europe's second renaissance.[10] Just as the first renaissance can best be understood by Leonardo da Vinci's ambition to build a bridge wherever he saw a river and by Blaise Pascal's fear in face of the dark open sky at night, Europe's second renaissance has been driven by hope and fear since its very beginning. The formative years after 1945 were only matched by the formative years for European integration that followed the fall of the Berlin Wall and the end to communist regimes in 1989/90.

The two most defining periods that constitute and frame European integration as we know it today were related to substantial crises and worries: it seems to be fair to say that "1957" was the European answer to "1945." The emergence of the European Economic Community was not only the response to war and destruction but also to its underlying crisis of hegemonic politics in Europe and the complete failure of past balance-of-power concepts. As for the European answer to "1989," any emerging consent is less clear. The eastward enlargement of the European Union in 2004 marked the peaceful and democratic unification of the continent, but it was followed by the subsequent crises of trust between "old" and "new" Europe. The signing of the European Constitutional Treaty in 2004 echoed the ambition of the political leadership to provide the enlarged EU with a political frame, but the treaty was rejected by popular vote in two of the EU's founding states. Still, one could propose the hypothesis that "1989" marked the beginning of the second founding of Europe, the search for a new rationale of European integration. Just as the formative period between 1945 and 1957 was strongly driven by external pressure, the effects of 1989 had a strong impact on the idea of Europe and the implementation pattern of European integration. The path that began with "1989" clearly did not come to an end with the formal decisions in 2004: in 2005, the reaction of the European Constitutional Treaty led to the latest crisis in EU integration. The second formative period of European integration had not been concluded yet.

The two formative periods of European integration have received very different interpretations as far as their success and effect are concerned. It is widely accepted that the Treaties of Rome and the creation of the European Economic Community in 1957 became the definite European responses to the end of World War II and the renaissance of parliamentary democracy in Western Europe after 1945.[11] As for the definite response to 1989/90, the jury is still out. The year 2004 marked the unification of Europe through the unprecedented eastward enlargement of the European Union, but a year later the realization of the first ever European Constitution failed. The unprecedented EU widening was not matched with a simultaneous deepening of integration. The eastward enlargement and the effort to constitutionalize the European Union can be understood as honest responses of the EU leadership to the fall of the Iron Curtain and to the quest for combining parliamentary democracy and constitutional authority on the national level with democratic transparency, efficiency and accountability on the EU level. Enlargement and constitution-making were and deserve to be considered the necessary and logical consequence of the revolutionary changes of 1989.[12] No matter the still unfinished business of enlargement to Southeastern Europe, 2004 was a pivotal year in the unification of Europe, setting a course that will continue for some time. No matter the disputes about the European Constitution and its eventual failure: the signing of the document in 2004 by twenty-five European countries and, after all, its ratification until 2007 by a majority of EU member states with a majority of Union citizens has accelerated the constitutionalization and politicization of the EU.[13] The effort of EU leaders to replace the aborted European Constitutional Treaty by a Reform Treaty until 2009 turned "2004" in a structural sense into a long and yet unfinished year. The double challenge of enlarging and widening the EU in the aftermath of the turning times of 1989/90 would remain subject to interesting and certainly controversial interpretations of historians and political scientists for a long time.

The year 2005 brought the constitutional debacle and hence a new crisis in integration. Ironically, the rejection of the European Constitution by a majority of voters in France and in the Netherlands in 2005 triggered the first more or less public constitutional debate in Europe. The negative referendums in France and the Netherlands have accelerated new dimensions of European integration. For example, more than ever, the idea of a Europe- wide referendum has been discussed across the EU.[14] With the proposition of a Reform Treaty, the EU leadership has contributed to a new and yet well-known application of the law of unintended consequences in order to make detours look like a path to higher levels of success. The constructivist effort to initiate a European demos continues.[15] For the time being, scholars will have to diagnose an emerging European constitutionalism without a Constitution.[16]

The outcome of past integration crises, one might be surprised to realize, has often strengthened the rationale for integration and the renewal of its form. Is it too far-fetched to argue that in the end crises tend to be Europe's most reliable fact but also the best partner for deeper integration?

Crises as Turning Points in European Integration

This thesis brings me to my third point. All crises in European integration since 1957 were possible only because the original post-1945 crisis had been resolved with far-sightedness: to resist Soviet expansion under the security umbrella provided by the United States through NATO had been the most successful test of Europe's resilience. After Europe's self-destruction, the path toward European integration and Atlantic partnership combined Europe's ability to reinvent itself with the Atlantic reinsurance guarantee for the new beginning. But neither the creation of NATO in 1949 or of the European Economic Community in 1957 nor any other year ever since marked the end of European integration crises. Several of the crises that were to follow the formative years marked relevant turning points in European integration history. Looking back at five decades of post-war Europe, one is inclined to conclude that there has never been more European integration than in the context or aftermath of crises. More empirical research would be necessary to substantiate the thesis. Its possible theoretical implications would be another matter for more substantial academic work. This book is not a stringent proof of my thesis and is not meant to be one. The subsequent essays in this publication are contributions to the discourse about push and pull factors that influenced some of the most relevant trends in European integration. Some of the examples discussed in more detail in the subsequent chapters in this book inspire the thesis of crises as engines in European integration, although none of the outcomes of the subsequent crises was the product of one-dimensional path dependencies:

- The crisis that broke out after the French National Assembly refused to ratify the European Defense Community in 1954 that France itself had launched two years earlier. Its ultimate solution was the creation of the European Economic Community in 1957.

- The failure to proceed with concepts of political integration after the governments of the six member states refused the proposals for political integration expressed in two Fouchet Plans in 1961 and 1962, which they had commissioned themselves. Its ultimate answer was a set of treaty revisions during the 1980s and 1990s establishing a pre-constitution for the EU.
- The Luxembourg Compromise which brought France back into the EEC institutions in 1965 after "la grande nation" had left the EEC tables over disputes on agricultural policies that had been initiated by France itself. Its ultimate effect, as slow as it turned out to be, was the gradual recognition of majority voting and the primacy of EU law even by the most rigid proponents of national sovereignty.
- The failure of the EEC to immediately implement the "Werner Plan" of 1970 precisely outlining the path toward monetary union and a common currency over the decade of the 1970s. It took new currency crises during the 1980s and 1990s to achieve the introduction of the EURO as ultimate response to the challenges outlined by Werner.
- The refusal of the Maastricht Treaty by the majority of Danes in a referendum in 1992 was considered to be the end to all hopes of a political union. The ultimate solution to this crisis was the pragmatic "invention" of dubious "opting-out clauses" for Denmark, which helped to bring the majority of Danes back on the path of integration by way of sending them to the voting booth a second time.
- The crisis over constitution-making that was brought about by the EU Heads of States and Governments in December 2003 when they were unable to find agreement on the draft European Constitutional Treaty, which the Constitutional Convention had presented to them in June 2003. The ultimate response to this crisis came in mid-2004 after postponing the decision for half a year: after face-saving compromises were reached, the European Constitutional Treaty could be signed in October 2004.
- Finally, the ratification crisis of the European Constitutional Treaty that broke out in 2005. In 2007, EU leaders agreed on a Reform Treaty meant to replace the original Constitutional project. Against all the odds, the resolution of this crisis by 2009, they argued, would eventually strengthen European institutions. It might also, some optimists thought, enhance the demand for a more transparent European public sphere.

The rationale of the European integration process has not lost credibility amidst the many currents of challenges and responses: building a Europe whole and free, based on democratic principles, defending human rights, supporting a market economy with strong elements of welfare state solidarity, gradually combining economic with political union and reconstructing global responsibility and respect for multilateralism in international politics with the United States as Europe's most indispensable partner. In short: contributing to a free world in which the European Union (like democracy), as Timothy Garton Ash has reminded us, "is not an end in itself. It is a means to higher ends."[17] In another sequence of his great, uncompromising and thoughtful new book *Free World* Garton Ash explained the gist of Europe's experience with freedom and the obligation emanating from it: "This enlargement of freedom is the great success story of Europe over the sixty years since the Second World War. It also provides a central purpose for the next twenty years."[18] The same holds true for the processes of deepening European integration. The only question I would add is: Why only for the next twenty years?

European and Transatlantic Adaptation Crises Intertwined

It is interesting to note—to add my fourth thought—that the important adaptation crises and turning points in European integration have been linked, one way or the other, to fundamental developments and adaptation crises in transatlantic relations. At first, the period from 1949 (the founding of NATO) until 1957 (the signing of the Rome Treaties) was crucial for creating what we have learned to call "the West." Then, since 1989 (and still continuing at the time of publishing this book in 2008), the second turning times of European integration have been intrinsically linked to important transformations in transatlantic relations. It would be a simplification to assume that the first defining period in building a common Atlantic civilization after World War II was one of pure harmony, while the second defining period since the end of the Cold War will go into history merely as one of transatlantic divorce. From the Berlin blockade to the Suez crisis, the transatlantic record of the 1940s and 1950s was mixed. So was the record during the period marked by the outbreak of four Wars of Yugoslavian Succession, two Iraq wars and, after all, the unique enlargement of NATO and efforts to define the transformation of the Greater Middle East as the new transatlantic project.[19] In 2007, the transatlantic partners were still in the midst of finding a new frame of mind for their future partnership in the management of global affairs. One of the lessons of past decades was evident: whenever transatlantic relations are in bad shape, European integration suffers.

The formative adaptation crises in transatlantic relations were interwoven with important adaptation crises and defining periods in European integration. Between 1949 and 1957 three complex adaptation crises amalgamated, before they finally defined both the new European and the new transatlantic architecture:

- The Cold War and Soviet expansionism—followed by the wars in Korea and Indochina as well as the Suez Crises, which made France and Great Britain painfully realize the limits of their global role—facilitated the American guarantee for Europe's security.
- Functional European integration through the Community of Coal and Steel turned out to be a highly successful way of matching a host of conflicting

integration ideas and national interests of rebuilding Western Europe as a society of affluence and freedom, based on a law-based Single Market.
- NATO as the strategic and military insurance policy for rebuilding Western Europe on the one hand, the Council of Europe as a loose community of European values and the European Economic Community as the first step to political integration in Europe on the other hand mutually reinforced a new and sustainable European peace order.

Between 1989 and 2007 (at the time of writing), again three decisive and interconnected adaptation crises shaped the future path of European integration and of the Atlantic community:

- The introduction of the Euro opened the perspective of currency parity between Euro and dollar, eventually leading to unprecedented strength of the Euro against the dollar. The underlying recognition of more or less economic parity between the US and the EU has been evident, for example, throughout trade negotiations in recent years, although the statistics of unemployment and innovation, growth and productivity still speak a different language.
- In spite of serious doubts and premature obituaries, the Euro-Atlantic institutions with twenty-six NATO members and twenty-seven EU members, both anticipating further enlargements, have not lost their role in the projection of stability beyond the Atlantic area. Their role remains unique in a world facing enormous opportunities as a result of globalization, but also serious new threats emanating from failed states, natural and man-made disasters, the modernization crisis of the Greater Middle East, the terrorist threat of Islamic totalitarianism and the proliferation of weapons of mass destruction.
- The "Internal Cold War of the West" over Iraq between 2002 and 2004 was more troublesome than the fallout of the four Wars of Yugoslavian Succession or differences about how to deal with a Russia returning to neo-authoritarian rule.[20] But ultimately, the transatlantic partners had to recognize their mutual dependency. Since 2006, the conflict over Iran's nuclear ambitions supported this healing process, which has been well under way since 2004, structurally an "unfinished" year also for transatlantic relations.

I do not want to overstretch the exercise of conceptualizing time lines and analogies. Some will be debatable or could even be implausible. Surely, it did not take my arguments to raise awareness for the link between defining periods in European and transatlantic adaptation crises. Yet it seems useful to encourage more research on the many links between the two political processes. During the most successful periods in European integration and transatlantic relations, crises eventually had been transformed into opportunities. The latest set of crises still has to stand this test of experience. On January 1, 2007, Romania and Bulgaria joined the EU and yet the enlargement process in Southeastern Europe had not been completed. In 2007, under the German EU presidency, a new effort was made to save the political substance of the European Constitutional Treaty, yet it was to take until 2009 to see the results of the Reform Treaty implemented. On all troublesome aspects of transatlantic relations, new pragmatism seemed to grow. Yet, in 2007, the need to find a solution to the Kosovo problem and the urgent pressure to make Iraq safe for democracy, to rescue Afghanistan from a return to Taliban rule, and to prevent Iran from provoking a new global crisis by building an atomic bomb were as burdening as ever throughout recent years.

While 2005 was the year that sent the EU into a coma, 2006 was a year of silent reflection. In 2007, the readiness for action and leadership reemerged. But it was still undecided in which way European political leadership would approach the future: by a set of cautious, timid, and parochial approaches defining European integration and transatlantic relations continuously from their limits or by returning to the much more promising attitude of defining European integration and transatlantic relations from their many opportunities. In theory, the answer seemed to be easy: since 1945, crises had always required courageous responses in order to turn into new opportunities. In reality, the constitutional debacle of 2005 was still waiting for a sustainable response that could help to reconnect the idea of European integration and the aspirations of European Union citizens.

Outline of This Book

It was no coincidence that the majority of Swiss voters said "yes" to the Schengen Agreement—that is to say to free border crossing—only hours after the "no" votes in France and in the Netherlands on the European Constitutional Treaty had shocked the EU's political class in mid-2005. According to Euro-Barometer and other opinion polls, also non-Swiss Europeans do not want less Europe: in their majority, EU citizens want more Europe (and, by the way, also a constitution), but often they want a better, a more democratic, and a more efficient Europe. They want a European Union that works and in which their citizenship matters. In the end, they want a European Union the Swiss would be ready to join.

This remark brings me to my last point, the logic and structure of this book. This collection of essays on turning points in European integration was written at the frustrating peak of the constitutional crisis Europe had entered with the negative referendums in France and in the Netherlands. The authors brought together in this publication used the period of silent reflection postulated by the EU leadership to look back. By raising questions about the constellation of several turning points in European integration, they combine the academic-technical with normative reflections and the commemorative-political. What might seem as a weakness in the structure of this book is in fact its strength as it echoes the diversity of the real puzzle that is the European Union. In the political arena, shock and helplessness were the prevalent reactions to the rejection of the European Constitution in France and in the Netherlands. The authors brought together in this book tried to understand the meaning of past crises for the process of European integration. While the main success stories of European integration have been well researched, this has not been the case as far as the failures, detours and crises along the way of five decades of European integration are concerned. The authors offer their scholarly knowledge to look into the impact of five decades of defining moments in integration. They do not speculate about the outcome of the latest crisis that escalated in 2005. But the common thesis of their chapters is telling: eventually, crises in the effort to integrate Europe have usually ended with a new level of strengthened integration. Although no determinism may indicate that this pattern must continue forever, the findings of this book invite skepticism about Euro-skepticism. The authors of this book are all Germans, as was the desire of the organizers of the lecture series that stood at the beginning of this project. But their methodology and perspective echo many of the prevalent currents of academic work on European integration beyond their home country.

Wilfried Loth, Essen University, discusses the meaning of World War II and the resistance movements in framing the parameters for imminent institutional integration after 1945. World War II, the biggest moral and material crisis of Germany and in Europe ever, became the watershed and a midwife for a unique experiment in the history of European politics and nation-states. Loth gives interesting insights into the intellectual framing of the idea of European integration in the interwar period and among resistance groups. The way to Europe was the fascinating and gradual transformation from an idea into political action and reality. With particular sensitivity he looks at the imminent post-World War II dilemma: the realistic possibility to begin European integration was limited to Western Europe while the hope to create the new Europe together with Central and Eastern European nations not only existed as an abstract vision, but was nurtured by interesting contributions from the region itself. The idea to position Europe between the two world powers at its fringes—the US and the Soviet Union—was as vivid in postwar Europe as the uncompromising ideal of a federal Europe, even in Britain.

Manfred Görtemaker, Potsdam University, discusses why and how the failure to organize European security through the European Defense Community in 1954 became instrumental in initiating the path that led to the signing of the Rome Treaties on March 25, 1957 and thus the founding of the European Economic Community. Görtemaker pays special attention to American contributions in the formation of the European integration project. These contributions were driven by the need to provide security for Europe. In the end, they brought about transatlantic security with Europe and a frame for economic integration in Europe. Therefore, Görtemaker argues, the failed European Defense Community was, in the end, not such a bad thing as it opened the way for a much more stable and lasting architecture combining European economic integration with transatlantic security commitments.

Jürgen Elvert, Cologne University, assesses the relationship between institutional deficits and structural worry on the one hand and institutional reforms and the implicit evolution of a proto-constitutional basis of European integration through treaty revisions on the other. He argues that the main institutional crises in the history of European integration—in the 1960s with the rejection of two Fouchet Plans on political union and the "empty chair crisis" following the withdrawal of France from EEC business and in 2005 after the rejection of the European Constitutional Treaty in France and in the Netherlands—were reflections of identity crises and widely spread uncertainty about the political finality of the integration project. Elvert links the most critical situations in European integration to the need for internal and institutional adaptation in the context of membership enlargement.

Jürgen von Hagen, Bonn University and for more than a decade my colleague as director at the Center for European Integration Studies, explains why currency crises were necessary in order to initiate the path toward the European Currency and Monetary Union. For many, to turn an idealistic idea into the irreversible reality of a solidly reinforced common market with a common currency has become the most remarkable and successful integration story of the second half of the past five decades. Von Hagen develops a strong argument around the theory of optimal currency areas and the concept of incentive compatibility constraints used by economists in order to assess benefits and costs of monetary union. According to his analysis, the shared gains of monetary union will remain constantly under pressure as long as they are not matched by fiscal and political union. Von Hagen predicts an increase in the conflict potential as socioeconomic heterogeneity in the monetary union increases. In the end, the enlargement of the EU to Turkey might trigger, he argues, the critical crisis leading either to a collapse of monetary union or its transformation into full fiscal and political union.

Wolfgang Wessels and Thomas Traguth, Cologne University, argue that, ever since the summit of the European Community in 1969 in The Hague, the triptych of "completing, widening, and deepening" has guided the evolution of European integration. The permissive consensus about this "magic triangle" has often been under pressure—not the least in the context of the Eastward enlargement of the European Union in 2004 and the subsequent crisis of the European Constitution. According to Wessels and Traguth, there is no evidence in support of the thesis that enlargement generates inevitably a "spill-back" in integration. To the contrary, they conclude, the three components of the "magic triangle" remain necessary and useful for mutually strengthening each others premises. To leave the question of a political finality of European integration open, vague and subject to interpretation has helped to overcome crises in balancing the triangle of completion, enlargement and deepening of integration whenever they occurred.

Mathias Jopp, Director of the Institute for European Politics in Berlin, and Udo Diedrichs, Cologne University, shed light on the paradoxical effect that the

EU's failure in preventing the four Wars of Yugoslavian Succession generated the first serious attempt to institutionalize and consolidate a Common European Foreign and Security Policy. "Learning from failure"—meaning that the European Union tried to gradually, almost incrementally catch up with changing geopolitical realities after 1989/90—came at a high prize, notably for the victims of Europe's first wars since 1945. Doing too little too late after the outbreak of violence in Yugoslavia produced an "expectation-credibility gap" that has almost become a constitutive criticism in analyzing the relationship between power projection and the subsequent perception of the factual global role of the EU ever since. Yet it cannot be denied that the European Union has gone a long way in a relatively short period of time in order to broaden competencies and instruments for a more political and increasingly global role, Jopp and Diedrichs stress, with reference to the treaty amendments and a broad series of remarkable operations the EU has conducted in a short period of time. It almost seems justifiable to say that the victims of Yugoslavia did not die in vain if the first European wars since World War II would go into history as the last wars of European unification. In order to reach global coherence and consistent political will, Jopp and Diedrichs conclude, the EU will have to take its own security strategy more seriously.

Michael Gehler, Hildesheim University, supports my initial hypothesis that the interplay of crisis and response has been constitutive for the development of European integration. The crisis over the ratification of the European Constitutional Treaty at the time of writing can be considered as nothing but another element in a long series of disputes related to the search for a European order. The stable and successful evolution of European integration since 1957, Gehler argues, allows for cautious optimism that the EU would eventually also come out of this latest constellation of seeming stalemate with a new sense of dynamics. In discussing the limits of one EU Presidency—the Austrian Presidency of the first half of 2006 being an insightful case study—to unlock the ever increasing complexity of crises in European integration, Gehler supports one of the possible remedies offered by the abortive European Constitutional Treaty: longer-term EU Presidencies in order to better manage the multi-level governance system that has evolved in the EU.

Hans-Gert Pöttering, President of the European Parliament between 2007 and 2009, discusses the perspectives of the European Union beyond its double crisis of the ratification of the European Constitutional Treaty and lack of confidence in EU activities expressed by many citizens across Europe. His contribution to this book is a document of interest to contemporary historians: Pöttering, Osnabrück University, was Chairman of the group of the European People's Party/European Democrats, the largest faction in the European Parliament, when he gave the "Konrad Adenauer Lecture 2006" at St. Antony's College Oxford. At the time of his lecture, which is published in this book for the first time, trust and confidence in the European Union had reached a new low point. In order to overcome the most recent crisis of trust and the new wave of Euro-skepticism, concrete, verifiable and successful actions of the European

Union were more necessary than ever. Pöttering analyzed the role of the European Parliament in the process of implementing economic reforms aimed at encouraging growth and modernization across the EU. He gives a favorable account of the effects of EU enlargement and underlines the continuous relevance of transatlantic relations. He concluded with confidence that only European solutions would be helpful in revitalizing the European economy, dealing with the challenge of demographic change and migration and positioning Europe as a respected world partner. His lecture at St. Antony's College was an indicative sign for a turning point within the crisis that had escalated in 2005: he could not give satisfying answers to all queries regarding the future course of European integration. But he did not stop at the red light switched on by referendum majorities in France and the Netherlands. He was prepared to look back, as all other authors of this book do, in order to better approach the uncertainties and opportunities of the future. A few months after addressing St. Antony's College, Pöttering was elected President of the European Parliament. His is the voice of an optimistic Euro-realism that avoids cynicism or frustration and goes ahead with "building Europe" as a long and daunting project that cannot be defined or derailed by one crisis alone.

This book originated in a lecture series at the European Studies Center of St. Antony's College Oxford during Hilary Term 2006. The German scholars who came together on that occasion did not dare to predict the outcome of the German EU Presidency in 2007 or even of the solution to the ratification crisis of the European Constitutional Treaty. But in spite of all their differences in methodology and perspective they echoed the permissive consent in Germany to contribute to a revitalized European spirit. The German government's EU Presidency of 2007 was driven by this aspiration. But from the Austrian case study in 2006 and the experience of most former rotating EU Presidencies it was clear that one six-month EU Presidency alone could not turn the wheel around in an overly complex European Union. The main issue would require years of political action and correction: to reconnect the aspirations, hopes, and fears of European citizens with the ambitions and proposals of their political leadership. Beyond the ratification crisis of Europe's first ever constitution, this challenge seemed to be at the heart of a fundamental revision of the rationale of European integration. European integration could no longer be pursued as an elite-driven project aimed at reconciling former enemies and overcoming cleavages caused by Europe's internal history. European integration would need to be rooted and "owned" by the EU's citizens if it were to achieve a new global role for Europe amidst globalization and a vast array of issues regarding the management of global affairs.

More than being a static showcase of German scholarship at Oxford, with the gratefully acknowledged support of the Stifterverband für die Deutsche Wissenschaft, this lecture series was meant to initiate a lively dialogue between German and British scholars on the future of Europe. By publishing these essays, we invite the lively discussions at St.Antony's to be continued elsewhere. We contribute to this dialogue by looking into the past, but we do it because we wish to see a future in which old Europe can contribute to a new world. After all, no one else will do this job for Europe. Academic research originating in Europe, I believe, is not exempt from this task.

Notes

1. See Ludger Kühnhardt, *Implications of Globalization on the Raison d'Etre of European Integration*, Oslo: ARENA, 2002.
2. Jan Zielonka (ed.), *Paradoxes of European Foreign Policy*, The Hague: Kluwer, 1998; see also Jan Zielonka, *Europe as Empire: The Nature of the Enlarged European Union*, Oxford: Oxford University Press, 2006.
3. I am grateful to Timothy Garton Ash and Kalypso Nicolaidis for their suggestions to clarify the underlying theoretical assumptions of my study.
4. Some other lessons are already widespread, obvious, and increasingly consensual: (a) The relationship between "integration" and "European identity" has never been static during the past five decades as some of those tend to suggest who are afraid of an EU that would be enlarged to the Balkans and to Turkey; (b) The relationship between "deepening" and "widening" has always turned out to be mutually reinforcing and not, as is sometimes suggested in the scholarly literature, mutually exclusive; (c) and finally, the debate about "supranationality" and "intergovernmentalism" has lost its fertility since the concept of multi-level governance in an unfinished federation of nation-states and Union citizens has been recognized as a new category of academic reasoning about the nature of the EU.
5. See Marlene Wind, *Europe Towards a Post-Hobbesian Order? A Constructivist Theory of European Integration, or How to Explain European Integration as an Unintended Consequence of Rational State-Action*, Fiesole: European University Institute, 1996.
6. Arnold Joseph Toynbee, *Studies of History: Abridgement of Volumes I-VI*, New York and London: Oxford University Press, 1947, p. 51.
7. Ibid, p. 63.
8. See Jeffrey T. Checkel, "Social Construction and European Integration," in: Thomas Christiansen, Knut Erik Jorgensen and Antje Wiener (eds.), *The Social Construction of Europe*, London: Sage Publications, 2001, pp. 50–64.
9. In his small and concise book *The Origins and Development of the European Union 1945–1995* (London: Routledge, 1996, pp. 7–33) Martin Dedman describes the three most influential approaches to the theory of European integration, although it remains questionable whether they can really be called 'theories' or should rather be referred to as comprehensive assessments of analysis: 1. Functional theory that dominates contemporary Political Science. It assumes that an increase in international cooperation and consequently in integration is the logical precondition for states to enhance their scope of action in the modern state system. The scholarly works of David Mitrany (*A Working Peace System: An Argument for the Functional Development of International Organization*, New York: Russel & Russel, 1943) and Ernst Haas (*The Uniting of Europe: Political, Social, and Economic Forces 1950–1957*, Stanford: Stanford University Press, 1958) laid the ground for this most influential integration theory. 2. Ideational approaches refer to the growth and influence of European federalist movements in the interwar period and during World War II. The erudite work of Walter Lipgens (*Documents on the History of European Integration*, 2 vols., Berlin and New York: de Gruyter, 1985 and 1986) has

contributed the best possible insights into their quest for a new normative beginning in building a European order. 3. Historical-systematizing research has focused primarily on the period from the Treaties of Rome until the Treaty of Maastricht. Alan S. Milward (*The European Rescue of the Nation State*, London: Routledge, 1992) in one of the most influential works of this nature has argued that integration occurs only when it is needed by the states that come together. Andrew Moravscik (*The Choice for Europe: Social Purpose and State Power from Messina to Maastricht*, Ithaca: Cornell University Press 1998) has elaborated on the theme that European integration strengthened the European nation-states. Today, the main new focus deals with "Europeanization" and its transforming impact on both integration mechanisms on the EU level and national structures in all possible variants; see Maria Green Cowles, James Caporaso and Thomas Risse (eds.), *Transforming Europe: Europeanization and Domestic Change*, Ithaca: Cornell University Press, 2001; Kevin Featherstone and Claudio M. Radaelli (eds.), *The Politics of Europeanization*, Oxford: Oxford University Press, 2003.

10. See David B. Abernethy, *The Dynamics of Global Dominance: European Overseas Empires, 1415–1980*, New Haven: Yale University Press, 2000.
11. See Wilfried Loth, *Der Weg nach Europa: Geschichte der europäischen Integration, 1939–1957*, Göttingen: Vandenhoek & Ruprecht, 1990.
12. See Timothy Garton Ash, *History of the Present: Sketches and Dispatches from Europe in the 1990s*, London: Allen Lane, 1999; Ludger Kühnhardt, *Revolutionszeiten: Das Umbruchjahr 1989 im geschichtlichen Zusammenhang*, Munich: Olzog, 1994.
13. For the text see European Union, *Treaty Establishing a Constitution for Europe*, Luxembourg: Office for Official Publications of the European Communities, 2005; see also Yves Meny, "Making Sense of the EU: the Achievements of the Convention," *Journal of Democracy*, 14 (2003), pp. 57–70; Michael Gehler, Günter Bischof, Ludger Kühnhardt and Rolf Steininger (eds.), *Towards a European Constitution: A Historical and Political Comparison with the United States*, Vienna: Böhlau, 2005; Marcus Höreth, Cordula Janowski and Ludger Kühnhardt (eds.), *Die Europäische Verfassung: Analyse und Bewertung ihrer Strukturentscheidungen*, Baden-Baden: Nomos, 2005; Ludger Kühnhardt, *European Union—The Second Founding: The Changing Rationale of European Integration*, Baden-Baden: Nomos, 2008.
14. See Simon Hug, *Voices of Europe: Citizens, Referendums and European Integration*, Lanham: Rowman & Littlefield, 2002; Frédéric Esposito, "The European Referendum: a Tool to Legitimate the European Integration Process?" in: Stuart Nagel (ed.), *Policymaking and Democracy: A Multinational Anthology*, Lanham: Lexington Books, 2003, pp. 15–37; Nina Eschke and Thomas Malick (eds.), *The European Constitution and Its Ratification Crises: Constitutional Debates in the EU Member States*, ZEI Discussion Paper C 156, Bonn: Zentrum für Europäische Integrationsforschung 2006.
15. See Lars-Erik Cederman, *Nationalism and Bounded Integration: What it Would Take to Construct a European Demos*, Fiesole: European University Institute, 2000.
16. See Thomas Banchoff and Mitchell P. Smith (eds.), *Legitimacy and the European Union: The Contested Polity*, London and New York: Routledge, 1999; Niclas Berggren and Nils Karlson, "Constitutionalism, Division of Power and Transaction Costs," *Public Choice*, 117.1/2 (2003), pp. 99–124; Michiel Brand, *Affirming and Refining European Constitutionalism: Towards the Establishment of the First Constitution for the European Union*, Fiesole: European University Institute, 2004; Günter Frankenberg, "The Return of the Contract: Problems and Pitfalls of European Constitutionalism," *European Law Journal*, 6.3 (2000), pp. 257–276; Oliver Gerstenberg, "Expanding the Constitution

Beyond the Court: The Case of Euro-Constitutionalism," *European Law Journal*, 8.1 (2002), pp. 172—94; Ingolf Pernice, "Multi-Level Constitutionalism in the European Union," *European Law Journal*, 27.1/6 (2002), pp. 511—29.
17. Timothy Garton Ash, *Free World: Why a Crisis of the West Reveals the Opportunity of Our Time*, London: Allen Lane, 2004, p. 246.
18. Ibid, p. 210.
19. See Ronald D. Asmus and Kenneth M. Pollack, "The New Transatlantic Project," *Policy Review*, 115 (2002), pp. 3–18; Charles Grant, *Transatlantic Rifts: How to Bring the Two Sides Together*, London: Centre for European Reform, 2003.
20. See Philip H. Gordon and Jeremy Shapiro, *Allies at War: America, Europe and the Crisis over Iraq*, New York: McGraw-Hill, 2004.

1
Sources of European Integration: The Meaning of Failed Interwar Politics and the Role of World War II

Wilfried Loth

When some sixty years ago in his famous Zurich speech of September 19, 1946, Winston Churchill called for the building of "a kind of United States of Europe," he was arguing in light of the failures of the past. As he said:

> The League of Nations did not fail because of its principles or conceptions. It failed because these principles were deserted by those States who had brought it into being. It failed because the Governments of those days feared to face the facts, and act while time remained. This disaster must not be repeated. There is therefore much knowledge and material with which to build: and also bitter dear-bought experience.[1]

It does indeed seem that this experience was the most important driving force behind the efforts to build a European community and promote European integration in the period after World War II. In order to understand the emergence of the first institutions of this European community, I would therefore like to invite you to consider this first major cycle of crises and responses: What were the "knowledge and material" that Churchill mentioned in his speech, and how were they used to build the kind of "European family" we now know?

Experiences of War

When the failure of the Treaty of Versailles became apparent, initiatives toward the unification of Europe were given new impetus. The success of the politics of revision and the rapid march to victory by National Socialist Germany in 1939–40 made it painfully obvious to the peoples of Europe that the European nation-states were no longer in a position to guarantee the safety of their citizens.

Alliances and pact systems of the conventional type no longer offered adequate protection against armed aggression. This realization gave added strength to demands for the creation of collective security structures which would do away with interstate anarchy at least in Europe. At the same time, all those nations which felt themselves threatened by the expansion of National Socialist Germany moved closer together.

In Great Britain, this development began to make itself apparent soon after the Munich Agreement of 1938. Authors such as Lord Lothian and Clarence Streit, who advocated a federation of the democratic states, gained a great deal of attention. Within a very short time, the "Federal Union" favoring this program had attracted more than ten thousand members and with the broad support of the academic and political establishment, had organized a series of conferences in 1939 and 1940, at which there was substantive discussion of the problems of a federative reorganization of Europe. In March of 1940, a Federal Union Research Institute was established at the University of Oxford and very quickly became the center of discussion.[2]

Churchill's famous union offer to France has to be discussed within the framework of this movement. On June 16, 1940, the British government followed the initiative of Jean Monnet (who oversaw the French efforts of coordinating the wartime supply with Britain) and General Charles de Gaulle (deputy secretary of the French War Department who had just arrived in London) by proposing a joint declaration that was to announce joint civil rights for British and French citizens and joint bodies for the conduct of war. From Churchill's perspective this was certainly a maneuver intended first of all to keep the French from signing a truce with the German victors. Yet there is no doubt that, had the French accepted, this proposal indeed would have led to joint war efforts; and on both sides, there were politicians and civil servants who wanted to continue institutional cooperation in peacetime.[3]

Subsequently, when Britain had been fighting entirely alone for more than a year against the German onslaught, the willingness of the British to enter into a permanent association with the continent had diminished perceptibly. Hopes for peace in the long term were now predominantly based around close cooperation with the US, and the country tended to see itself as growing into the role of one of the three world powers that would be called upon to safeguard peace in the future.[4] Conversely, in those places where the German occupation inspired resistance, the experience of the failure of the League of Nations was deepened by that of national fragmentation and disintegration. Under these conditions, the rejection of the principle of the nation-state was formulated in a correspondingly radical fashion, and the appeal of federalist ideas became broader as soon as the defeat of the Nazis began to seem plausible. "In one point, my convictions are profound and unshakable, whatever the world may say," wrote the French socialist leader Léon Blum in early 1941 in one of the Vichy government's prisons. "If this war does not at last give rise to fundamentally stable international institutions, to a really effective international power, then it will not be the last war." Like Blum, dozens of resistance writers and the overwhelming majority of resistance programs formulated what was required for this kind of effectiveness: the restriction of national sovereignties in favor of a superstate with its own institutions and leadership. "The international body must have the institutions and the powers it needs to do what it is created to do; in other words, it must be boldly and openly set up as a super-state on a level above national sovereignties."[5]

The longer the struggles of the war lasted, the more the thinking of the elite within the resistance was shaped by the experience of an increasing dissolution of power vis-à-vis the new world powers as well as by the war itself and by the general collapse it caused. While Europe had largely exhausted its resources in the conflict, the United States had more than doubled its production volume. This finally allowed the yardstick of economic productivity to be extended beyond the confines of European nation-states, and fundamentally called into question the competitiveness of the countries of Europe, and therefore also their independence. Due to the key military decisions of the war, the United States at the same time rose to be the leading military power in the world, while the Soviet Union emerged as far and away the strongest military force on the European continent. This not only robbed the old states of the continent of a great deal of their previous influence over world politics, but actually placed them increasingly within the power of the war's two main victors. Europeans came to realize that they needed to pool their resources if they were to have any hope of holding their own against the new world powers in the future.[6]

The readiness to find supranational solutions was further reinforced by the fact that many resistance fighters regarded totalitarian suppression by fascists as the ultimate consequence of the adoration of the principle of the nation-state's sovereignty. In the struggle against the extreme fascist form of power politics and nationalism, they rediscovered the community of traditional European values. What drove them to resist was less the struggle against foreign domination than the revolt against the suppression of human rights. This caused them to move toward one another across philosophical, social and national divides, and to seek ways to avoid a repetition of the unleashing of the nation-state's power. Ernesto Rossi and Altiero Spinelli addressed this in the summer of 1941 in light of long discussions with fellow inmates on the Italian prison island of Ventotene: "No longer is the 'nation' considered to be the historical product of the communities of man that find their state to be the most efficacious form of organizing collective life." The nation-states' striving for dominance, they asserted, necessarily leads to totalitarian regimes. The peoples of Europe must therefore do away with the continent's division into sovereign nation-states in order to combat the exploiters of the old order. A "federal reorganization of Europe" was the essential prerequisite for the development of modern civilization, a process that had been completely shut down in the era of totalitarianism.[7]

The revolutionary dimension of this European movement became even more apparent among the representatives of the socialist left. The development of productive forces led them to conclude that a socialist revolution in Europe required a federative reorganization; at the same time, the socialist left emphasized the necessity of this radical change as a prerequisite for a European peace order. This applies to Austro-Marxists such as Oskar Pollak[8] as much as to those young leaders of left-wing German socialist groups in exile such as Willi Eichler, Richard Löwenthal, and Willy Brandt,[9] and the southern French resistance groups "Libérer et Fédérer" and "L'Insurgé" of Alexandre Marc and Marceau Pivert.[10] They all assumed that the anti-fascist uprising offered a chance for socialist revolution. However, the engagement for a federative new order also made most of them open to pragmatic partial solutions that could be realized in a compromise with non-socialist forces. This resulted not only in the partial renewal of democratic socialism, particularly in France and in Germany, but also, as a closely connected phenomenon, in the growing commitment of these parties to a "Federation of all European Peoples."[11]

The longer the war lasted and the more evident the bestiality of the National Socialist regime became, the clearer became the need for federative structures to solve the German problem as well. "Hatred cannot banish hatred, nor violence put an end to violence," wrote Léon Blum as early as 1941. "There is only one way to resolve the contradiction, to make Germany harmless in a peaceful and stable Europe, and that is to incorporate the German nation in an international community."[12] To eliminate the social roots of German imperialism, it was essential that there be a controlled reform of German society by the victors. This tutelage, as Claude Bourdet put it in the French resistance newspaper *Combat* in March of 1944, "cannot be justified and will not be accepted unless it is followed by the renunciation, by all the nations of Europe, of part of their national sovereignty in favor of the European federation." Without the prospect of development within the federative community of Europeans, the coercive measures of the victors threatened to produce only a new movement bent on revenge.[13]

It goes without saying that these arguments also struck a chord with those Germans who were thinking about the future of their nation after the defeat of the Third Reich. The democratic resistance could conceive of a future for Germany acceptable to all European nations only in a federative international order. As the prospects of an uprising against the National Socialist regime disappeared, its supporters tried to draw the attention of the Allies to the link between democratization and federalization. The conservative resistance around such men as Ludwig Beck, Ulrich von Hassell and Carl Goerdeler was initially oriented toward the traditional conceptions of a Central Europe dominated by Germany. Many of its supporters, however, became more modest as time passed. A good number, such as Goerdeler in particular, allowed themselves to be won over to the necessity of economic integration and controlled disarmament and in the end, they were drawn to the concept of a federated Europe "in which neither Germany nor any other power would claim predominance."[14]

Taken together, the experiences of World War II brought about a broad European unification movement by 1943. Some uncertainties remained regarding the geographic borders of a united Europe and its relationship with a global peacekeeping organization. Within the movement, there were different notions of its position toward the Soviet Union and the role of the Germans within a united Europe; there were also differences on social conceptions and strategies. The supporters of the movement renounced traditional power politics and the political implementation of its ideals to different degrees, and they also varied in their pronouncements regarding the necessity of certain regional alliances. However, beyond the limits of national and philosophical outlooks, they agreed (often even using quite similar arguments) on the inadequacy and the dangers of the nation-states' outdated system of order and on the necessity of federative solutions. This consensus was shared among the majority of the politicians in exile as well as the vast majority of the resistance fighters in the occupied countries from France to Poland, although not among a minority of conservatives or the communist resistance. Britain did not join the movement either given that trust in its own forces increased again after its having previously been drawn to federative solutions; and neither did the Nordic states, which traditionally followed the British orientation. For continental Europe in the narrower sense, however, there was a basis for developing an alternative for the restoration of the broken system of nation-states.

Governments and Negotiations

Most European politicians had fled to London as the Germans overran their homelands and had formed governments in exile, which initially focused on regional alliances of adjacent countries. Such alliances seemed to be the most urgent and also the most likely to be realized. In any event, the politicians in exile felt themselves primarily responsible for achieving this. If they succeeded in creating such regional alliances, then this might also help promote the emergence of a federative order for the whole of Europe.[15]

The most specific and detailed planning was developed by the representatives of the exiles and resistance of Eastern Europe. As early as November 11, 1940, the Polish government in exile under General Władysław Sikorski and the provisional Czech government under President Eduard Beneš had issued a joint declaration of their intention "to enter, as independent and sovereign states, into a closer political and economic association" which was to be joined by "other countries in that part of the European continent."[16] On January 23, 1942, the two governments concluded a formal agreement in which they undertook to form a Polish–Czechoslovakian "confederation" after the war. A few days earlier, on January 15, the Yugoslav and Greek governments in exile had also signed a confederation agreement, in which they committed themselves to the formation of joint bodies for the determination of joint foreign, economic and defense policies. The great majority of those belonging to the Eastern European resistance, drawn mostly from the ranks of the political center and the socialist left, saw in this agreement the prelude to a federalization of the Eastern European region within an overall European context. A number of figures turned their attention to a combination of Eastern–Central European federation, Danube federation and Balkan federation; others, including Sikorski, wanted to gather the whole of Eastern–Central and Southeastern Europe into one federation. Beneš himself took a rather skeptical view of the notion of federation but, while he was being forced to fight in London for the recognition of his government in exile, did at least accept the idea of the confederation project.

It was the representatives of the Belgians in exile in particular who articulated ideas about a regional merger in the western areas of the European continent. Paul-Henri Spaak, who held the post of foreign minister in the government in exile, put forward the case for an association of Belgium, the Netherlands, Luxembourg and France in the economic, political and military spheres; it was intended as a means of allowing these states, supported by their colonial possessions, to hold their own in world politics alongside the great powers. This Western European grouping was also intended as a means of maintaining friendly and increasingly close relations with the other federations and the great powers. Paul van Zeeland, former prime minister (and later foreign minister), pressed for a customs and monetary union in Western Europe. And Louis de Brouckère, former president of the Socialist Workers International, stressed the need for the integration of German industry into the European economic association too, which was to be organized from the west of the continent.[17] Similar arguments were put forward by Count Carlo Sforza—as foreign minister of pre-fascist Italy one of the foremost Italian figures in exile—for a Central European federation from Poland to Serbia and for a Latin federation of France and Italy, which might later also encompass the other Mediterranean states.[18]

After relocating from London to Algiers in the early summer of 1943, the French government in exile under General de Gaulle reached agreement on the project for a regional federation in the west. De Gaulle remained skeptical of Britain's willingness to participate in such a union. It was also the case that he could not properly conceive of the involvement of the Germans on an equal footing, as Jean Monnet was proposing.[19] Otherwise, however, de Gaulle allowed himself to be persuaded that a process of federation in Western Europe represented a necessary pre-condition for the economic well-being of France and that the role of France as a great power could be assured only in this way. On October 30, 1943, he instructed the Liberation Committee to study seriously the "project for a Federation of Western Europe." France, Belgium, the Netherlands, and Luxembourg were to form the core of this federation; the committee was also to consider carefully whether this federation could be expanded to the south, whether the attachment of the Rhine-Westphalian industrial basin was a good idea, and whether there was a possibility of an association of this federation with Britain.[20]

The integration of the regional federations into a greater Europe was discussed for the first time at a round of meetings organized by Sikorski at the headquarters of most of the governments in exile in London. At his invitation, representatives of Poland, Czechoslovakia, Norway, Belgium, the Netherlands,

Luxembourg, Greece, and Yugoslavia as well as the "Free France" Committee met to air their views on the organization of a "European community." The negotiations lasted for the whole of 1942, and, in the process, it became apparent that there was considerable agreement on the need to surrender sovereignty to the community and for the participant states to be organized democratically. It was also clear, however, that it was no longer feasible to decide on the overall structure of Europe without the involvement of the new world powers and that the problem of securing peace could in any event no longer be solved predominantly on the European level.[21]

When it came to winning over the great powers to the idea of a federative new order in Europe, the Europeans soon encountered difficulties, however. Of the "Big Three," only Churchill took a clearly positive attitude to the initiatives for unification. In a welcoming address to the Fifth Congress of the Pan-European Movement, organized in March of 1943 in New York by Richard Count Coudenhove-Kalergi, the British prime minister held out the hope that "under a world institution embodying or representing the United Nations, and some day all nations, there should come into being a Council of Europe." They must endeavor, Churchill said, to create "a real effective League, with all the strongest forces concerned woven into its texture, with a High Court to adjust disputes, and with forces, armed forces, national or international, or both, held ready to impose these decisions."[22] This European Council, as he described it in August that year at a meeting with President Franklin Roosevelt in Quebec, was to form, together with an Asiatic and an American council, one of the three regional sub-organizations of the future United Nations. He also pressed for smaller states, especially in the Danube region and beyond, to be incorporated into compatible associations and federations.[23] He was thereby evidently thinking of keeping Germany under control and at the same time avoiding a power vacuum, which the Soviet Union could have unilaterally exploited.

Joseph Stalin did not fundamentally reject the concept of the three regional organizations. However, he did insist at the Tehran Conference in November of 1943 that the United States as well as the Soviet Union be members of the European Council, as well as of the Asiatic one. A European Council without Soviet participation seemed to him too insecure vis-à-vis the risk posed by Germany as well as the anti-Soviet tendencies in Eastern Europe, and might even emerge as an instrument for the formation of an imperialist power block under British leadership. He categorically rejected the plans for a regional federation in Eastern Europe. After the Soviets' experience with the Eastern European states, he considered direct Soviet control of the region utterly essential. Accordingly, efforts toward an Eastern European federation were simply diversionary maneuvers that had to be rapidly suppressed.

Roosevelt in turn wanted to hear nothing of a regional council for Europe, either with or without American participation. As he told Stalin quite openly at Tehran, he did not believe that he could get the one past the US Congress, and the other—a European council without American participation—seemed to him to harbor the risk of the US being kept out of European affairs, thus giving a new lease of life to American isolationism. Moreover, regional councils ran counter to the views of US Secretary of State Cordell Hull. The left wing of the Democratic Party feared that they would only provoke new conflicts and barriers against the unhindered access of the American economy to the world market. Plans for a European alliance, as had been presented by experts from the State Department and the peace councils of the churches, were thus definitively rejected by the Roosevelt administration in August/September of 1943.[24] The American president was also concerned with securing the co-operation of Stalin beyond the end of the war. In an entirely realistic assessment of the development of power relationships, he was convinced that future world peace would depend on that cooperation above all else.

Thus the chance of realizing plans for an Eastern European federation disappeared. Once the Soviet leadership had made its rejection apparent, Beneš, still reticent on the federation idea, informed the Czechoslovak Council of State in November of 1942 that he considered the time "not yet ripe" for the realization of the federation project with Poland. When Stalin broke off diplomatic relations with the Polish government in exile in May of 1943, Beneš likewise ended the negotiations with the Poles.[25] In the other circles of Eastern European exiles, support for federation plans rapidly dwindled too; to pursue them in light of the Soviet attitude seemed neither sensible nor realistic. Following Sikorski's death in an air crash in July of 1943, discussions among the governments in exile in London were not pursued any further.[26]

The other federation plans remained open. At the negotiations relating to the future world peace organization, the possibility of forming regional subdivisions was established in its essentials (taking shape in Article 52 of the United Nations Charter). No specific conclusions for Europe were drawn, however.[27] Instead, the Allies agreed to occupy and administer a defeated Germany together. The creation of a pan-Europe federation was therefore postponed; this could become a reality only if the victorious powers succeeded, after the occupation of Germany, in agreeing on a jointly responsible integration of the Germans into the European context.

More feasible was progress in bringing Western Europe into an alliance. In early 1944, the French government in exile proposed to the British that they work together for the integration of Western Europe; this was to provide Europeans with a greater degree of independence and, in particular, would also make possible the joint control of the West German industrial areas. In the late autumn of that year, Paul-Henri Spaak, representing the Belgian government, approached the British with a similar proposal. In London, however, there was hesitation about being brought into such an association with continental Western Europeans. This project, too, was thus left hanging.[28] Without British participation, the smaller Western European states did not want any connection with France. Spaak accordingly put an end to the plan for a Franco–Belgian customs union, which he himself had been promoting earlier. As long as the union with Britain was not going to come about, the only customs union he considered acceptable would be one limited to Belgium, the Netherlands, and Luxembourg.[29]

The decision was then made. On September 5, 1944, the governments of Belgium, the Netherlands, and Luxembourg undertook—in what was known as the Benelux Agreement—to form a customs union after the end of the war. Negotiations between the Benelux representatives and the French government about the extension of the union to France were no more than dilatory. As differences in the course of financial policy among the participant countries began to become apparent, the parties concerned had to be content with an agreement (signed February 23, 1945) on economic consultation between Belgium and France, to which Luxembourg and the Netherlands then acceded.[30]

"Third Force" or Western Integration?

The challenge to go further—once the agreements had been reached on the creation of the United Nations, the forming of a four-power administration for occupied Germany, and the Benelux Customs Union—was in the first instance taken up after the end of World War II by representatives and members of the democratic left. They had in mind the Europe of the "Third Force", a united Europe that would be in a position to mediate between the US and the Soviet Union and which would thus strengthen the international community. The advancement of the left in the first postwar elections, and particularly the victory of the British Labour Party on July 25, 1945, made this program seem highly promising. Great Britain, it was hoped, would take the lead in creating such a Europe, combining the advantages of the American and Soviet social systems, avoiding their respective disadvantages, and thus serving as a guiding light for both of them.[31]

Of course, it was primarily the socialist parties that welcomed the notion of the "Third Force" in France and in Germany as well as parts of the Italian socialist camp, the Austrian Socialist Party, and the Dutch Partij van de Arbeid. In Britain, it was the forces of the Labour Party's left wing that signed Richard Crossman's "Keep Left" Manifesto in the spring of 1947. Numerous leftwing Catholics also favored the project, such as the supporters of *Esprit* in France and the *Frankfurter Hefte* in occupied Germany. The new Christian democratic parties adopted the notion at least in part. In Germany, Jakob Kaiser made his mark with the "bridge" concept, primarily emphasizing the mediating function of a united Germany within a close, mutually supportive group intended "to bring all of Europe toward such social forms that allow for a new and lasting understanding."[32]

Reminiscences of "Third Force" notions were also to be found within circles that were less interested in a socialist reorganization of European societies than in a pragmatic kind of self-assertion, prosperity, and use of the remaining chances for strengthening the United Nations. In London, *The Economist* pleaded for the close association of the states of Western Europe, beginning with a free trade zone and common bodies for defense planning, custom politics, and reconstruction, which were to serve as the "core" of the federation of Europe.³³ In France, Raymond Aron suggested that close cooperation between France and Britain would bring Europe closer to what he considered the difficult but at the same time indispensable transcending of the old nation-states in favor of a European order.³⁴ Hubert Beuve-Méry, the publisher of Le Monde, welcomed Britain's apparent loss of power, which he considered the prerequisite for the "hope for the necessarily slow and difficult creation of a third organization in the world, comparable in its importance to the US and the Soviet Union"; "vis-à-vis America and Russia," this organization would need to maintain "equal efforts for understanding and equal independence" from each power.³⁵

At first, however, only a few Europeans welcomed the concept of integrating Western Europe within a Western bloc. Nor could it easily be harmonized with the objectives of preventing another world war or securing the self-determination of as many Europeans as possible; and by the same token, it did not fit the prevailing leftist orientation in domestic politics. It really could be justified only if one accepted that Eastern Europe and the Soviet Zone of Occupation in Germany for the time being were lost to Soviet tyranny. And it was only the fear of the extension of that Soviet tyranny beyond the eastern half of the European continent that made a Western bloc an urgent necessity.

The most prominent spokesman of this Western bloc concept became Winston Churchill, who in the Zurich speech mentioned above called for the creation of "a kind of United States of Europe" that was to defend against the "approach of some new peril, tyranny, or terror." At the core of this united Europe, Churchill envisioned "a partnership between France and Germany." He thought Britain should remain outside the European construct and among the "friends and sponsors of the new Europe." He did, however, also say that "we" (that is, the British) "must proceed to assemble and combine those who will and those who can."³⁶ Following the Zurich speech, Churchill's colleague and son-in-law Duncan Sandys set about creating a "United Europe Movement."³⁷

The response to Churchill's initiative was largely negative, however. A majority of the political forces in Western Europe, as before, did not want to contribute toward anything that might promote the division of the continent into eastern and western halves. Committed federalists, who had banded together at the end of 1946 to form the European Union of Federalists (EUF), were decidedly unwilling to adhere to the Western bloc concept: At their first joint working meeting in Amsterdam from April 12 to 15, 1947, they declared: "What we want is a Europe which shall be an open society, friendly to both East and West, prepared to co-operate with all and capable of incorporating a federal Germany without danger."³⁸

Churchill's notions only became more attractive when Stalin launched a vigorous campaign against the Marshall Plan in the fall of 1947. That campaign did not only strengthen the view in Western Europe that it was impossible to cooperate with the Soviet Union in the foreseeable future, but it also gave impetus to those observers who saw in Soviet policy an aggressive strategy aimed at extending control over the entire continent. Hence, the movement for the unification of Western Europe was given a double boost. Those whose hopes were centered on a mediator role as the Third Force no longer needed to take the Soviet Union into account; at the same time, for many Europeans, a form of unification providing defense against the Soviet menace became a matter of urgency. And, since it followed from the Soviet rejection of the Marshall Plan that only the Western Occupation Zones of Germany would be incorporated into the common reconstruction program, a united Western Europe was now needed more than ever for the integration of the West Germans. Unilateral control of the Germans was incompatible in the long term with the principle of common reconstruction.[39]

While the governments of Western Europe negotiated with one another and with the US about the terms of the Marshall Plan, and the communists in the Western European countries demonstrated against its adoption, the unification of Europe became a matter of public debate even more strongly in the second half of 1947. "Begin in the West" was the slogan of the federalists at their congress at the end of August 1947.[40] Duncan Sandys then gave notice of the convening of a European congress in the following spring at which all the leading politicians of Western Europe were to gather.

When the congress met at The Hague from May 7 to 10, 1948, it turned out to be less representative than Sandys had portrayed. The Labour Party had refused to participate in an undertaking conducted by the Conservative opposition, and the socialists of the continent had showed solidarity with their British comrades by staying away. There was thus no mention of the idea of the "Third Force" in the declarations of the congress. Among the seven hundred participants, there were, however, leading politicians from almost all the countries of Western Europe. The will to unite had clearly been demonstrated, and the governments of Western Europe were unable to ignore it. If one also counts the remaining supporters of the "Third Force" not participating in the Hague congress, one can speak of a clear majority for the Western European union—at least in those countries that later were to form the "Europe of the Six."[41] It was a majority seeking not only safety from the Soviet threat: other important aspects included the integration of Germany, a lasting peace order, at least in Western Europe, economic prosperity, and independence from the US. The European unity movement was indeed based on the experiences of the instability of Versailles and the catastrophes of World War II.

Notes

1. Walter Lipgens and Wilfried Loth (eds.), *Documents on the History of European Integration*, vol. 3.: *The Struggle for European Union by Political Parties and Pressure Groups in Western European Countries 1945–1950*, Berlin and New York: de Gruyter, 1988, pp. 662–66.
2. John Pinder, "Federal Union 1939–1941," in: Walter Lipgens (ed.), *Documents on the History of European Integration*, vol. 2.: *Plans for European Union in Great Britain and in Exile 1939–1945*, Berlin and New York: de Gruyter, 1986, pp. 26–155.

3. Max Beloff, "The Anglo-French Union Project of June 1940," in: Max Beloff, *The Intellectual in Politics and Other Essays*, London: Weidenfeld & Nicolson, 1970, pp. 172–99; Avi Shlaim, "Prelude to Downfall: the British Offer of Union to France, June 1940," *Journal of Contemporary History*, 6 (1974), pp. 27–63; Elisabeth du Réau, "Jean Monnet, le Comité de coordination franco-britannique et le projet d'Union franco-britannique: les moyens de vaincre le nazisme (septembre 1939—juin 1940)," in: Gérard Bossuat and Andreas Wilkens (eds.), *Jean Monnet, l'Europe et les chemins de la Paix*, Paris: Publications de la Sorbonne, 1999, pp. 77–96.
4. Philip M.H. Bell, "Discussion of European Integration in Britain 1942–45," in: Lipgens, *Documents*, vol. 2., pp. 205–67.
5. Léon Blum, *A l'échelle humaine*, Paris, 1945; extracts from the English translation in Lipgens, *Documents*, vol. 1., pp. 278–84, here 281 ff. On the context, see Wilfried Loth, *Sozialismus und Internationalismus: Die französischen Sozialisten und die Nachkriegsordnung Europas 1940–1950*, Stuttgart: Deutsche Verlags-Anstalt, 1977, pp. 23–44; on the postwar planning of the resistance movements in general, see Lipgens, *Documents*, vol. 1.
6. For a general assessment of the results of World War II, see Wilfried Loth, "Weltpolitische Zäsur 1945. Der Zweite Weltkrieg und der Untergang des alten Europa," in: Christoph Kleßmann (ed.), *Nicht nur Hitlers Krieg. Der Zweite Weltkrieg und die Deutschen*, Düsseldorf: Droste, 1989, pp. 99–112.
7. Lipgens, *Documents*, vol. 1.: 471–84, here 474 and 478. Similar argumentation can be found, among other places, in the first memorandum by Helmuth von Moltke of April 24, 1941, ibid., pp. 381–88, and in the manifesto of the French Resistance group "Combat" of September 1942, written by Claude Bourdet, Henri Frenay, and André Hariou, in: ibid, pp. 291–93.
8. Oscau Paul (i.e., Oskar Pollak), *Underground Europe Calling*, London, 1941; a short extract in Lipgens, *Documents*, vol. 2., pp. 636–38.
9. See Klaus Voigt (ed.), *Friedenssicherung und europäische Einigung: Ideen des deutschen Exils 1939–1945*, Frankfurt am Main: Fischer, 1988, pp. 31–124.
10. See Walter Lipgens, "Ideas of the French Resistance on the Postwar International Order," in: Lipgens, *Documents*, vol. 1., 264–361, here pp. 289–91 and p. 346.
11. As formulated in the "Directions on International Politics" adopted in October 1943 by the Organization of German Social Democratic Organizations in Great Britain; Klaus Voigt, *Friedenssicherung*, pp. 105–7. See Rainer Behring, *Demokratische Außenpolitik für Deutschland. Die außenpolitischen Vorstellungen deutscher Sozialdemokraten im Exil 1933–1945*, Düsseldorf: Droste, 1999; Boris Schilmar, *Der Europadiskurs im deutschen Exil 1933–1945*, Munich: Oldenbourg, 2004.
12. Lipgens, *Documents*, vol. 1., p. 283.
13. Claude Bourdet, "Future Allemagne?" *Combat*, no. 55, March 1955, English translation in Lipgens, *Documents*, vol. 1., pp. 342.
14. Carl Goerdeler, "Peace plan late summer–autumn 1943," English translation in Lipgens, *Documents*, vol. 1., pp. 430–32; for the general development, see Lipgens, "Ideas of the German Resistance on the Future of Europe," in: ibid., pp. 332–55.
15. On the postwar planning of exile governments, see Lipgens, *Documents*, vol. 2.
16. Text in *The Times*, November 12, 1942. See Lipgens, "East European Plans for the Future of Europe: The Example of Poland," *Documents*, vol. 1., pp. 609–58; Feliks M. Goss and M. Kamil Dziewanowski, "Plans by Exiles from East European Countries," in Lipgens, *Documents*, vol. 2., pp. 353–413; Feliks Gross, "Views of East European Transnational Groups on the Postwar Order in Europe," ibid., pp. 754–85; Józef Łaptos and Mariusz

Misztal, *American Debates on Central European Union 1942–1944. Documents of the American State Department*, Brussels: P.I.E. Peter Lang, 2002.
17. See José Gotovitch, "Views of the Belgian Resistance on the Future of Europe," in: Lipgens, *Documents*, vol. 1., pp. 215–43; idem, "Views of Belgian Exiles the Postwar Order in Europe," in: Lipgens, *Documents*, vol. 2., pp. 491–554, here pp. 507–9.
18. Presented for the first time in a lecture at Westminster College in Fulton, Missouri in 1941; see Ariane Landuyt, "Ideas of Italian Exiles on the Postwar Order in Europe," in: Lipgens, *Documents*, vol. 2., pp. 491–554, here pp. 507–9.
19. Memorandum of August 4, 1943, quoted in Jean Monnet, *Mémoires*, Paris: Fayard, 1976: 262–64; on the presentation within the committee, see Hervé Alphand, *L'étonnement d'être. Journal 1939–1973*, Paris: Fayard, 1977, p. 168.
20. Text of the circular in René Massigli, *Une comédie des erreurs, 1943–1956*, Paris: Plon, 1978, p.41. See Wilfried Loth, "Die europäische Integration nach dem Zweiten Weltkrieg in französischer Perspektive," Helmut Berding (ed.), *Wirtschaftliche und politische Integration im 19. und 20. Jahrhundert*, Göttingen: Vandenhoeck & Ruprecht, 1984, pp. 225–46, here pp. 227–29, p. 233.
21. See the report by Paul Henri Spaak, *Memoiren eines Europäers*, Hamburg: Hoffmann und Campe, 1969, p. 117. A detailed reconstruction of these talks is still lacking.
22. Charles Eade (ed.), *The War Speeches of the Rt. Hon. Winston S. Churchill*, vol. II, London: Cassell, 1952, pp. 425–37.
23. On this and the following point, see Keith Sainsbury, *The Turning Point. Roosevelt, Stalin, Churchill and Chiang-Kai-Shek, 1943: The Moscow, Cairo and Teheran Conferences*, Oxford: Oxford University Press, 1985.
24. See Harvey A. Notter, *Postwar Foreign Policy Preparation 1939–1945*, General Foreign Policy Series 15, Washington: State Department, 1949; the most important documents are in Walter Lipgens, *Europa-Föderationspläne der Widerstandsbewegungen 1940–1945*, Munich: Oldenbourg, 1968, pp. 417–67.
25. Piotr S. Wandycz, *Czechoslovak-Polish Confederation and the Great Powers 1940–1943*, Bloomington: Indiana University Publications, 1956, pp. 75–88.
26. Gross, *Views of East European Transnational Groups*, p. 759.
27. Frank Donavan, *Mr. Roosevelt's Four Freedoms: The Story behind the UN Charter*, New York: Dodd, Mead, 1966.
28. See Massigli, *Comédie*, p.48; Paul-Henri Spaak, *Memoiren*, pp. 122–25; Albrecht Tyrell, *Großbritannien und die Deutschlandplanung der Alliierten 1941–1945*, Frankfurt am Main: Metzler, 1987, pp. 108–14.
29. Paul-Henri Spaak, *Memoiren*, pp. 128–30.
30. Kersten, Albert E., "Nederland en België in London, 1940–1944. Werken aan de na-oorlogse betrekkingen," *Colloquium over de geschiedenis van de Belgisch-Nederlandse betrekkingen tussen 1815 en 1945. Brussel 10–12/12/1980. Acta*, Ghent: Erasmus, 1982, pp. 495–520; Richard T. Griffith and Frances M.B. Lynch, "L 'échec de la 'Petite Europe': Le Conseil tripartite, 1944–1948," *Guerres Mondiales et conflits contemporains*, no. 152, 1988, pp. 39–62.
31. See Loth, *Sozialismus*, pp.137–75; Jonathan Schneer, "Hopes Deferred or Shattered: The British Labour Left and the Third Force Movement, 1945–49," *Journal of Modern History*, 56 (1984), pp. 197–226; Wilfried Loth, *Der Weg nach Europa: Geschichte der europäischen Integration 1939–1957*, Göttingen: Vandenhoek & Ruprecht, 1990, pp. 28–47; idem, "From the 'Third Force' to the Common Market: Discussions about Europe and the Future of the Nation-State in West Germany, 1945–57," in: Dominik Geppert (ed.), *The Postwar Challenge 1945–1958*, Oxford: Oxford University Press, 2003, pp. 192–209.

32. Speech to the executive board of the CDU in the Eastern Zone, February 13, 1946, quoted in Loth, "Third Force," p. 194.
33. "Western Association–I. New Model in Europe?" *The Economist*, June 2, 1945, pp. 722–24, reprinted in Walter Lipgens and Wilfried Loth (ed), *Documents on the History of European Integration*, vol. 3.: *The Struggle for European Union by Political Parties and Pressure Groups in Western European Countries, 1945–1950*, Berlin and New York: de Gruyter, 1988, pp. 652–56.
34. Raymond Aron, *L'âge des empires et l'avenir de la France*, Paris: Défense de la France, 1945, English extracts in Lipgens and Loth, *Documents*, vol. 3., pp. 31–34.
35. *Le Monde*, July 31, 1945. On September 8, 1945, *Le Monde* stated that the group of Western European states would serve as a "bridge" between East and West.
36. Lipgens and Loth, *Documents*, vol. 3., pp. 663–66. For an analysis, see Walter Lipgens, *A History of European Integration 1945–1947: The Formation of the European Unity Movement*, Oxford: Clarendon Press, 1982, pp. 317–22.
37. Ibid., pp. 332–34.
38. *Federal News*, 147(June 1947), pp.11–13.; see Lipgens, *History*, pp. 361–85.
39. Loth, *Weg nach Europa*, pp. 48–68.
40. Lipgens, *History*, pp. 569–85.
41. See Alan Hick, "The European Movement," in: Walter Lipgens and Wilfried Loth (eds.), *Documents on the History of European Integration*, vol.4.: *Transnational Organizations of Political Parties and Pressure Groups in the Struggle for European Union 1945–1950*, Berlin and New York: de Gruyter, 1990, pp. 319–435, here pp. 333–67.

2
The Failure of EDC and European Integration

Manfred Görtemaker

When, on August 30, 1954, the French National Assembly refused to ratify the treaty on the establishment of a European Defense Community (EDC), the French "veto" was widely interpreted as a fateful setback in the process of European integration. Bitter disappointment mixed with a gloomy outlook to the future. "The European Defense Community has broken down in the face of French opposition," Ludwig Erhard, the German Vice-Chancellor and Minister for Economic Affairs in the German Federal Republic, noted in September 1954: "The integration tide is no longer running high, and we may well ask ourselves whether we shall have to put away any thoughts of European collaboration and consider the spirit of togetherness as dead."[1]

In a more recent analysis of *The Struggle for Europe*, published in 2003, US historian William I. Hitchcock still referred to the failure of EDC as a "fiasco," but added that it "did not squelch new proposals for widened economic integration."[2] Indeed, the "fiasco" of military integration was overcome quickly by West Germany's entry into NATO, and proposals for a customs union between the members of the European Coal and Steel Community (ECSC) provided the basis for structural and institutional economic integration, which eventually led to the creation of the European Economic Community (EEC) in 1958. What seems to have gone largely unnoticed, however, is the fact that the failure of EDC was far less an impediment than a precondition for gradual progress toward a more unified Europe. The crisis of 1954, originally deemed a blow to the idea of Europe, soon turned out to be a wake-up call for those who for several years had adhered to the illusion that a European political and military union could be established overnight. Now, with the rejection of EDC, it became clear that it was imperative to move ahead more slowly and with the care necessary after the experience of two major wars in one generation that had upset the nations of the European continent so much.

The Lessons of War

In fact, the lessons of war can hardly be overstated. If it is correct—and I believe it is—that the idea of European integration emerged long before 1945, even before 1789,[3] but that it took two world wars for the European vision to gain momentum, it seems fair to say that the integration of Europe needed, indeed depended upon, the catalytic force of crises to prosper. Without the two wars and their subsequent economic misery and political unrest, progress might never have been achieved. They provided the fuel that allowed integration to move ahead or, to be more precise, to move at all.

This argument is strongly supported by the events of World War I, seen by many as the "prime catastrophe" of the twentieth century, and the failure of the Paris Treaties of 1919 to ensure peace, when first steps toward European unification were undertaken. The disillusionment with US President Woodrow Wilson's policy of establishing the League of Nations as a global organization to contain conflict through negotiations led Count Richard N. Coudenhove-Kalergi, a citizen of the former Austrian-Hungarian Empire, to believe that the Wilsonian promise of a new order was not being fulfilled and that a European solution was needed to ban the threat of renewed conflict and war.[4]

Even before Coudenhove-Kalergi, the founder of the Italian FIAT Company, Giovanni Agnelli, and the economist Attilio Cabiati rejected the projected League of Nations and argued in favour of a European union with a strong central government. They argued that "without hesitation we believe that, if we really want to make war in Europe a phenomenon which cannot be repeated, there is only one way to do so and we must be outspoken enough to consider it: a federation of European states under a central power which governs them. Any other milder version is but a delusion."[5]

But it was Coudenhove-Kalergi, not Agnelli or Cabiati, who took the initiative by propagating and organizing a movement for the unification of Europe. In 1923, which he felt was "the darkest and most discouraging year ... since the World War,"[6] after French and Belgian troops had occupied the German industrial territories at the Ruhr to enforce their demand of reparation payments agreed upon in the Versailles Treaty, Coudenhove-Kalergi launched the Pan-European Union to promote the cause of European integration. In view of the Ruhr crisis he noticed an increasing "weariness of Europe on the part of America, Asia, Russia and England," and thus proposed a federalist system of European states to achieve what he called "the stabilisation and liberation of the new Europe grown out of the World War."[7]

Hence the legacy of the Great War and the Ruhr crisis contributed to the starting of European integration. French Foreign Minister Aristide Briand and his German colleague Gustav Stresemann were clearly influenced by such ideas when they pushed for reconciliation among their nations and, in 1925, concluded the Locarno Treaty. The following year, the Hungarian economist and member of the International Committee for a European Customs Union, founded in 1924,

Elemér Hantos, outlined a customs union as the most promising road toward integration,[8] while the Bolshevik leader Leon Trotsky pleaded for a "Soviet United States of Europe" as early as in 1924.[9] Yet it was Foreign Minister Briand, the most pro-European of statesmen, who put forward the first proposal by a European government for European Union in 1929. After further study and consultation of twenty-seven European governments, Briand submitted a "Memorandum on the Organization of a Regime of European Federal Union," dated May 17, 1930, in which he argued that "the proposal taken under consideration ... found its justification in the very definite sentiment of a collective responsibility in face of the danger which threatens European peace, from the political as well as the economic and social point of view."[10] Commenting on the memorandum, Edouard Herriot, a former Prime Minister of France, strongly supported Briand's policy in his book *The United States of Europe*, published in 1930.[11]

Yet the idea to stop aggression and the use of force in Europe by weakening, indeed abandoning, the traditional nation-state was soon to be buried by the same forces it sought to eliminate. The rise of Nazism during the 1930s left little, if any, room for the vision of a new Europe dominated by understanding among nations, conflict management and economic evolution. The Nazi concept of German hegemony and a racial restructuring of Europe, including the mass murder of Jews, rather prompted the collapse of the European movement that had developed during the 1920s, despite some consideration that continued to be given to the idea in resistance circles and among several European governments. During World War II, with the decline of Europe and the rise of the United States of America and the Soviet Union to global empires, a "European solution" seemed to become an even more distant perspective.[12]

Rather than extinguishing the European flame, however, the war again spurred support for the European vision, which was believed to be an antidote to the forces of nationalism. Newly inspired by the catastrophe caused by the failure of the system of nation-states, as they saw it, various groups of federalists began to coordinate their activities and eventually, in December 1946, founded the European Union of Federalists (UEF). In preparation for the UEF, at their Hertenstein Conference in September 1946, the federalists left no doubt, however, that their vision of Europe was meant to be an all-European approach, when they rejected a concept put forward by former British Prime Minister Winston Churchill to form a West European bloc against the emerging communist threat in the east. In a speech in Zurich, made at the same time as the Hertenstein meeting, Churchill had demanded that "we must build a kind of United States of Europe," and, as a first step, had proposed to form a "Council of Europe:" "In all this urgent work," Churchill had stated, "France and Germany must take the lead together. Great Britain, the British Commonwealth of Nations, mighty America, and I trust Soviet Russia ... must be the friends and sponsors of the new Europe and must champion its right to live and shine."[13] Naturally such rhetoric, although expressing not the principles of traditional

British balance of power politics but new ideas of European integration, sounded divisive from a federalist point of view, as the policy of the federalists was aimed at unifying the whole of Europe, not just the western part of it. To be sure, within less than a year the world had changed when the beginning of a "Cold War" between East and West made a united Europe unfeasible and forced the UEF to adopt much of Churchill's concept.

The Role of the United States

The second most important element in fostering the idea of European integration, next to the experience of two world wars within one generation, was the pressure exerted by the United States. Until 1945, US President Franklin D. Roosevelt as well as the US Congress had rejected the idea of European federal integration, favouring a universal peacekeeping institution, i.e., the United Nations Organization, instead. Two years later, however, when the wartime cooperation between the United States, Great Britain and the Soviet Union had ended, and Roosevelt's "one world" vision had given way to the reality of a divided world in which Western liberal democracies were confronted with the grim perspective of an ever increasing threat of Soviet-dominated communism under the leadership of Joseph Stalin, the White House and Congress were forced to adjust their position accordingly.

In view of the "Iron Curtain" that was now separating Europe's East from the West, as Winston Churchill had claimed in Fulton, Missouri, in June 1946, America's new President Harry S. Truman gradually acknowledged the fact that postwar Europe was very much in need of American support to resist Soviet pressure. In a speech in Stuttgart on September 3, 1946, US Secretary of State James F. Byrnes therefore called for closer cooperation among the Western occupation zones in Germany, while President Truman himself promulgated the "Truman Doctrine" on March 10, 1947, openly describing the East–West conflict as a struggle between two ways of life, the democratic and the totalitarian. Such views were very much in line with US diplomat George F. Kennan's belief that, due to the very nature of revolutionary communist ideology and expansionist Russian power politics, the wartime coalition that had proven so successful in defeating Nazi Germany could no longer be perpetuated and should therefore be replaced by a policy of "containment."[14] Kennan's basic assessment was shared by the influential journalist Walter Lippmann, who subsequently coined the phrase of a "Cold War" between East and West. Although Lippmann did not hesitate to criticize Kennan's, as he saw it, all too optimistic view that "Soviet power ... bears within itself the seeds of its own decay" and that "Soviet Russia might be changed overnight from one of the strongest to one of the weakest and most pitiable of national societies," he also argued that the Soviet threat could not "be charmed or talked out of existence," but needed to be "confronted with power, primarily American power, that it must respect."[15]

Yet what could realistically be done to counter a possible Soviet advance into Western Europe at this stage? In the spring of 1947, the launching of distinctive American programs, both economic and military, were as easy to demand as they were difficult to achieve; in fact, they seemed rather vague and distant perspectives. The most logical first step, therefore, appeared to be the unification of Europe, as had been proposed by the European movement since the 1920s. Among the first Americans who openly advocated European integration were Senators J. William Fulbright and Elbert D. Thomas. Within two weeks after the promulgation of the Truman Doctrine, on March 21, 1947, they introduced, together with Representative Hale Boggs, concurrent resolutions in the Senate and in the House stating that "Congress favours the creation of a United States of Europe within the framework of the United Nations." The resolutions calling for European "political unification," "economic integration," and "cooperation and unity" passed with a large majority and were widely publicized in the American press.[16] Among the journalists who supported the idea was, of course, Walter Lippmann of the *New York Herald Tribune*.

Thus it was hardly surprising that the European Recovery Program (ERP), which was introduced by Secretary of State George C. Marshall on June 5, 1947, was also based on the assumption that US financial support would depend upon the willingness of the European nations—even if they did not realize it at the beginning—to overcome their historic mutual mistrust and enter a period of cooperation, indeed integration, by collaborating gradually in certain institutions and processes. This "functionalist" approach was reflected in the Organization for European Economic Cooperation (OEEC), formed in 1948, whose policy was guided by the Allied experience gained during the war that "integration, both European and worldwide, might best be achieved not by confronting the rights and privileges of the sovereign states head-on, but by pragmatic and selective integration."[17]

The Economic Cooperation Administration (ECA), which ran the European Recovery Program from Washington, also pressed on Europeans the need for European unification and supranational institutions. In the autumn of 1949, ECA Chairman Paul G. Hoffman literally blackmailed the French to come up with some proposal for European integration by threatening to halt financial aid if his demand was not met by the spring of 1950. In a speech to the OEEC's Council on October 31, 1949, Hoffman urged Europeans to form "a single large market within which quantitative restrictions on the movement of goods, monetary barriers to the flow of payments, and eventually, all tariffs are permanently swept away." In order to build "an expanding economy in Western Europe through economic integration," he suggested adapting existing organizations or creating "new central institutions." This, he said, would greatly improve Europe's competitive position in the world. Heeding the State Department's concerns that public advocacy of detailed American blueprints for European unification might be construed in Europe as an attempt to snatch the initiative away from Europeans, Hoffman refrained, however, from mentioning ECA's plans for a European central bank and a trade commission.[18]

As a result of the American pressure, in a historic declaration at the Quai d'Orsay on May 9, 1950, French Foreign Minister Robert Schuman eventually proposed "the pooling of coal and steel production ... for the setting up of common foundations for economic development as a first step in the federation of Europe."[19] The "Schuman Plan," which led to the creation of the European Coal and Steel Community (ECSC) on April 18, 1951, and marked the beginning of European economic integration as well as, equally important, Franco-German rapprochement, had been conceptualized by Jean Monnet, who then served as general commissary for the French Plan of Modernization and Equipment, and had persuaded Schuman to endorse his proposal.[20] Monnet, however, was by no means an isolated French expert who acted on his own, but he was closely connected with many friends on both sides of the Atlantic, among them Henry A. Byroade at the German Desk in the US State Department and John J. McCloy, then the American High Commissioner in Germany. The influence of such friends could be felt not only in Monnet's concept of the Schuman Plan, but even more in the case of the "Pleven Plan" for a European Defense Community (EDC) a few months later, which was also drafted by Monnet, again in close contact and cooperation with his American counterparts.

For the time being, however, the Schuman Plan set the stage. Since coal and steel production were essential ingredients for building the machines of war and were located mostly in Germany and France, the proposal "that Franco-German production of coal and steel as a whole be placed under a common High Authority, within the framework of an organisation open to the participation of the other countries in Europe," meant that the threat of war would be essentially diminished. "The solidarity in production thus established," Schuman stated, "will make it plain that any war between France and Germany becomes not merely unthinkable, but materially impossible."[21]

All of this happened in the framework of OEEC and in the process of implementing the Marshall Plan. Thus the achievements of the Schuman Plan were prompted not only by the horrors of two world wars, but by American pressure as well. Without such pressure, it seems highly unlikely that the French would have come forward with a proposal that effectively put their arms industry under European, including German, control. Instead, the French would almost certainly have pursued a line similar to the position of the British Cabinet, whose Ministers argued on June 22, 1950, that they "were not ... opposed in principle to some integration of the coal and steel industries of Western Europe. They must, however, reject any proposal for placing these industries under the control of a supranational authority whose decisions would be binding on Governments."[22] Following this approach, the integration of Europe would not have happened—not at the time, to be sure—as the national governments would have retained their right to interfere at any given moment. But this was not what the Americans wanted. In their need for strong allies to counter the Soviet threat, they felt it necessary to promote integration on a more intense level and thus forced the Europeans to unite.

The European Defense Community

On June 25, 1950, North Korean forces invaded South Korea.[23] The outbreak of the Korean War prompted the US administration and Congress to dramatically increase the defense budget and to give priority to rearmament rather than economic prosperity. To US Secretary of State Dean Acheson and to many Europeans, like German Chancellor Konrad Adenauer, the aggression in Korea appeared as a prelude to a communist onslaught on Western Europe. Monnet, recalled George Ball, "was quick to see the implications." The Americans would intervene and "American intervention would not only jeopardize the Schuman Plan, it would create serious problems for European unity. It might well stir up an atmosphere of panic in Europe while increasing American insistence on a larger role for Germany in the defense of the West."[24]

Monnet was right in every respect. On June 30, Truman authorized military intervention in Korea. Four weeks later, the US High Commissioner to Germany, John J. McCloy, declared German rearmament necessary to provide a contribution to Western defense, and Secretary of State Acheson argued that Germany's participation in the defense of Europe must no longer be "secondary but primary." Korea, Acheson said, "speeded up evolution."[25] The question now was no longer whether Germany should be rearmed, but how this could be achieved. Once again it was Jean Monnet who came up with the answer, as he wrote the speech that French Prime Minister René Pleven delivered at the French National Assembly on October 24, 1950, proposing the establishment of an integrated military force in the framework of what was later called the European Defense Community (EDC).[26]

Yet the basic idea of EDC did not originate with Monnet, but was developed in a memorandum entitled "An Approach to the Formation of a European Army," drafted by Henry Byroade at the German Desk of the US State Department. In August 1950, Byroade exchanged several cables on the matter with McCloy in Germany, who then met with Monnet in Monnet's house in Houjarray, some forty kilometers outside Paris, where the eventual framework of the European Defense Community was conceptualized.[27]

Before Pleven could deliver his speech, however, the content of the US proposal was substantially altered in an internal debate in the French government. In particular, the French did not agree with the size and organization of German forces envisaged in the US plan, insisting on a scaling down of German troop levels and command structures. When Pleven eventually presented his concept, President Truman and Secretary of State Acheson reacted with "consternation and dismay," deeming it "hastily conceived without serious military advice and ... unrealistic and undesirable." The Pleven Plan seemed "designed for infinite delay on German participation." The European framework would have to be established first, and there was no timetable for a European military and political structure to be created. Even worse, "the second-class status accorded Germany was all too plain."[28]

This was actually a fair description of the French motives, but there were few alternatives. As early as in the fall of 1950, German membership in NATO and the establishment of a German army sufficiently strong to deter a Soviet attack was not really an option that most Europeans could agree with. Thus a protracted struggle began—first on the formulation of a reasonable EDC treaty, then on ratification. The struggle not only prevented the Europeans from coming to terms with their own military defense; the struggle also diverted the attention for effective European integration.

So, on the one hand, the defeat of the EDC proposals on August 30, 1954, by the French National Assembly came as a great disappointment to supporters of European integration. Among them was Chancellor Adenauer, who called this day "a black day for Europe," as the failure of EDC also involved the rejection of the draft statute for a European Political Community (EPC) and the Bonn Treaty on German sovereignty, which would have effectively ended the Allied occupation regime in the Federal Republic of Germany.[29] On the other hand, one could ask to what extent the French veto made new initiatives in the integration process easier or, to be more precise, to what extent it even helped to pave the way for European economic integration. The answer seems obvious: EDC was the right project at the wrong time. It came either five years too late or fifty years to early. Therefore the failure of EDC created the vacuum necessary for new steps toward integration in non-military fields. With the EDC debate still in progress, it had hardly been practicable to pursue other plans for integration. When the question of a German contribution to the defense of Western Europe was eventually resolved in October 1954 with the signing of the Paris Treaties, which provided for the restoration of German political sovereignty as well as Germany's entry into NATO within the framework of the newly created West European Union (WEU), a major stumbling block to further European integration was finally removed. New initiatives for increased economic integration became feasible again, and surprisingly quickly they turned into reality.

Relance européenne: the Relaunching of Europe

Thus the disappointment over EDC spurred new support for the resumption of the sectoral approach toward European integration. On August 30, 1954, European integrationists had painfully noticed the distance between the continuing reality of national traditions and the much aspired-to goal of political unity. More than most other Europeans, the officials and parliamentarians in European institutions felt in their daily work the frustration stemming from deficits in the integration process. Therefore, as early as in September 1954, the President of the High Authority of the European Coal and Steel Community (ECSC), Jean Monnet, and the Belgian Foreign Minister Paul-Henri Spaak proposed an extension of the authority of the ECSC to pursue integration in "limited but decisive fields."[30] In December, a Special Commission was established by the Common Assembly of the ECSC to study how this could be done.

In the Commission, the Belgians and the Dutch quickly took the lead. Yet there were considerable differences of opinion. While the Belgians argued that specific sectors of the economy should be covered, mainly transportation and energy sources, such as gas, electricity, and the atom, the Dutch favoured overall economic integration instead. Most prominently, the Dutch Foreign Minister Jan Willem Beyen did not believe in the sectoral or functional approach. During the negotiations over the European Political Community in 1953, Beyen had already presented a plan for a General Common Market, which eventually became part of the EPC and was rejected by the French National Assembly alongside EDC. Now, in early April 1955, in a letter to Spaak, Beyen renewed his criticism of the sectoral approach, arguing that it had "the tendency to solve problems in one sector to the detriment of other sectors or the interests of consumers." In addition, sectoral integration would only "lead to the exclusion of foreign competition." Therefore the best avenue of integration was, he maintained, "to create a supranational community with the task of bringing about the economic integration of Europe in the general sense, reaching economic union by going through a customs union as a first stage."[31]

The differences about how to proceed with European integration were also reflected in the policy of France and Germany, and even within the ECSC itself. France, with a long tradition of protectionism and afraid of open competition with the more dynamic German economy, strongly supported the limited Belgian approach, while Germany, with an economy largely oriented toward exports, favoured wider trade liberalization over the sectoral approach. German Economics Minister Ludwig Erhard in particular, a classical "free-trader," strongly urged his European colleagues not to confine economic integration to those countries willing to participate in narrow institutional arrangements. However, Erhard was opposed by the German Vice-President at the High Authority of the ECSC and then Adenauer's most likely successor as Chancellor, Franz Etzel, as well as Walter Hallstein, State Secretary at the German Foreign Office. Both Etzel and Hallstein strongly believed in institution-building as the best way to continue with European unification. Within the ECSC, the President of the High Authority, Jean Monnet, also gave priority to the continuation, or resumption, of the sectoral approach over integration. Since atomic energy seemed by far the most promising area for integration, he felt that it might be a good idea to form a separate organization (Euratom) for the development of a European atomic energy industry, which then might become a catalyst of the European idea.[32]

Beyen disagreed. On April 21, 1955, he made his plan for a Common Market public and thus forced Spaak, who until then had been "somewhat fearful of such an ambitious scheme," to follow suit.[33] Two weeks later, on May 5, 1955, a joint memorandum of the three Benelux countries, which blended the Dutch and Belgian ideas, combining the sectoral and common market approaches, was presented to Monnet by Spaak, Beyen, and the Prime Minister of Luxembourg, Joseph Bech. The paper outlined a coherent strategy for Europe's future: above all, it asked for further economic integration through common institutions. A series of sectoral initiatives in the field of transportation and energy, with special emphasis on the formation of an atomic community, would be complemented by first steps toward a Common Market. An ever closer economic cooperation, the memorandum concluded, would be the engine and pioneer of subsequent political unification.[34]

The move of the Benelux countries was publicly welcomed by Monnet who told the ECSC Assembly on May 9 that he viewed the sectoral and the overall approaches as "equally valid" and "mutually non-exclusive."[35] On May 14 the Assembly unanimously adopted a resolution asking the foreign ministers of the six ECSC nations to establish an intergovernmental committee to develop and formulate concrete steps for further integration on the basis of the Benelux memorandum.[36] This was done at a special meeting of the ECSC Council of Ministers at Messina on June 2–3, 1955, under the chairmanship of Joseph Bech. The committee, later to be headed by Spaak, was charged with a report that would look into the viability of both a common market, including a unifying customs policy by setting a common external tariff rate, and an atomic energy agency to coordinate nuclear research and development and establish a common market for fissionable materials.

The weekend meeting at Messina, a small provincial town at the northeastern tip of Sicily, was almost entirely overlooked by the world's media. The success of the meeting, Peter Stirk and David Weigall have stated quite correctly, took everyone by surprise, not least the foreign ministers of the Six who took part.[37] In fact, "Messina produced no sharp electric shock signalling a new determination to resume the process of uniting Europe."[38] But such a *relance européenne* was exactly what happened when the Spaak committee and various subcommittees met at the Chateau de Val Duchesse outside Brussels in the following months to explore possible avenues of economic integration. Of course, there was, as always, a time of crisis, when technical difficulties mounted and made the formulation of a single plan questionable. Yet, with the assistance of a small group of experts, among them the German diplomat Hans von der Groeben and Pierre Uri, one of the closest collaborators of Jean Monnet, a report was eventually produced in the spring of 1956, which contained the essence of the European Economic Community (EEC) and Euratom, and was then used as a basis for negotiating the Rome Treaties. "The object of a European common market," the report stated, "should be to create a vast area with a common political economy which will form a powerful productive unit and permit a steady expansion, an increase in stability, a more rapid rise in the standard of living, and the development of harmonious relations between the Member States."[39] The report was accepted by the foreign ministers of the Six in May 1956 in Venice, and the Spaak committee was asked to draw up formal treaties.

In essence, the Spaak report advocated two major goals:

1. Functional integration in the field of atomic energy, which was seen as the most promising area of transnational cooperation, while oil, electricity, gas, and transportation were regarded as less important.

2. The creation of a customs union with a common external tariff—as opposed to the realization of a free trade area—as a first step toward overall economic integration.

This compromise, combining functional and institutional integration with the eventual goal of a common market, hardly mirrored the difficult circumstances under which it was reached. Crises occurred on several levels and in different countries. In Germany, Economics Minister Erhard, favouring free trade over integration, was as strong an opponent as many others in the Federal Republic who were concerned with the prospect of deepening German division in the case of increased West European integration. In France, most officials as well as the public rejected the idea of a customs union, let alone a common market, as they still feared the strong German economy and global competition; only Foreign Minister Christian Pineau and Prime Minister Guy Mollet were "favourably disposed" toward the proposals of the Spaak report.[40] The British were even more negative. Russel Bretherton, a Board of Trade official, who served as an "observer" on the Spaak committee, opposed every single aspect of the envisaged economic integration and soon left the committee with his famous parting words, which made quite plain his, and the British, disgust about the talks and their intentions:

> The future treaty which you are discussing has no chance of being agreed; if it was agreed, it would have no chance of being ratified; and if it were ratified, it would have no chance of being applied. And if it was applied, it would be totally unacceptable to Britain. You speak of agriculture, which we don't like, of power over customs, which we take exception to, and of institutions which frighten us ... au revoir and bonne chance.[41]

Germany and France, however, unlike the British, continued to work with the Spaak committee, despite many reservations. In the French case, it was mainly Euratom, not the common market, which kept France in the negotiations. In June 1956, Spaak was told by the French that "the signature of Euratom is the only means of then bringing about ratification of the common market by the parliament." For France, the access to atomic energy, and eventually the development of an atomic bomb, actually appeared to be "the right of entry into the club of great powers."[42] Therefore the French Government left no doubt that France reserved for itself the right to develop nuclear weapons, and the only question was how European dependence upon the United States for supplies of uranium could be reduced. The proposed European Atomic Energy Community, which also provided for joint financing of an isotope separator for enriching uranium, could be a possible answer. This was crucial to winning over the National Assembly in the vote of July 1956, which allowed the French government to proceed not only with the negotiations on Euratom but also with the talks on the common market.[43]

The German case was different, almost the adverse of that of French. Above all, there was fear of a French attempt to bring the German nuclear energy industry under French control. Monitoring the development of the German atomic industry was in fact one of the reasons why France insisted upon Euratom's ownership of fissile material. This was not what the Germans wanted. They strongly resisted any priority on Euratom over economic integration and insisted, as did indeed most other West European countries, upon linkage between the two treaties, suspecting that if France obtained agreement on Euratom it would allow the negotiations on the common market to stagnate.[44] In addition, the German Minister for Atomic Energy, Franz Josef Strauss, fought very hard to keep the ownership of fissile material private in order to prevent any French attempt to control, via Euratom, German industry.[45]

Eventually, the treaty establishing the European Economic Community turned out to be significantly more important than the treaty on the formation of the European Atomic Energy Community, both signed on March 25, 1957, in Rome. Spaak's careful but decisive guidance had shifted the negotiations in the direction of a common market, prescribing above all a customs union between the six member states, i.e., the elimination of customs duties and of quantitative restrictions in regard to the importation and exportation of goods between member states, and a step-by-step introduction of a common external tariff vis-à-vis all nonmember states. In addition, the treaty envisaged the inauguration of a common agricultural policy, a common transport policy, the abolition of the obstacles to the free movement of persons, services and capital between the member states, and the establishment of a system ensuring that competition should not be distorted in the common market. The institutions of the community, mainly the Council of Ministers and the European Commission, were charged with the application of procedures that would make it possible to achieve a balance in the economic and financial development of the members states and to create a European Social Fund in order to harmonize the standard of living throughout the community, while a European Investment Bank would facilitate the economic expansion of the community through the creation of new resources.[46]

The carefully worded 248 articles of the EEC treaty, which went into effect after ratification on January 1, 1958, were obviously designed to allow an evolution of the European Economic Community with an uncertain goal, but most likely a political union or, eventually, maybe even a "United States of Europe." In the treaty itself, however, there was no clear definition of any goal. Article 2 only stated: "It shall be the aim of the Community, by establishing a Common Market and progressively approximating the economic policies of Member States, to promote throughout the Community a harmonious development of economic activities, a continuous and balanced expansion, an increased stability, an accelerated raising of the standard of living and closer relations between its Member States." Only the preamble expressed the will to "establish the foundation of an ever closer union of the peoples of Europe."[47]

Britain and the Free Trade Area

Yet, even without a clear definition of its eventual goal, the formation of the European Economic Community put pressure on those who had excluded themselves, above all Great Britain. The British counterproposal of a Free Trade Area (FTA), initially presented as a "complement" to the Benelux initiative and tabled at the meeting of the ECSC Council of Ministers in Messina in June 1955, appeared to be too weak on integration and was therefore rejected by most "Europeans" in the ECSC. It was limited to the industrial sector, it did not include agriculture, and tariffs would only be progressively limited over a ten-year period within the FTA, but would not be affected in regard to the rest of the world, which would continue to be subject to GATT commitments. When the talks on the EEC were about to be concluded in February 1957, the British Government once again put forward its FTA proposal, but at the same time made clear why Britain could not join a European Customs and Economic Union, referring mainly to "the United Kingdom's interests and responsibilities in the Commonwealth."[48]

Among the Six, France took the lead in opposing the FTA concept. In 1958, Foreign Minister Maurice Couve de Murville summed up the French attitude in an interview with the BBC's Michael Charlton:

> We believed that the good direction was the Common Market and not the Free Trade Area. I would say, philosophically, because the Common Market was more in our tradition than Free Trade. France has never been a free-trade country, and it believes more in organisation. The Common Market was not only free trade for industrial production but also a future agriculture common policy; and that's a thing to which we were very much attached, for the reason simply that agricultural production is important in our country. So we could not accept the British idea. We accepted the Common Market, and inevitably a sort of conflict was to appear between Britain and the Common Market countries.[49]

By now, virtually all "Europeans" throughout the Six, notably the first Commission President, Walter Hallstein, and Monnet's Action Committee, had turned against the British FTA plans, fearing that an extension of the Free Trade Area to all of Western Europe would destroy the cohesion of the common market. Consequently, there was no longer any chance for Britain to expand the Free Trade Area into EEC territory. Thus the British Government narrowed its objectives and formed a smaller industrial FTA in April 1958—the European Free Trade Association (EFTA)—encompassing the Scandinavian states, Britain, Austria, Portugal, and Switzerland, later also Iceland and, as an associate member, Finland.[50] Thus Europe was divided a second time after 1945. The Cold War between East and West was now complemented by a trade rift between EFTA, i.e., Britain, and the EEC. A new crisis developed that would overshadow European politics for more than a decade to come, with French President Charles de Gaulle at center-stage. But that is another story.

Conclusions

To make a long argument short, it can be assumed that only the failure of EDC created the necessary leeway to proceed with economic integration in Europe, moving slowly and gradually from a sectoral approach to the idea of a common market and, eventually, political union. In fact, crises and catastrophes have always played a role in the development of European integration. Without the impact of two world wars the impetus for integration would not have existed, and without the pressure exerted by the United States in view of the Soviet threat during the Cold War progress would not have been achieved. As a matter of fact, the Schuman Plan was a direct result of US demands, while EDC was caused, more indirectly but clearly, by the communist aggression in Korea. Yet only the rejection of the EDC Treaty in the French National Assembly on August 30, 1954, and the crisis that ensued from the French veto provided the "shock" necessary to launch a new initiative in European integration that eventually led to EEC and Euratom. Crises, in other words, turned out to be the most significant catalysts of change in the history of European unification. They certainly played this role in the early stages of European integration after World War II, and there is every reason to believe that the future will not be much different from the past.

Notes

1. Ludwig Erhard, *The Economics of Success*, London: Thames & Hudson, 1963, p. 155.
2. William I. Hitchcock, *The Struggle for Europe: The Turbulent History of a Divided Continent, 1945–2002*, New York: Doubleday, 2003, p. 154.
3. For a general overview see Peter Krüger, *Das unberechenbare Europa: Epochen des Integrationsprozesses vom späten 18. Jahrhundert bis zur Europäischen Union*, Stuttgart: Kohlhammer, 2006, pp. 19–34. See also Michael Gehler, *Europa: Ideen, Institutionen, Vereinigung*, Munich: Olzog, 2005, pp. 72–79. Among others, Gehler refers to William Penn's "Essay toward the Present and Future Peace of Europe" of 1693, proposing a "European Reichstag" or federal parliament with a European army and the right to majority rule, and to Abbé Charles Irenée de Saint-Pierre's "Projet pour rendre la paix perpétuelle en Europe" of 1712–13, aimed at establishing a "European Senate," a permanent assembly with delegates sent from all European sovereigns, and a common European legal system in the Roman tradition.
4. See Richard N. Coudenhove-Kalergi, *Pan-Europe*, New York: Alfred Knopf, 1926. The book was first published in German in 1923.
5. Giovanni Agnelli and Attilio Cabiati, *Federazione europea o lega delle nazioni?* Turin: Fratelli Bocca, 1918. Quoted in *The Federalist*, 31 (1989), p. 71.
6. Richard N. Coudenhove-Kalergi, "Three years of Pan-Europe. Supplement," in: Coudenhove-Kalergi, *Pan-Europe*, p. 197.
7. Ibid.
8. Elemér Hantos, "Der Europäische Zollverein," *Weltwirtschaftliches Archiv*, 23 (1926), pp. 229–38.
9. Leon Trotsky, "The Premises for the Proletarian Revolution" (1924), quoted in *Europe and America: Two Speeches on Imperialism*, New York: Pathfinder, 1971, p. 30.

10. Aristide Briand, "Memorandum on the Organisation of a Regime of Federal Union," *International Conciliation*, Special Bulletin June (1930), pp. 327–53.
11. Edouard Herriot, *The United States of Europe*, London: Harrop, 1930, pp. 286–87.
12. See, as an example of this skepticism, the *Ventotene Manifesto* by Altiero Spinelli and Ernesto Rossi, formulated in August 1941: "Germany's defeat would not automatically lead to the reorientation of Europe in accordance with our ideal of civilisation ... Most probably, the British leaders, perhaps in agreement with the Americans, will try to restore the balance-of-power politics, in the apparent immediate interests of their empires," Altiero Spinelli and Ernesto Rossi, *The Ventotene Manifesto*, London: Altiero Spinelli Institute, (1941), pp. 385–86.
13. Winston Churchill, "Speech to the Academic Youth," Zurich, September 19, 1946, quoted in: A. Boyd and F. Boyd, *Western Union*, London: Hutchinson, 1948, pp. 141–42, online at http://www.europa-web.de/europa/02wwswww/202histo/churchil.htm (last visited August 1, 2006).
14. "Mr. X," The Sources of Soviet Conduct, *Foreign Affairs*, XXXV, No. 4 (July 1947), pp. 566–82. Reprinted in: George F. Kennan, *American Diplomacy 1900–1950*, Chicago and London: The University of Chicago Press, 1951, pp. 107–28.
15. Walter Lippmann's criticism first appeared in a series of articles that appeared in the *New York Herald Tribune* in 1947 and was then republished in full under the title, *The Cold War: A Study in U.S. Foreign Policy*, New York: Harper & Brothers, 1947.
16. 62 Statutes 137, Title I, U.S., Congress, House, Congressional Record, 80th Cong., 2nd sess., 1948, pp. 3645–46. See also Pascaline Winand, *Eisenhower, Kennedy, and the United States of Europe*, Houndmills and London: Macmillan, 1993, p. 20.
17. David Weigall and Peter M.R. Stirk (eds.), *The Origins and Development of the European Community*, Leicester and London: Leicester University Press, 1992, pp. 23–24.
18. Winand, *Eisenhower*, pp. 20–21.
19. Robert Schuman, Declaration of May 9, 1950, quoted in: Pascal Fontaine, *Europe—A Fresh Start: The Schuman Declaration 1950–90*, Luxembourg: Commission of European Communities, 1990, pp. 44–46.
20. Jean Monnet, *Memoirs*, New York: Doubleday, 1978. See also Jean Monnet, *Amérique—Europe: Relations de Partenaires Nécessaires à la Paix*, Lausanne: Fondation Jean Monnet, 1963, and Jean Monnet, *Les États-Unis d'Europe ont Commencé*, Paris: R. Laffont, 1955.
21. English version of the Schuman Plan in *Documents on American Foreign Relations*, vol. 12., Princeton: Princeton University Press, 1951, p. 85.
22. Extract from the conclusions of a meeting of the British Cabinet, June 22, 1950, quoted in: R. Bullen and M. Pelly (eds.), *Documents on British Policy Overseas*, series 2, vol. 1., London: HMSO, 1986, p. 210–13.
23. For details, based on new sources, see William Stueck, *Rethinking the Korean War: A New Diplomatic and Strategic History*, Princeton, NJ: Princeton University Press, 2002. For a most comprehensive analysis of various aspects, see Spencer C. Tucker (ed.), *Encyclopedia of the Korean War: A Political, Social, and Military History*, 3 vols., Santa Barbara, CA: Abc-Clio, 2000. See also Rolf Steininger, *Der vergessene Krieg: Korea, 1950–1953*, Munich: Olzog, 2006, pp. 29–40.
24. George Ball, *The Discipline of Power*, Boston: Little, Brown, 1968, p. 49.
25. Dean Acheson, *Present at the Creation*, New York: W.W. Norton, 1969, p. 132.
26. See "The Pleven Plan for a European Defense Community (EDC), 24 October 1950," in: D. Patijn (ed.), *Landmarks in European Unity*, Leiden: Europa Institute, 1970, pp. 73–85.
27. See John J. McCloy, Telegram No. 962 for Acheson and Byroade, August 3, 1950, in: Record Group 466, Top Secret General Records, Box No. 2, File August 1950, John J.

McCloy Papers, National Archives; Henry A. Byroade, Telegram No. 943 (Eyes Only for McCloy), August 4, 1950, ibid. The files reveal that Secretary of State Acheson was fully informed about Byroade's initiative, which he obviously approved.
28. Dean Acheson, *The Struggle for a Free Europe*, New York: W.W. Norton, 1971, pp. 142–43; FRUS 1951, vol. 3., part 1, 1981, Circular Telegram, The Secretary of State to Certain Diplomatic Offices, Washington, January 29, 1951, pp. 760–62.
29. Konrad Adenauer, *Erinnerungen 1953–1955*, Stuttgart: Deutsche Verlags-Anstalt, 1966, p. 289.
30. Pascal Fontaine, *Le Comité d'Action pour les Etats-Unis d'Europe de Jean Monnet*, Lausanne: Center de recherche européennes, 1974, p. 27.
31. Ibid., pp. 29–39. See also Pierre Gerbet, *La Construction de l'Europe*, Paris: Notre Siècle, 1983, p. 197.
32. Peter M.R. Stirk and David Weigall (eds.), *The Origins and Development of European Integration: A Reader and Commentary*, London and New York: Pinter, 1999, p. 125.
33. Winand, *Eisenhower, Kennedy, and the United States of Europe*, p. 73.
34. See Curt Gasteyger, *Europa zwischen Spaltung und Einigung 1945–1990*, Cologne: Verlag Wissenschaft und Politik, 1990, p. 151.
35. Gerbet, *La Construction de l'Europe*, p. 198.
36. Winand, *Eisenhower*, p. 73.
37. Stirk and Weigall (eds.), *The Origins and Development of European Integration*, p. 126.
38. William Diebold Jr., *The Schuman Plan: A Study in Economic Cooperation, 1950–1959*, New York: Praeger, 1959, p. 664.
39. Quoted in Walter Lipgens (ed.), *45 Jahre Ringen um die Europäische Verfassung: Dokumente 1939–1984. Von den Schriften der Widerstandsbewegung bis zum Vertragsentwurf des Europäischen Parlaments*, Bonn: Europa-Union Verlag, 1986, p. 391.
40. Stirk and Weigall, *The Origins and Development of European Integration*, p. 127. See also Robert Marjòlin, *Architect of European Unity: Memoirs 1911–1986*, London: Weidenfeld and Nicolson, 1989, p. 285.
41. Quoted in Percy Cradock, *In Pursuit of British Interests: Reflections on Foreign Policy under Margaret Thatcher and John Major*, London: John Murray, 1997, p. 122.
42. *Documents diplomatiques français: Depuis 1954*, vol. 1, Brussels: Peter Lang, 2005, doc. 308.
43. Stirk and Weigall (eds.), *The Origins and Development of European Integration*, p. 128.
44. Ibid., p. 128. See also Hanns Jürgen Küsters, "Walter Hallstein und die Verhandlungen über die Römischen Verträge 1955–1957," in: Wilfried Loth, William Wallace and Wolfgang Wessels (eds.), *Walter Hallstein: Der vergessene Europäer?* Bonn: Europa-Union Verlag, 1995, pp. 91–97.
45. Stirk and Weigall (eds.), *The Origins and Development of European Integration*, p. 128.
46. "The Treaty of Rome Establishing the European Economic Community, March 25, 1957," in: *Common Market Law: Text and Commentaries*, London: Stevens and Sons, 1962, pp. 206–303.
47. Ibid., p. 206.
48. *British Memorandum to the Organization for European Economic Co-operation regarding a European Free Trade Area, 7 February 1957*, London: HMSO, 1957, pp. 433–36.
49. Quoted in Michael Charlton, *The Price of Victory*, London: British Broadcasting Corporation, 1983, p. 226.
50. Stirk and Weigall (eds.), *The Origins and Development of European Integration*, p. 129.

3

The Institutional Paradox: How Crises Have Reinforced European Integration

Jürgen Elvert

On June 17, 2005, a visibly deeply disappointed President of the European Council, Jean Claude Juncker, commented on the failure of the Brussels summit in the following words: "Europe is not in a state of crisis, it's in a state of profound crisis."[1] To a certain extent Juncker's statement was the answer to an analysis which the then German Foreign Minister Fischer had given a fortnight earlier, in a speech at the American Academy in Berlin, saying that Europe was, with regard to the failed European constitutional referendums in France and the Netherlands, in a difficult situation but certainly not in a crisis.[2] The worldwide media echo on Juncker's statement, which was backed by other comments given by the then German Chancellor Schröder and the French President Chirac, gave the impression of reporting on something new. Juncker had not at all told a secret. In fact, the summit crisis of June 2005 only marked, for the time being, the peak of a series of critical events in that year, which, for the European integration process, would turn out to be another *annus horribilis*. Subsequently, the number of scholarly analyses—of greater or lesser lucidity—on the critical state of the Union mushroomed all over Europe,[3] and in March 2006 a famous Internet search machine fed with the phrase "European Union in Crisis" counted a total of 50,200,000 hits within 0.30 seconds.

A Profound Crisis

Thus, currently the European Union is indeed facing a serious crisis, which finds expression not only in the probable failure of the constitutional treaty as a consequence of the French and Dutch referendums but also in the obvious disorientation among members of the political caste in the Union's member states on the future direction of the integration process, and, thirdly, in drastically shrinking public support for the European project in many member states. A Eurobarometer survey of July 2005 produced devastating results: only 46 percent of all EU citizens expressed their confidence in the EU Commission, only 52 percent in the European Parliament. The results for Germany were even worse: in July 2005 only 37 percent of the Germans expressed their trust in the EU Commission, 46 percent in the European Parliament. These figures made the formerly determinedly Europhile Germans the nation with the lowest degree of confidence in European institutions within the whole EU apart from the British.[4] This is not the place to discuss in detail the reasons for this drastic forfeit of support for the EU from its own citizens. It must be stated, however, that the future of the European project in general is currently at stake—"Nationalism has Now become the Enemy of Europe's Nations" was the headline of an article by Anthony Giddens and Ulrich Beck, in which the authors openly discussed the possibility of an abolished EU—as a kind of worst case scenario and by way of caution, it must be added.[5]

Much has been said so far about the current crisis of the EU without a clear definition of the word. Originally, "crisis" as a technical term is related to medicine, meaning a "malfunction" or a "critical period" and identifying a turning point, from which the patient's condition will either improve or drastically deteriorate. Therefore, a crisis must be considered a very decisive moment, not only in a patient's life, but, generally spoken, for institutions, too.[6] On this background, the word "crisis" is used in this chapter to identify "a severe or existential crisis," threatening the EEC's, EC's or EU's very existence. With regard to the aforesaid we must separate these existential crises from all those well-known but only putative critical situations of the 1970s, 1980s and 1990s, when, especially during summits, certain delicate or even difficult matters required night-long negotiations, only to be solved by compromise. Apart from a few exceptions, these summits were not running the risk to either find a way out of the crisis or to threaten the very existence of the European Community or Union. For that reason certain collectively remembered crises will have to be debunked as mere critical situations without being an existential threat for European integration. From this point of view, the number of real existential crises seems to be manageable. And there can be no doubt, too: the current constitutional crisis is among them.

The general outline of this book indicates the idea that crises, especially existential crises can, against the background of historical experience, be seen as a kind of propulsion for the integration process, a motive power that has generated the energy that was needed to set forward the European integration process. From this angle the depth of a crisis can be taken as a gauge for the integration dynamic: the deeper the crisis, the more dynamic the integration process. As a matter of fact, there seems indeed to be some circumstantial evidence to support this assumption—the failure of the Pleven Plan and the European Defense Community (EDC), which led to the *relance européenne* and thus to the Treaties of Rome, the failure of the Fouchet Plans growing into the Elysée Treaty as the centerpiece of the future French–German motor in particular and deeper political cooperation among the member states in general, the Euro-sclerosis of the 1970s paving the way to the Single European Act and the Maastricht Treaty. The latter was the starting point for the ratification crisis, again producing enough energy not only to digest the third enlargement but to prepare the ground for the fourth enlargement and the constitutional treaty itself. All told, the integration process appears like a sometimes painful but generally purposeful process, which will one day flow into a fully united and integrated Europe, a Nirvana for Europhiles and hell for Euro-skeptics—in spite of all crises, which only seem to be a threat for the very existence of integrated Europe, but in fact are only expressions of its integrative dynamics.

However, history tells us that this perception of the integration process is only an intellectual construction, being the result of the—at least from the scholarly point of view—relative short-livedness of the probe. Thus, the idea that crises reinforced integration should better be considered a rather provocative working hypothesis. It must be tested whether or not this hypothesis is justified. This test run will be as follows. In a first step the integration process from the foundation of the Coal ands Steel Community to the present day must be divided into shorter periods of topical coherence. Secondly, it must be tested whether either our collective memory or scholarly research is associating crises with these periods. Thirdly, it must be checked whether these crises were existential crises in the strict sense of the word, or if they simply were critical situations in the course of certain decision-finding processes or not crises at all. Fourthly, it must be controlled whether a direct impact of the crises on the integration process can be detected. And, fifthly it must be either verified or rejected that the crisis under consideration was the sole impact factor on the reinforcement of integration dynamics or whether or not this reinforcement depended on certain additional factors to come into effect.

Step One: Three Phases of the European Integration Process

This chapter suggests a tripartite division of the European integration process from 1952 to the present day. The first phase is identified as the "phase of implementation," extending from the ECSC's foundation in 1952 to the consummation of the first enlargement in 1973. The second "phase of reconciliation" ranges from 1973 to the consummation of the Treaty of Maastricht in 1993, and the third "phase of Europeanization" covers the period from 1993 to the present day.[7]

The "phase of implementation" (1952–73) is earmarked by the conveyance of certain sovereign rights of a group of Western European democracies to a supranational institution. Although all Western and Northern European democracies had been invited to participate, some of them preferred self-exclusion for domestic or external reasons. The readiness to reduce national sovereignty in favour of a supranational institution was generated by a general consensus among the participants of the ECSC scheme that only an integrated Europe would be able to overcome the previous cleavages caused by nineteenth century nationalism and would safeguard the participants' security interests against Germany and thus help to solve the German problem. During the "phase of implementation" all major decisions on the direction and components of the integration process had been made. This refers to the supranational character of the European institutions as well as to the principle that an increasingly integrated economy should pave the way to a deepened political cooperation among the participating states. From its very beginnings this phase is also characterized by an internal dispute about the *finalité politique* of integrated Europe. When there was an early majority among Euro-politicians in favour of a federalist finality, counterbalanced by intense French intervention in favour of a confederate or intergovernmental *finalité*, the first enlargement, especially British and Danish accession to the EC, backed the confederate side, thus helping to leave the question of the *finalité politique* open. Therewith the groundwork of the Maastricht Treaty of 1992 was laid out, giving the EU its actual "in-between shape" with certain supranational and certain intergovernmental elements. Another decisive element of this phase with a strong forwardly directed dimension was the EC Commission's decision to rule out membership of nondemocratic states in spite of the opposed insistence of certain individual member states. There can be no doubt that the exclusion of authoritarian states from the integration process put pressure on the authoritarian governments in Greece, Portugal, and Spain, thus contributing at least to a certain extent to their final collapse in the 1970s. After all, in the context of negotiations on the first EC enlargement, the participants agreed on a procedure that would show the way forward to all subsequent enlargements by setting up the rules for the applicants, who had to accept the *acquis communautaire* in total to safeguard the state of integration subsequent to the referring accessions. The rules had been introduced by the original six at the Hague summit of 1969 to safeguard the original integrative consensus and had been accepted by the acceding states as a prerequisite for taking up negotiations although they did not inevitably share the original consensus.

The "phase of reconciliation" (1973–93) is characterized on the one hand by the attempts to realize the decisions of the Hague summit referring to the maintenance of the general integrative consensus against the background of the forthcoming and all subsequent enlargements. The line of thought was easily laid out: the potentially negative side effects of the widening of the Community should be absorbed by a deepening of its institutional structures. The institutional deepening was to be realized by a three-track approach: the extension of European institutional competences in combination with an improved apparatus for political cooperation and the completion of the Economic and Monetary Union. On the other hand this phase witnesses the conversion of the formerly authoritarian political systems in Greece, Portugal, and Spain into democracies of

Western quality. The modernization of these states and its societies was to a significant extend initiated and moderated by European Social Democrats, who thus helped to integrate Western European Social Democracy into the European project and thus to overcome the long-lasting cliché presenting the integration process as a primarily capitalist, Catholic, and conservative venture. And thirdly global reconciliation must be mentioned here as well, putting an end to the systemic conflict. Therefore, reconciliation is detectable in at least four contexts: the context of deepening the EC's structures, the context of broadening political support for the integration process, the context of modernizing formerly authoritarian states, and the context of global détente. The stages of this phase are easily detectable: the monetary policy in the 1970s, the Greek, Portuguese, and Spanish accession in 1981 and 1986, the Single European Act of 1987, which prepared the Treaty of Maastricht of 1993, German reunification in 1990 and the collapse of the Soviet Union in 1991, marking the end of the post-World War II setting, which had been established in the late 1940s and which had stimulated the formulation of the general integrative consensus as one of the impulsive forces of European integration.

The "phase of Europeanization" (since 1993) is characterized by a significant fusion of national and European politics, which did not replace the traditional nation state by a European federation but has created a mixture of national and European resources, competences, and responsibilities, set up in a multilevel system of growing complexity and opacity.[8] This is my understanding of the word "Europeanization," notwithstanding other definitions and usages. While my approach to the word relies to a large extent on Wolfgang Wessels's thought, other possible definitions were pointed out by Kevin Featherstone. He was able to show that "Europeanization" as a technical term has, to a large extent, only been in use since the early 1990s. With regard to the usage of the word he also set up a catalogue of eight different headings for "Europeanization," ranging from the identification of historical processes to the impact of foreign relations as a Europeanizing factor within the European Union.[9] Taking the fusion of national and European competences as one characteristic for the phase of Europeanization, a further differentiation of the Maastricht Treaty can be taken as another. A third characteristic of this phase is the third enlargement, which completed the Western European integration by the accession of those states that had previously preferred self-exclusion due to their policy of nonalignment during the Cold War. Their accession in combination with a certain "Euro-phoria" after pulling aside the Iron Curtain cleared the way for a third characteristic feature of EU's Europeanization. EU membership had been regarded as highly attractive for the newly established democracies in Central and Eastern Europe in the early 1990s for several reasons. Their governments considered the EU a new point of reference after several decades of predominant Soviet influence: EU membership thus became a benchmark for the countries' Westernness in general and Europeanness in particular. Expected economic benefits under the auspices of, for examples, the European cohesion fund were another incentive to apply for accession. A third one was the expected help for the modernization and transformation of the applicants' societies. These and other expectations had been nourished from the outset by the governments of several EU member states as well as by representatives of several EU institutions since the early 1990s. The road to the fourth EU enlargement was thus chosen around 1990 and the task accomplished in 2004, thus within a significantly short time, without acknowledging four decades of totally different development and socialization. To absorb pressure on the EU's structures and to minimize the risk of overstretching them by opening the doors for ten or more new member states, the Convention drafting a European Constitution was appointed. Its task was to cast the existing constitutional elements of the *acquis communautaire* into the paragraphs of a written constitution to strengthen the endangered structures of the Union. However, the ongoing debates about the European constitution may suffice here to underline the fact that the European Union of today has come to a point from where it is no longer possible to carry on regardless patching together apparently nonfitting parts if we want to keep the integration process running. Beck and Giddens's aforementioned warning seems ample proof that there is a serious danger of a breakup of the EU under the impact of previous and ongoing enlargements.

Steps Two and Three: Identification and Classification of Crises

To identify actual or perceived crises in the three phases of the integration process, at first sight a long list seems to be available in the records of the integration process. On closer inspection, however, a clear assignment can be done which identifies many collectively remembered crises as merely expressions of discontent with certain stages of the integration process or as accumulations of technical problems while pushing ahead the European project. Many of these perceived crises have furthermore been introduced into the debate on the state of the integration process by staunch Euro-skeptics to back up their respective points of view. Thus, the number of existential crises of the integration process can be reduced drastically. As a matter of fact, during the first phase of implementation only two crises seem to be acceptable in the above-mentioned sense as a threat to the existence of an integrated Europe: the failure of the EDC scheme in 1954 and the identity crisis of the 1960s, evoked by strongly deviating conceptions of the *finalité politique* of the integrated Europe in France on the one side and in most other EEC member states on the other. It showed up on at least three interrelated occasions: it stimulated the controversy about the Fouchet Plans of the early 1960s, it fed the more or less synchronic French resistance against British EEC membership, and it discharged in the Empty Chair crisis of the mid-1960s.

With regard to the second phase of reconciliation from 1973 to 1993, at first sight there in fact seems to be a long list of crises: the negative referendum in Norway on EC membership in 1972; the feckless attempts of harmonizing economic and monetary cooperation in the first half of the 1970s, under the impact of the oil price crisis of 1973; the difficulties in coordinating domestic and external political cooperation during the 1970s in spite of contrary manifestations given at European summits. "Eurosclerosis" has become the collective noun for all these critical forms, although economists had originally coined it in the 1970s only to identify the sluggish economic performance of the common European market. However, a more thorough investigation of these critical moments produces a different picture, especially if compared with the European programme as it was set up during the Hague summit of 1969 and a series of subsequent conferences, dealing with the question of how to develop the future shape of the European community. Two main topics had been on the European agenda of the 1970s and 1980s: the introduction of new steering machinery for political cooperation and the induction of an economic and monetary union as the backbone of the integration process. Reviewing the handling of these matters in the background of the achievements of the late 1980s and early 1990s, especially the Single European Act (SEA) and the Treaty of Maastricht, it mirrors a policy of trial and error, due to a lack of historical models. There simply was no benchmark that could have been used by European policy makers in the early 1970s as a gauge for a rapid and purposeful completion of their political tasks. Instead, many domestic and external factors—such as national reservations toward widening the EC's competences or the global economic turbulences caused by the oil price shock—turned it into a difficult and delicate matter. Nevertheless, the self-imposed duties were successfully completed in the late 1970s and during the 1980s: the European Monetary System (EMS) of 1978 created an EC-wide system of definite but adaptable parity of currencies for all EC members except Great Britain. In combination with the introduction of the ECU, the EMS cleared the way for the Social, Economic, and Currency Union of the 1990s. The necessity for harmonizing not only economics but domestic and foreign policies, too, was acknowledged in the Single European Act of 1987, which prepared the ground for the Maastricht Treaty, defining the European Union as a mixture of supranational and intergovernmental elements, according to the principles of subsidiarity. These had already been laid out in the late 1940s, prior to the induction of the integration process. With regard to the aforesaid no existential crises can be identified that would have endangered the process of integration during the phase of reconciliation between 1973 and 1993. On the contrary, European politics had been stimulated by an obviously given and broadly accepted consensus that the integration process should be carried on, not only to enlarge but also to deepen the structures of the European Community, as had been laid out in the proceedings of the Hague summit of 1969.

The results for the third phase of Europeanization since 1993 are different again. Scholarly literature as well as the collective memory is listing another series of crises: the ratification crisis due to the negative Danish referendum on the Maastricht Treaty of June 1992, the difficulties bearing upon the implementation of the treaty which required the additional major agreements of Amsterdam and Nice, the negative Irish referendum on the Nice Treaty, and, finally, the constitutional crisis caused by the negative French and Dutch referendums during the process of ratification. On closer inspection, most of these critical moments or crises seem to be manifestations of yet another existential crisis, which again has something to do with either identity of the still unsatisfactory state of discussion on the *finalité politique* of the integration process with regard to both its internal structures, the balance between supranational and intergovernmental competences, and its geographical dimension. The Euro-phoria of the early 1990s had obviously tempted the European political decision makers, spoilt by their integrationist successes between 1987 and 1992, to dare too much too quickly. They simply ignored the fact that there is a huge difference between completing the framework for political and economic cooperation of the EC-12 with nearly forty years of expertise in integration matters on the one hand and the bloating of the EU by fifteen and more new members within fifteen years, especially as the Central and Eastern European newcomers to the European Union looked back on completely different historical experience during the four decades between the late 1940s and the late 1980s.

Many warning voices could be heard during the 1990s, pointing out the incalculable risks of such an uncontrolled enlargement and promoting alternative ways to integrate the Central and Eastern European applicants either by legislating a frame treaty between the EU and the candidate states, which would have allowed a controlled growing into the Union, or the creation of an EU with a staggered depth of integration, ranging from a larger outer free trade area to a thoroughly supranational integrated European nucleus. However, all these warnings and alternatives had been of no avail, as the political decision makers put all their hope in the constitutional treaty and its curative effects on the EU structures, running the risk to become overstretched. Instead, the constitution was rejected in summer 2005 by the French and Dutch, who obviously were not prepared to follow the Euro-politicians on their way to a more and more enlarged Europe of growing complexity and opacity. The current crisis therefore must be considered another identity crisis. But, while the identity crisis of the 1960s was more or less a crisis of the European political elite, torn between de Gaulle's intergovernmental *Europe unie* and Monnet's supranational *Europe unifié*, the actual crisis is deeply rooted in the European public mind. It is a clear proof of the failure of the European political elite to take the citizens of Europe along on their way to an integrated Europe of, as it seems, doubtful shape and size.

Steps Four and Five: the Crises' Impact on the Integration Process

To recapitulate, three existential crises were identified—the EDC crisis of 1954, the first identity crisis of the 1960s, and the present second identity crisis. With regard to the EDC crisis it is relatively easy to expose its impact on the integration process. The French National Assembly refused to deal with the topic "ratification of EDC" on August 30, 1954. Less than two months later the Treaties of Paris were signed, channelling all the European defense structures into NATO, and in

June 1955 the conference of Messina started the *relance européenne*, which was fully accomplished on March 25, 1957, when the Treaties of Rome were signed. At first sight these data are the cornerstones of a remarkable progress in European integration—threatened by total failure in August 1954, the framework for a fully integrated economic area of the six founder states was completed less than three years later. However, it ought not to be overlooked here that there had been some important additional factors that acted as catalysts and supported the integration process. First of all, the EDC failure required immediate action as the growing tensions between East and West urgently called, at least from the Western point of view, for a completion of the Western European security structures, including the integration of the Federal Republic of Germany. As the military components of the EDC had been heavily criticized from the very beginning and because the whole concept was only enforceable as the political framework for future military cooperation in Western Europe, its failure was noticed with a kind of relief by many observers and political decision makers all over Europe. They had always preferred the NATO solution which now was easily to be realized. On the other hand, the EDC concept was considered by many Europhiles another important step toward closer integration. Especially Article 38 of the EDC Treaty, which set up the rules for future political cooperation in supranational Europe, was considered with much interest.

Therefore compensation seemed to be necessary which was suitable not only to safeguard the still fragile ECSC scheme but to enforce the French—German reconciliation as a precondition for European security and prosperity. As economics had enabled the induction of the ECSC as the first step to supranational European institutions, this track seemed to be resilient enough to be used again. Characteristically enough, it had been the heads of states of Belgium, Italy, the Netherlands, and Luxembourg who, under the guidance of the prominent Belgian politician Paul-Henri Spaak, put pressure on the ECSC members to further deepen and broaden the supranational structures of integrated Europe. By embracing Western Germany they wanted to stop further unilateral French action for the sake of their nations' security. Obviously enough, the original consensus, which had ignited the integration process in 1952, was still powerful enough to overcome the EDC crisis by paving the way for the Treaties of Rome.

We know today that especially the French government only gave in with bad grace and due to lack of political alternatives, especially against the background of the Suez disaster. However, a backlash had to be expected. While the economic side of the European Communities, after the implementation of the Treaties of Rome, worked remarkably smoothly, the *finalité politique* of the integration process remained controversial. While the French governments, especially after the election of Charles de Gaulle for president, staunchly favoured an intergovernmental approach, a majority of Euro-politicians led by Walter Hallstein, the first president of the EEC Commission, Jean Monnet and others supported the deepening of the Communities' supranational structures. Under these circumstances and under particularly in consideration of the imponderables of a prolonged discussion of the EC's political structures, de Gaulle wanted to do things properly and instructed his confidant Christian Fouchet to present to the European institutions a concept on the *finalité politique* of the integration process. The two Fouchet Plans of November 1961 and January 1962 subsequently saw the European integration area post-1961 as an intergovernmental union of states. Hallstein, Monnet, and many leading politicians in the other member states had good reasons to assume that Fouchet's Europe would have established a moderate French political hegemony in the European integration area, whereas they preferred a union of the peoples along stronger supranational lines which would strengthen the original integrationist idea.

Against this background they thoroughly welcomed the perspective of an enlarged Europe that arose subsequent to the applications for membership in the early 1960s. Especially the prospect of British EEC membership seemed to be inviting, as Great Britain would have been the only member state strong enough to balance imminent political predominance by France. These different points of view mark the area of crisis that prevailed in European integration politics throughout the 1960s and beyond. President de Gaulle on the one side, failed to establish his "Union d'États" due to heavy resistance from the European supranationalists; he succeeded, however, due to his boycott of European institutions—the so-called Empty Chair crisis of the mid-1960s—with the integration process being carried on in general and along supranational lines in particular. However, due to the indubitable successes of the early integration process, especially in the field of the economy but also with regard to the emerging French–German détente under the European roof and beyond, he did not go to the extreme of risking the complete breakup of integrated Europe but preferred a standstill instead. Characteristically, his successor Pompidou tried at least for a while to continue de Gaulle's politics under changed conditions: shortly after his election to the post of French President he signalled his approval of British, Danish, Irish, and Norwegian EC membership, hoping that especially British membership would support the French intergovernmental preferences with regard to the European integration process's *finalité politique*. On the other side, the adherents of deeper integration along supranational lines refrained from cherishing the illusion that a federal Europe was realizable within only a few years and pinned their hopes on the normative powers of institutional facts by focussing on enlarging the competences of the existing European institutions and extending the supranational elements of the *acquis communautaire*.

Conclusions

Thus, the identity crisis of the 1960s did not reinforce the European integration process, but what it did was to separate the desirable from the manageable. Obviously enough, none of the maximum demands had been realizable as they would have threatened the very existence of the integration project. Therefore a compromise had to be found to overcome the crisis. And, as we know today, within the limits drawn by compromise, the integration process could be continued, in fact quite successfully, if we take into account the enormous progress that was made in the phase of reconciliation of the integration process between 1973 and 1993. The Treaty of Maastricht, as well as the text of the constitutional treaty, with its mixtures of supranational and intergovernmental elements, clearly mirrors the diversity of opinions on the *finalité politique* of an integrated Europe. It has also clearly marked the cornerstones on which one day the European house could be completed.

With regard to the current crisis it seems too early to dare make a historiographic evaluation. But to a certain extent the initial situation of the crisis is somehow comparable with the identity crisis of the 1960s, if in a much more complex setting. The number of member states has grown up to twenty-five, with at least two more members on the doorstep, the global setting has changed dramatically and, last but not least, integration has reached a density that, from the point of view of the 1960s, must have seemed difficult to imagine. But again the crisis reminds us that some central questions concerning the integration process have remained unanswered so far and that some central aspects have not been adequately dealt with. With regard to the latter, the current public discontent with the state of the integration process, as it is reflected by the French and Dutch referendums as well as by recent Eurobarometer surveys must be taken as proof for the failure of European policy makers to take the European public with them on their way to an integrated Europe. This insight corresponds, apart from some other shortcomings, to at least some extent with the still disputed final design of the European house. The increased number of member states, including their various expectations of their individual benefits from membership and their individual ideas of the EU's ideal operating methods has contributed a lot to the growing opacity of the European project. And, when eastern enlargement has already heavily disturbed the labour market in large parts of Central Europe, the question of the final size of the European house must be asked, too. Many of the French and Dutch questioned on the reasons for their negative votes have among other arguments mentioned the current discussion about further enlargements. Especially with regard to the Turkish problem, the social dimension overlaps the cultural dimension.

Thus, the current crisis of the European integration process will, like the previous crises, most likely not directly reinforce the integration process. Hopefully, it will remind European policy makers that, with particular regard to the changed composition of the EU and the changed global setting, a reevaluation of the EU's role in today's global context is overdue. From the points of view of both public acceptance by the Europeans and its ability to work the EU's *finalité politique* to be aimed at should be more than a mere "cosmopolitan project" along Beck and Giddens's line of thought.[10] With regard to the traditional antagonism between supranationalists and intergovernmentalists the structure to be established could be made out of a more intensely integrated nucleus of states like the euro zone and a less deeply integrated margin, probably organized along free trade area lines. In any case and as a precondition, a European self-ascertainment must take place, taking into consideration the EU's remarkable success after the end of the bipolar system. As a matter of fact, the EU has reunited Europe after the fall of the Berlin Wall and has influenced political change in the Ukraine and in Turkey.[11] Thus, the current crisis could in fact and at least to some extent help to reorient the integration process and to lead it into safer and more manageable waters. It definitely must return there, as a standstill of the integration process would in fact run the risk of an abolishment of the European project. This, however, cannot be taken as a serious alternative to the continuation of the construction work of the European house.

Notes

1. See www.edition.cnn.com/2005/WORLD/europe/06/17/eu.summit/index.html.
2. See www.spiegel.de/international/0,1518,358905,00.html.
3. See for example Janis A. Emmanoulidis, *Overcoming the Constitutional Crisis*, München: Centrum für angewandte Politikforschung, 2005; Jürgen Elvert, *Zur gegenwärtigen Verfassung der Europäischen Union: Einige Überlegungen aus geschichtswissenschaftlicher Sicht*, ZEI Discussion Paper C 148, Bonn: Zentrum für Europäische Integrationsforschung, 2005; Romain Kirt, *Macroshift: Die Europäische Union in der Modernisierungskrise*, Esch-sur-Alzette: Le Phare, 2005; Nina Eschke and Thomas Malick (eds.), *The European Constitution and its Ratification Crisis: Constitutional Debates in the EU Member States*, ZEI Discussion Paper C 156, Bonn: Zentrum für Europäische Integrationsforschung, 2006.
4. See Eurobarometer 63, Die öffentliche Meinung in der EU, July 2005, pp. 17–28.
5. Ulrich Beck and Anthony Giddens, "Nationalism has Now Become the Enemy of Europe's Nations", *The Guardian*, October 4, 2005.
6. Kirt, *Macroshift*, p. 7–8.
7. An extensive comment on the suggested tripartite division of the European integration process was given in Jürgen Elvert, *Die Europäische Integration*, Darmstadt: Wissenschaftliche Buchgesellschaft, 2006.
8. Wolfgang Wessels, "Zur Debatte um einen europäischen Staatenbund: Sechs Thesen der Fusionstheorie," in: Roman Herzog and Stephan Hobe (eds.), *Die Europäische Union auf dem Weg zum verfassten Staatenverbund: Perspektiven der europäischen Verfassungsordnung* (Schriften des Rechtszentrums für Europäische und Internationale Zusammenarbeit RIZ Bd. 22), Munich: Verlag C.H. Beck, 2004, pp. 200–3. The fusion-theory was introduced in 1996 in Dietrich Rometsch and Wolfgang Wessels (eds.), *The European Union and Member States: Towards Institutional Fusion?* Manchester: Manchester University Press, 1996.
9. Kevin Featherstone, "Introduction: In the Name of Europe," in: Kevin Featherstone and Claudio M. Radaelli (eds.), *The Politics of Europeanization*, Oxford: Oxford University Press, 2003, pp. 6–12.
10. See Beck and Giddens, "Nationalism has Now Become the Enemy of Europe's Nations."
11. Ibid.

4

Through Crises to EMU: Perspectives for Fiscal Union and Political Union

Jürgen von Hagen

According to popular critique of European monetary integration, often voiced in the 1990s and still part of the public debate today, the stability of a monetary union requires a political and a fiscal union among the member states. In this context, fiscal integration is commonly understood as the implementation of a tax and transfer system of a significant size spanning the European Monetary Union (EMU) member countries. Political integration is understood to mean the creation of more competent and effective political institutions at the center of the EMU. Steps in both directions, fiscal and political union, would push the EU in the direction of a European Federal State.

According to the popular critique, the Treaties of Maastricht and Amsterdam failed to recognize this requirement and the Treaty of Nice did not do enough to rectify that failure.[1] The European constitutional project would have been an opportunity to make up for the lack of fiscal and political integration, at least partially, but it failed, first in the European Summit of December 2003 and then, after some repair work, in the French and Dutch referendums in 2005. Thus, if the critique is right, the continuing lack of political and fiscal union poses a threat to the viability of the EMU.

The reasoning behind this critique is often based on historical analogies: historical monetary unions that where not connected with fiscal and political union, such as the Scandinavian and the Latin Currency Unions, ultimately vanished, while monetary unions created together with political unions, such as Germany after 1871, exhibited greater stability. But these arguments are not convincing. The Scandinavian and the Latin Currency Unions were rather loose agreements to standardize coinage among the participating countries. Beyond that, they had no implications for monetary policy, which was dominated by the prevailing gold standard, anyway, and are not comparable to the EMU. The monetary union of the German Reich, which was completed with the foundation of the Reichsbank in 1875, shows the fallacy of the argument in that the German Reich itself was not a stable entity. If anything, the example proves that political union does not guarantee the stability of a monetary union.

In this chapter, I discuss the links between economic, monetary, fiscal, and political union from a perspective of political economy. I argue that the sustainability of cooperative arrangements among sovereign states, like economic and monetary unions, is threatened by crises emerging from two conflict potentials. The horizontal conflict potential results from the uneven distribution of the benefits and costs of economic and monetary integration among the member countries. The vertical conflict potential results from the possibility of abuse of resources and political powers by the center of the union.

In the second part of this chapter, I argue that steps to increase fiscal and political integration can be used to contain the horizontal conflict potential, but at the same time they increase the vertical conflict potential. Since the stability of the union depends on the force and the interaction of both conflict potentials, the claim that the stability of a monetary union needs political and fiscal union cannot always be correct. Whether or not it is, depends on which conflict potential is more important.

In the third part of this chapter, I review the history of monetary integration in Europe, arguing that it owes its existence to repeated situations in which the prospect and promise of monetary union were used to resolve crises resulting from this horizontal conflict potential.

In the fourth part of this chapter, I argue that, due to the nature of their interaction, neither political nor fiscal integration in Europe is likely to proceed in small steps in the future. A more likely scenario is that the EMU will be faced with a severe crisis that will make the expected payoffs from a large step in that direction sufficiently big to be attractive for all member states.

The final part of the chapter offers two conclusions. First, the very failure of the EU's constitutional project, which was built on the idea of small steps forward, may have been just the right move to make EMU sustainable instead of exposing it to excessive conflicts arising from the vertical dimension. Secondly, given EMU, fiscal and political union might be pushed forward by an external crisis calling the benefits of monetary union into question. Turkey's entrance to the EU might provide the occasion.

Horizontal and Vertical Conflict Potentials in Economic Unions

Every form of economic cooperation among sovereign countries raises two basic questions. First, are the total benefits from cooperation large enough to outweigh total costs? This is a question of collective rationality for the group of participating countries. Secondly, assuming that all other countries stick to the agreement to cooperate, is the individual payoff from cooperating larger than the payoff from deviating from the cooperative agreement for each country? This is the question of individual rationality or "incentive compatibility." Since both questions and their answers relate to expected benefits and costs, the relevant benefits and costs need not materialize immediately, but they must be sufficiently large in expectation—with appropriate discounting of an uncertain future. In order to lead to a stable arrangement, the answer to both questions must be yes. If the answer to the first question is no, the group as a whole will agree not to cooperate. If the answer to the first question is yes, but the answer to the second question is no, an agreement to cooperate will be made, but the cooperation will turn out to be unstable as individual countries will deviate from it.

The benefits from and costs of cooperation may change over time, as circumstances and expectations may change. If, over time, the answer to the first question becomes negative, the cooperative arrangement will fall apart by agreement of the members. The history of the Bretton Woods System, which had achieved a remarkably high degree of monetary and fiscal integration in the 1960s, is a case in point. Once the benefits from fixed exchange rates centered on the US dollar had evaporated, the member states agreed to end the arrangement, leaving only those parts intact that they continued to consider useful.

If, over time, the answer to the first question remains positive, but the answer to the second question becomes negative, one or more members will want to withdraw from the arrangement. It may be that the remaining members will just let them do that. However, it is also possible that this would reduce the value of the cooperation for the remaining members such that they want to continue it and keep all members in the group. A crisis emerges, in which the former threaten to end the cooperation and the latter struggle to find a way to keep them on board. Obviously, such a solution demands an increase in the expected benefits for the former country or countries.

There are several ways how this can be achieved. The first is to increase the scope of the cooperative arrangement to include aspects of economic policy that were not previously subject to cooperation. The second is to find mechanisms to redistribute the benefits from cooperation among the members, i.e., to implement side payments large enough to keep the relevant members in. The third is to use coercion, i.e., to make deviations and withdrawal sufficiently costly, for staying in to become the preferred alternative even if the net benefits from cooperation are negative.

The history of European integration offers examples of all three, and monetary integration often played a role in these crises. As we shall see below, the EU repeatedly used monetary integration to raise the expected benefits from cooperation sufficiently to prevent potential deviants from withdrawing from the union or reducing the level of cooperation. Thus, monetary union emerged through a series of conflicts and crises.

Monetary Integration History from Rome to Maastricht

A first instance to consider is the writing of the original Treaty of Rome. The immediate purpose of the treaty was to establish cooperation in a small number of very specific fields of economic policy, i.e., the regulation and governance of the coal and steel industries in the member states, the civil use of nuclear energy, internal trade, and agricultural policy. From a purely economic perspective, policies in these fields did not touch in important ways on matters of monetary policy. Nevertheless, the treaty included some provisions for monetary policy and, thus, present the first steps toward monetary integration in Europe. Article 104 defined external equilibrium, full employment, price stability, and external stability of the currencies as the common, general objectives of economic policy in the Community. Article 103 declared that the member states would regard their macroeconomic policies as a matter "of common concern." Article 107 defined the member states' exchange rate policies as "a matter of common concern" and sanctioned the use of foreign exchange and capital controls by the member states. Under the conditions of the Bretton Woods System, exchange rates, foreign exchange, and capital controls were the core business of monetary policy. Article 105 called upon the member states to coordinate their economic and monetary policies and to facilitate cooperation among the relevant national authorities. As early as 1959, the European Parliament called for the creation of a common monetary institution patterned after the US Federal Reserve System, while important Community politicians endorsed the formation of some form of exchange rate union among the member states. In the European Exchange Rate Agreement of 1958, the member states agreed to keep the exchange rates of their currencies within bands narrower than those implied by the Bretton Woods System.

Why the interest in monetary integration if neither macroeconomic policy nor financial market integration was part of the original scope of European integration? There are two parts to the answer:

- First, the founders of the EC did not want European integration to stop at the stage of trade integration. The Treaty of Rome, in its preamble, affirmed that the founding nations were "determined to lay the foundations of an ever closer union among the peoples of Europe." By including provisions for a minimal degree of monetary integration, the founders may have wanted to establish a basis for subsequent efforts to expand the scope of European integration in the direction of monetary integration. Given the unequal strength of economic development among the founding countries, they may have perceived that the gains from trade integration would automatically be shared equally. Although there were as yet no clear ideas about how macroeconomic policy coordination would work among the member states and, hence, no specific mechanisms were devised for its purpose, monetary policy was, in the Keynesian thinking of the day, regarded as an important tool to boost growth and employment and the potential benefits from monetary integration may have seemed large for some.

- Secondly, some of the member states may have perceived that the benefits from cooperation in the immediate fields were not sufficiently large and secure without a minimal degree of monetary integration. After all, the memories of the deleterious competitive devaluations of the 1930s, when countries had used exchange rate policies to gain competitive advantages in international trade were still vivid in the 1950s. Thus, some members may have feared that others would abuse their exchange rates to undermine the agreement to eliminate bilateral tariffs and establish a customs union and a common agricultural policy.

It is noteworthy, however, that further steps in the direction of monetary integration in the early years of the EC were taken outside the formal EC institutions. For example, the Committee of Central Bank Governors, which was set up in the early 1960s to make cooperation in the field of exchange rate policies more concrete, was not an EC body. Germany in particular was very reluctant to increase the degree of monetary integration formally within the EC framework. The reason is easy to see: as the country with the strongest currency among the Six, Germany's incentive compatibility constraint required limits on monetary integration to assure that the quality of its currency was not diluted.

The relevance of monetary integration within the existing structures of cooperation became clear very quickly in the early 1960s nevertheless. Specifically, the functioning of the Common Agricultural Policy (CAP), which determined the prices of agricultural goods in nominal terms throughout the EC, depended critically on exchange rate fixity. It was soon realized that changes in the central parities would cause enormous strains in the CAP framework. In view of this, it became fashionable in Community circles to call the EC a de facto monetary union, since exchange rate changes were thought to be too harmful to happen. With the benefit of hindsight, Tsoukalis later called this attitude "agricultural illusion."[2]

When the exchange rate stability of the Bretton Woods System crumbled, the crisis anticipated emerged. The devaluation of the French franc and the revaluation of the DM in the late 1960s severely damaged the relations between France and Germany in particular. The French government combined the parity change with the introduction of so-called Monetary Compensation Amounts, which protected French farmers from the consequences of the devaluation and undermined the price mechanism of CAP. Germany followed suit. Tsoukalis (1977) reports that these breaches of the CAP framework were widely regarded as precipitating the collapse of the EC.[3]

The prospect of deeper monetary integration became the key to resolving the crisis. The French president Pompidou and the German chancellor Brandt jointly proposed Economic and Monetary Union as an official goal of the EC at the Council of The Hague in December 1969, and the Council endorsed their proposal. Brandt and Pompidou's initiative gave impetus to the Werner Report, which was adopted by the European Council in 1970 and laid out a road map to monetary union by 1980.

It foresaw a first stage of creating machinery for policy coordination (1971–74), a second stage during which exchange rate realignments would be cooperative and exchange rate policies supported by a European Monetary Cooperation Fund, and a centralized monetary policy implemented by a Community central bank in the third stage. As before, Germany in particular insisted that monetary integration was not brought into the formal framework of the Treaty, implying that the costs of withdrawing from it would be smaller than otherwise.

The Werner Plan fell victim to the economic and financial turmoil of the 1970s, which brought the process of monetary integration to a halt. The European exchange rate system (the "snake") soon deteriorated to a "Greater DM zone" of small currencies pegged to the DM, which the lira and the French franc were forced to leave.

The late 1970s saw another period of growing dissatisfaction with European integration. US leadership in world politics and economics was on the decline, the world economy was threatened by instability from volatile oil and raw materials prices and external imbalances, and Europe did not have enough to offer to assume international leadership. Looking back at the period, Germany's Chancellor Schmidt (1990) later wrote:

> We [Schmidt, Giscard d'Estaing, and Barre] knew that the European economies were unable to shield themselves individually against the turbulences of the world. Therefore, we wanted unification and joint success. ... The conduct of monetary and exchange rate policies in the US and the dependence of the European countries' monetary policies on the dollar, on dollar interest rates, and dollar speculation had been particularly harmful.[4]

In a famous speech in Florence in 1977, the president of the Commission, Roy Jenkins, criticized the European approach for being a gradual *politique des petits pas* and advocated a big leap forward to build a unified Europe. Again, monetary integration became the key to the solution. Again, the solution came as a French–German initiative.

In 1978, the French president Giscard d'Estaing and the German chancellor Schmidt launched their initiative for a new European Monetary System (EMS) as the launching pad for monetary union. The EMS implemented a formal mechanism for cooperative exchange rate realignments and mechanisms for short-term financial support for the weaker currencies of the system and the pooling of foreign exchange reserves. The system was designed explicitly to be symmetric in the sense that its governance would be shared by all participating countries and the burden of adjustment to deviations from the average monetary policy stance would be shared between the relatively weak and the relatively strong economies. In this way, the system would produce a more equitable distribution of the benefits among the participants and avoid the system being "dominated" by a notoriously strong DM. This was important in order to make the system agreeable to France. At the same time, the EMS mechanisms were again kept outside the Treaty, and the Bundesbank received an assurance from the German government that it would be allowed to withdraw unilaterally from the system if the exchange rate peg ever seriously threatened price stability in Germany. This possibility of withdrawal made sure that the incentive compatibility constraint was kept for Germany's monetary authority.

During the 1980s, the EMS turned out to be less symmetrical than it was originally devised to be. In particular, it did not cause the Bundesbank to soften its commitment to low inflation. A large part of this was due to the fact that Europe's traditionally more inflation-prone economies, France and Italy, moved to a more price-stability-oriented monetary policy during that decade, and, consequently, found it much less painful to peg to the DM. In fact, toward the end of the decade, it became fashionable among economists to speak of the EMS as a mechanism by which Italy and France could acquire credibility for their new commitment to low inflation.[5] This, however, meant that the Bundesbank lost some if its credibility.[6] While Bundesbank policies dominated short-term interest rate movements within the system, it did not do so in the medium run.[7]

The next critical situation arose with the fall of the Berlin Wall. France and Britain initially opposed German unification, fearing that an even larger German economy would bias the benefits from European integration more in the German direction, and that Germany, the largest financial supporter of the EU, might become less interested in the EU once its problem of national unity had been solved. Both expectations called the incentive compatibility constraint for Germany's partners in the EU into question. In the negotiations that followed, monetary union again was decisive. France in particular agreed to a rapid German unification in exchange for a firm commitment by Germany to go ahead with European monetary union. The Maastricht Treaty finally brought monetary integration into the European Treaty framework, raising the cost of withdrawal from monetary cooperation for all member states including Germany, whose public and whose independent central bank never liked the idea of EMU.[8] The road map laid out in the Treaty finally led to the beginning of EMU in 1999.

Our short review shows that the prospect and, eventually, the beginning of monetary union in Europe several times served as the key to overcoming crisis or critical points in the development of the EU. Each time, it was used to raise the expected benefits from economic cooperation in Europe to preserve the existing cooperation among the member states. The start of EMU in 1999, of course, implies that this role of monetary integration has been exhausted. Future crises will need expansions of the scope of European integration in other areas to fulfil that role, unless one is willing to assume that the cost of leaving the EU (or certain parts of economic cooperation in Europe) is already so large that no strain can be large enough to break the individual incentive compatibility constraint.

Meanwhile, economic integration has progressed in other areas, too. The completion of the Single Market has largely perfected the integration of goods markets and financial markets. A network of various forms of "open coordination" in fields like labour market policy, research policy, and others, has emerged, but the commitment required from the member states to participate seriously in "open coordination" remains low,[9] and there are no signs that the member states want to move forward in this direction. The recent ill fate of the Service Directive suggests that there is no willingness to integrate services and labour markets beyond the status quo either. This leaves fiscal and political union as the fields of expansion in the future.

EMU and What Next?

With this in mind, we can consider the economic rationale for complementing the Single Market with a monetary union, and the role of fiscal and political union in this context.

The first issue leads to the relationship between economic and monetary union. Does the European Single Market need the common currency in order to function properly? A detailed discussion of this question would go beyond the scope of this chapter. Suffice it to say that the debate over the relationship between exchange flexibility and international trade has come full circle in the last sixty years. The Bretton Woods System was introduced in the hope that exchange rate stability would allow the member countries to maintain a high level of international trade. However, during the 1950s and 1960s, governments increasingly used trade restrictions to rectify external imbalances caused by exchange rate misalignments, as the exchange rates themselves were difficult to change. After the breakdown of Bretton Woods and the introduction of flexible exchange rates, and in view of the large appreciation of the dollar in the early 1980s, calls for import restrictions were voiced increasingly in the US. The result was an attempt to stabilize exchange rates by means of coordinated foreign exchange market interventions.

A review of this debate leads to the conclusion that the problem is not so much exchange rate flexibility per se, but the possibility of persistent exchange rate misalignments.[10] Whether the probability of such misalignments occurring is higher under regimes of fixed or flexible exchange rates remains a matter of debate in international economics. Economic union requires a view on this question, because it reduces the options to two, i.e., a common currency or completely freely floating exchange rates. The reason is that, with completely liberalized capital movements within the EU and between the EU and the rest of the world, systems of fixed but adaptable exchange rates, such as the European Monetary System, are no longer sustainable. With flexible exchange rates, persistent exchange rate misalignments are the more likely the more foreign currency markets are dominated by "noise traders," i.e., traders not acting according to economic fundamentals.[11] With fixed exchange rates and in a monetary union, persistent real exchange rate misalignments are the more likely the more government regulations of product and labour markets prevent prices and wages from adjusting quickly to their equilibrium values.

Beyond this, the economic advantages and disadvantages of a common currency are the subject of the theory of optimal currency areas.[12] According to the theory, the greatest advantage of a common currency is in the reduction of transaction costs in international trade. The use of a common currency saves the cost of exchanging currencies, of hedging currency risk in international trade and finance, and of computing relative prices quoted in different currencies. Thus, by eliminating trade barriers arising from currency exchange, monetary union contributes to the integration of markets and eliminates competitive distortions. In doing so, monetary union generates efficiency gains and, hence, real income gains.

Furthermore, the use of a common currency contributes to the integration of capital markets among the participating countries, improving the allocation of capital in the Single Market. This contributes to real economic growth in the areas where the levels of capital are relatively low. Note, however, that the benefits from capital market integration are not the same for all members, if there are differences in the initial capital endowments of the participating economies. As capital flows from capital-rich to capital-poor countries, the marginal productivity of labour declines in the former and increases in the latter. Workers in the capital-rich countries face downward pressure on their wages and, unless wages are sufficiently flexible, rising unemployment. In contrast, workers in capital-poor countries enjoy rising wages.

Monetary union also implies the convergence of inflation rates among the participating countries. For countries with relatively weak central banks before the start of the monetary union, a credible, low-inflation policy by the common central bank generates another economic benefit from monetary union.

The main economic disadvantage of monetary union stems from the loss of exchange rate flexibility as a mechanism to adjust to economic shocks affecting the member countries in asymmetrical ways. This can be illustrated by a simple example. Suppose that the aggregate demand for the products of a country declines exogenously, causing a fall in employment in this country. With flexible exchange rates, this entails a depreciation of its currency, which will improve the competitiveness of its products in external markets and reduce the demand for foreign products in its home markets. This relative price effect causes the demand for its products to go up and thus mitigates the initial negative shock. Thus, flexible exchange rates smooth the adjustment to asymmetrical economic shocks. Without the adjustment of the exchange rate, and unless wages and goods prices are sufficiently flexible, negative asymmetrical shocks will lead to deeper recessions with higher unemployment.

The most important alternative adjustment mechanism is factor movements. In our example, the movement of labor from the country hit by the negative shock to countries hit by positive shocks would reduce unemployment in the first and avoid over-employment in the latter. However, since the movement of people is costly, labor migration is an efficient response only in the case of permanent shocks. Thus, the importance of flexible exchange rates to adjustment to asymmetrical shocks is larger for shocks occurring at business cycle frequency than for long-term differences in economic development.

The existence of nominal government debt adds another aspect to this discussion. Governments can use—and have used—monetary policy to counteract sovereign debt crises, e.g., by reducing the real debt burden by surprise inflation. In principle, this is possible in a monetary union, too, but with different costs and benefits. A member state faced with a debt crisis will demand a more inflationary monetary policy to achieve a reduction in the real value of its debt. The central bank can provide such a rescue operation either ex ante, by keeping interest rates low, or ex post, by monetizing government debt which the member state concerned would not be able to sell in the market otherwise. The consequences are the same, i.e., a rising rate of inflation in the common currency area. Agreement on such an operation will be easy if all member states face a similar degree of (excessive) public indebtedness. Otherwise, member countries with different debt burdens will demand different degrees of monetary expansion, and this will lead to conflicts among the member states.

This short review shows that the net benefits from monetary union depend crucially on the degree of heterogeneity of the member states in terms of their exposure to asymmetrical shocks, the degree of government regulation and intervention in product and labor markets, price and wage flexibility, and the indebtedness of their governments. Increasing heterogeneity has two main consequences:

- First, it reduces the expected pay off from monetary union for all member states.
- Secondly, it makes the distribution of benefits across the members more uneven and, in doing so, raises the probability that individual members perceive that the net benefit is negative for them even if it is positive for the union as a whole. This problem of an uneven distribution of the benefits constitutes the horizontal conflict potential of the monetary union. If the distribution becomes too uneven, tensions will arise among the member countries that may lead to a falling apart of the monetary union. This conflict potential rises with increasing heterogeneity and an increasing degree of monetary integration.

As pointed out by the literature on optimal currency areas, the horizontal conflict potential of a monetary union can be mitigated by fiscal integration, i.e., the creation of fiscal adjustment mechanisms. When price and wage flexibility are insufficient to provide adjustment to asymmetrical shocks, fiscal mechanisms can do the work. Returning to our example above, a transfer of income from countries experiencing positive asymmetrical shocks to the country hit by a negative asymmetrical shock could stimulate aggregate demand and prevent unemployment from rising in the latter. Such transfers could be implemented in an interpersonal way, e.g., through a monetary union-wide unemployment insurance, or in an intergovernmental way, through payments among the member governments. They could be organized horizontally, i.e., on the basis of direct payments among the members states, or vertically, i.e., on the basis of payments to and from a central authority.[13]

Furthermore, fiscal integration would include the harmonization and coordination of the systems of social insurance among the member states, including the regulation of labor markets, to reduce the existing regulatory asymmetries and improve the functioning of the monetary union. Finally, fiscal integration may include the implementation of a common stabilization policy at the level of the monetary union to complement the common monetary policy. This, again, could be achieved by way of coordinating the individual fiscal stabilization policies at the national level, or by creating a common fiscal stabilization fund of sufficient size.

This potential role of fiscal integration to reduce the horizontal conflict potential among the member states of a European monetary union was recognized already by the *MacDougall Report* (1977), which evaluated the implications of monetary union for fiscal policy in the context of the Werner Plan.[14] The report noted that all existing monetary unions (meaning large federations) had fiscal mechanisms of equalization to address asymmetric economic developments. Reviewing the experience of existing federations, the report concluded that a European monetary union should have a central authority with a budget of at least 7 percent of the common GDP to be able to cope with asymmetrical shocks successfully.[15]

The alternative way to manage the horizontal conflict potential is by increasing the degree of political integration. The latter operates through the relinquishing of national sovereignty of the members states to the union they form, and with the creation of central political powers that can hold the union together even if the diverging economic interests are pulling it apart. The stronger the central power, the larger the horizontal conflict potential it can manage successfully.

Monetary policy is a powerful instrument of economic policy with important short- and long-run macroeconomic and distributional effects. Experience suggests that the political administration of a cooperative arrangement among countries will seek to acquire the power over such economic policy instruments to use them in its own interest. Similar reasoning applies to the instruments of fiscal integration. In a fiscal union, the central administration will try to gain influence over the common fiscal transfer mechanisms and instruments and over the common budget, to use them to promote its own interests. The more fiscal instruments the union possesses, and the more vertically these are organized, the larger will be the volume of resources redistributed within the union and the larger will be the scope and the incentive for the central administration to acquire power over them. Thus, as in any form of cooperative arrangement, political integration creates a principal agent problem. The more power is allocated at the center of the union, and the more powerful the instruments of monetary and fiscal policy the center commands, the greater the temptation for the central administration to use them for its own purposes.

This possibility of abuse of the central power constitutes the vertical conflict potential in a monetary union. If, from the point of view of the member countries, the central administration abuses its powers against their interests, their incentive to leave the union increases. The larger the degree of political integration, the larger the vertical conflict potential. Since the scope for abusing the resources and powers at the center can be reduced by mechanisms of accountability to the member states, accountability reduces the vertical conflict potential. Furthermore, for a given degree of political integration, the vertical conflict potential rises when the degree of fiscal integration increases vertically, because this gives the central administration more resources to command. This implies that political and fiscal integration endangers the cohesion of the monetary union by increasing the vertical conflict potential.

From Monetary Union to Fiscal and Political Union

We are now ready to characterize the relationship between monetary, fiscal, and political integration. Given a degree of heterogeneity among the member states (D), an increase in monetary integration (M) leads to an increase in the horizontal conflict potential (H). This can be mitigated by more fiscal integration (F) or political integration (P). Thus, we have:

$$H = H(\underset{+}{D}, \underset{+}{M}, \underset{-}{F}, \underset{-}{P})$$

This relationship is at the heart of the claim that the stability of a monetary union needs fiscal and political union. Increasing the degree of monetary integration leads to an increase in the horizontal conflict potential, which can be offset by increasing fiscal and political integration.

Figure 4.1 illustrates the relationship in the HH curve. The curve gives the relationship between monetary and political integration for given degrees of heterogeneity among the member states, a given degree of fiscal integration, and a given force of the horizontal conflict potential. In light of the arguments above, increasing monetary integration requires increasing political integration. Note that scenarios above the HH curve are more stable from the perspective of the horizontal conflict potential; there is excess political integration. Scenarios below the HH curve, in contrast, are unstable. For given degrees of heterogeneity and fiscal integration, the degree of political integration is insufficient to keep the union together given the degree of fiscal integration and heterogeneity among the member states. Moving below the curve is moving toward crisis.

For a given degree of monetary and fiscal integration, increasing political integration leads to an increase in the vertical conflict potential (V), and the more so the more advanced fiscal and monetary integration already are. This can be mitigated by appropriate mechanisms of accountability of the center, A. This is expressed by the relationship:

$$V = V(\underset{+}{M * F * P}, \underset{-}{A})$$

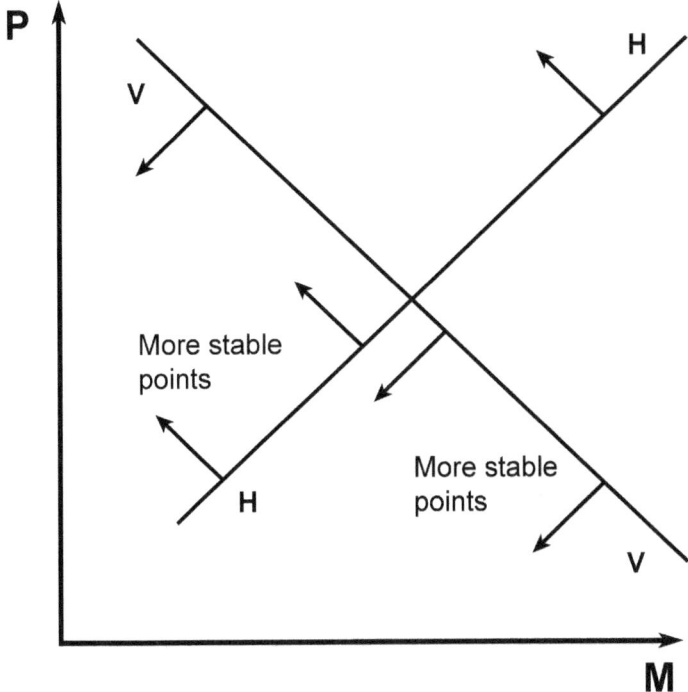

Figure 4.1

We illustrate this relationship by the VV curve in Figure 4.1. If the degree of monetary integration goes up, political union must decrease to keep the vertical conflict potential the same. Otherwise, the vertical conflict potential will increase. Scenarios below the VV curve are thus more stable from the perspective of the vertical conflict; points above the curve are less stable.

We are now ready to consider the effects of an increase in fiscal integration for a given degree of monetary and political integration. From the point of view of the horizontal conflict, this will stabilize the union. In Figure 4.2, the HH curve shifts down and to the right, increasing the range of horizontally stable scenarios. At the same time, however, fiscal integration increases the vertical conflict potential. This is expressed in a shift of the VV curve down and to the left. The area of stable scenarios becomes smaller from this perspective. Thus, increasing fiscal integration has both stabilizing and destabilizing effects. It can improve the sustainability of the union or worsen it, depending on whether the horizontal or the vertical conflict potential grows by a larger amount. A similar reasoning holds for any increase in P given F.

A further assessment, therefore, needs additional assumptions about the relative effects on the horizontal and the vertical conflict potential. Experience

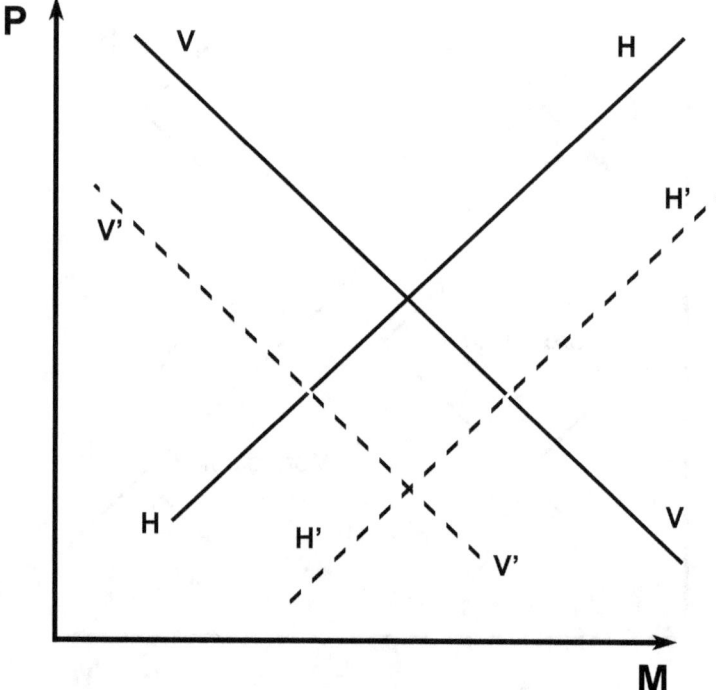

Figure 4.2

with international cooperative arrangements suggests that these relative effects depend on the initial conditions. The fewer and weaker the common fiscal and political institutions shared by a group of countries, the greater the aversion against steps in this direction. In contrast, if the public is already used to the existence of a strong central power, as in a mature federation, attempts to increase the fiscal and political powers of the central administration will meet much less resistance. This suggests that the vertical conflict potential grows with decreasing marginal rate if political and fiscal integration are increased.

At the same time, it seems plausible to argue that starting from a low level of political and fiscal integration, small increases in either one will do little to reduce the horizontal conflict potential in a monetary union. This is also reflected in the MacDougall Commission's recommendation of a central Community budget of 7 percent of GDP. This suggests that the horizontally stabilizing effect of an increase in political and fiscal integration is small initially and grows larger as steps in this direction become larger.

Under such circumstances, the effect of limited steps increasing the degree of political or fiscal integration depends on the initial position. If the existing fiscal and political institutions are weak, the increase in the vertical conflict potential will dominate at first. The union becomes less stable. Only if the degree of

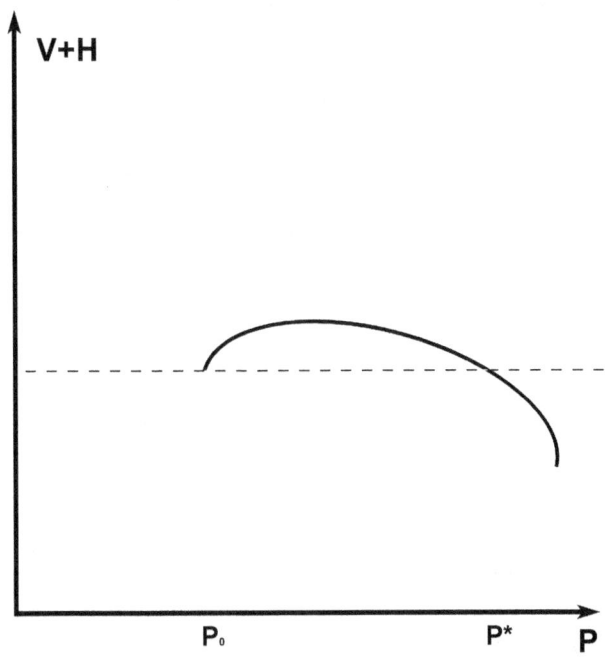

Figure 4.3

political and fiscal integration reaches a minimum level will further steps in this direction have a stabilizing effect.

This is illustrated in Figure 4.3. The figure shows the total conflict potential of the union for a given degree of monetary integration and increasing degrees of political and fiscal integration. Only if the critical level of (P*F*) is reached do limited steps in the direction of political and fiscal integration make the union overall more sustainable. A policy of small steps, complementing the monetary union with only a little political and fiscal integration at first, is, therefore, worse for its sustainability than either no steps in that direction or one large step passing the critical level. The existence of a critical level explains why, in practice, we have observed true monetary unions only with high degrees of political and fiscal integration so far, while arrangements with weak fiscal and political elements have only produced small degrees of monetary integration.

Waiting for the Next Big Crisis

This analysis suggests two points. First, it may explain why the project of a European constitution failed. While the draft constitution added a few steps in the direction of political union, it did not do enough to cross the critical level, and it did not add sufficient mechanisms of accountability to reduce the perceived vertical conflict. If voters were risk-averse and shunned the expected increased instability, they were right to reject the proposed constitution.

Secondly, a large step in political or fiscal integration is unlikely to occur, unless it produces sufficiently large expected benefits from the perspective of the member states. This may occur in two ways: a political crisis outside the EU that would raise the benefits of closer political cooperation among the member states, or a severe economic crisis within the EU that would make EMU as it is unattractive for some of its members and would give political union the same role to play as monetary union played in the past, i.e., to provide enough benefits to stay in the EU. Either way, much as it emerged from a series of crises, monetary union would be completed through a crisis.

What does an increase in the heterogeneity of the member countries due to an enlargement of the monetary union imply in this context? In Figure 4.1 or Figure 4.2, an increase in heterogeneity leads to a shift upwards and an increase in the slope of the HH curve, as a given degree of monetary integration implies more horizontal conflict and every increase in the degree of monetary integration leads to stronger increases in the horizontal conflict potential. In Figure 4.3, this means that the critical level P^*F^* shifts to the right.

Thus, enlarging a monetary union with an intermediate level of political and fiscal integration would endanger its stability more than if the union had either very low or very large degrees of political and fiscal integration already. Obviously, the enlargement would have to be by a large economy for these shifts to be significant. Turkey might be a candidate for such a scenario. For some, bringing Turkey into the EU and EMU is a clever way of trying to bring any future movements in the direction of fiscal and political union to a halt. Indeed, our analysis suggests that bringing Turkey into the EU might produce a reduction in fiscal and political integration to preserve the stability of the union. But this is not the only possibility suggested by our analysis. The other is to take a large step toward a much more developed political and fiscal union to manage the greater economic heterogeneity. At this point, it is impossible to predict which one would happen if Turkey were allowed to enter the EU. If it is a crisis, it may well push the EU forward a long way toward fiscal and political union.

Notes

1. See, for example, Hans Tietmeyer, "Europäische Währungsunion und Politische Union— das Modell mehrerer Geschwindigkeiten," *Deutsche Bundesbank: Auszüge aus Presseartikeln*, 66 (1994), p. 1; Martin Feldstein, "Europe's New Challenge to America," *The New York Times*, May 7, 1998; Paul de Grauwe, "On Monetary and Political Union," Catholic University of Leuven: mimeo, 2006.

2. Loukas Tsoukalis, *The Economics and Politics of European Monetary Integration*, London: George Allen & Unwin, 1977.
3. Ibid.
4. Helmut Schmidt, "Die Bürokraten ausgetrickst" and "Kampf gegen die Nationalisten," *Die Zeit*, August 24 and August 31, 1990.
5. Francesco Giavazzi and Marco Pagano, "The Advantage of Tying One's Hand: EMS Discipline and Central Bank Credibility," *European Economic Review*, 32 (1988), pp. 1055–82.
6. Michele Frattianni and Jürgen von Hagen, "German Dominance in the EMS: The Empirical Evidence," *Open Economies Review*, 1 (1990), pp. 67–87.
7. Michele Fratianni and Jürgen von Hagen, "The European Monetary System 10 Years After," *Carnegie Rochester Conference Series on Public Policies*, 32 (1990), pp. 173–241.
8. In fact, one may doubt that central bankers in Europe ever liked monetary unification, since it was going to take away the clout they enjoyed as the heads of national central banks. As explained in Frattianni and von Hagen, "German Dominance in the EMS," the Delors plan for monetary union masterfully overcame this potential opposition by giving the committee of central bankers the opportunity to write the blueprint of the EMU.
9. Susanne Mundschenk and Jürgen von Hagen, "The Political Economy of Policy Coordination in Europe," *Swedish Review of Economic Policy*, 8 (2002), pp. 11–41.
10. Barry Eichengreen, "A More Perfect Union? On the Logic of Economic Integration," Frank D. Graham Memorial Lecture, Princeton University: mimeo, 1995.
11. Paul de Grauwe and Marianna Grimaldi, "Exchange Rate Puzzles: A Tale of Switching Attractors," *European Economic Review*, 50 (2006), pp. 1–33.
12. Robert Mundell, "A Theory of Optimal Currency Areas," *American Economic Review*, 51 (1961), pp. 657–65; Paul de Grauwe, *The Economics of Monetary Union*, Oxford: Oxford University Press, 2005.
13. See, for example, Charles Goodhart and Stephen Smith, "Stabilization," *The Economics of Community Public Finance: European Economy Reports and Studies*, 5 (1993), pp. 417–56; Jürgen von Hagen and George Hammond, "Regional Insurance Against Asymmetric Shocks—An Empirical Study for the EC," *The Manchester School*, 66 (1998), pp. 331–53; Ken Kletzer and Jürgen von Hagen, "Monetary Union and Fiscal Federalism," in: Charles Wyplosz (ed.), *The Impact of EMU on Europe and the Developing Countries*, Oxford: Oxford University Press, 2001, pp. 17–39.
14. *MacDougall Report: Report of the Study Group on the Role of Public Finance in European Integration*, 2 vols, Brussels: European Commission, 1977.
15. Note that the MacDougall Commission was considering a monetary union among no more than nine member states at the time, and these states were arguably exposed to much smaller asymmetries than the members of the current EMU. That is, the Commission would probably have recommended an even larger central Community budget had it known the composition of the current EMU.

5
Opportunity or Overstretch? The Unexpected Dynamics of Deepening and Widening

Wolfgang Wessels and Thomas Traguth

The evolution of the European construction over the last five decades is a subject of high interest and causes both fascination and frustration. We start with a puzzle. On the one hand, it is not surprising to find that the breakdown of large federations is often accompanied by the creation and resurgence of smaller political units possessing proud national histories and identities. It is, however, somewhat counter to this conventional wisdom to observe that more and more nation states of Europe have been transferring or sharing their sovereignty—at least partially—thereby shifting some kind of loyalty to a new center. Much in the sense of Delors's famous *"objet politique non-identifié,"* this political construct defied any simple characterization until today. Given such fascination, it is frustrating to realize that academic analysis is still struggling to fully explore and explain such an evolution.

A major issue is the relation between deepening and widening. For a deeper look we shall use the concept of "imperial overstretch." first advanced by Paul Kennedy in the 1980s[1] and originally developed for the US. It also can be taken as an inspiration for the current debate on the outer borders of the EU and further attempts at institutionally strengthening the Union. Based on this premise, it is often argued that the sum of engagements, responsibilities and liabilities the EC/EU has taken on board outweigh its economic and political capacity to shoulder this burden and deliver the means necessary to achieve the self-set goals.[2] The capability-expectations gap[3] created by the EU will, according to this logic, increase with every round of enlargement and consequently result in overstretch. In this chapter, we shall consider different dimensions of possible overstretch in the EU but also opportunities that were and are used by European actors. Widening thus might turn out to give unexpected dynamics for deepening.

Conventional Wisdom: Two Lines of Argument

For this vital debate on the future destiny of Europe we can start by confronting two opposing lines of argument (see Graph 6.1, especially lines c and d).

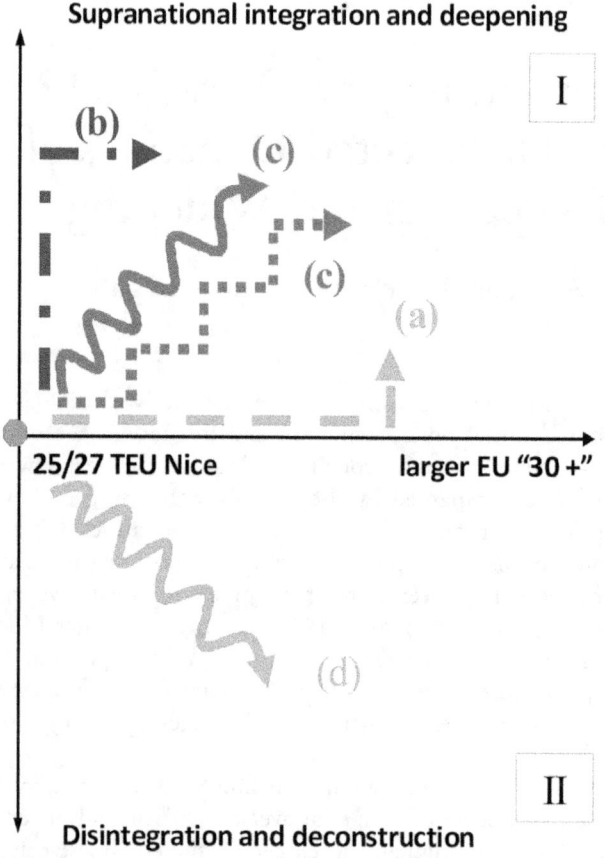

Graph 5.1: Scenarios of Integration
(a) Linear enlargement strategy: enlargement including minimal institutional adjustments without constitutional extension and upgrading.
(b) (Federal) community strategy: deepening first in order to be able to enlarge.
(c) Coupling option: close connection between enlargement and deepening – deepen and enlarge step by step or spirally.
(d) Intergovernmental approach: enlargement leads to disintegration.

Source: Adaptation of Anne Faber and Wolfgang Wessels, "Wider Europe, Deeper Integration? A Common Theoretical and Methodological Framework for EU CONSENT," Paper for the Kick-off Meeting, November 18, 2005, Brussels, online at http://www.eu-consent.net/content.asp?contentid=740.

A conventional school of thought might propose the argument of the "vicious spiral" (see line d in Graph 5.1) suggesting that continuous widening of the Union amounts to overstretch, which necessarily leads to disintegration and deconstruction of the status quo. The increased heterogeneity resulting from successive waves of accession by new member states weighs heavily on the institutional capacity of the EU to act efficiently and effectively by reducing the likelihood of reaching consensus necessary for decision making. From this point of view, particularly the last round of enlargement up to twenty-five to twenty-seven members should be the most appropriate test case for substantiating or disproving this line of argument.

The extrapolation of such an analysis can lead to the following prognosis: first, in institutional terms, with a country as large and singular as Turkey ranking high on the candidate list, any further widening of the EU will tend to exacerbate such trends toward disintegration; secondly, in terms of political culture, the absence of a clear delimitation of the future EU's outer borders and an ever greater societal and normative heterogeneity within the EU polity may result in the withdrawal of loyalty to the common institutions by some members. Thus, the democratic deficit, and with it the legitimacy gap, would widen even more.

The opposite line of argument suggests the dynamics of a "virtuous spiral" (see, for example, line c in Graph 5.1) in what has been described as "an ever closer union among the peoples of Europe."[4] Widening through enlargement and deepening through Treaty revisions are perceived as closely linked milestones, "history making decisions,"[5] and "critical junctures"[6] in the history of European integration. This method of incremental or "step by step" integration and enlargement has proven to be the feasible strategy, or rather compromise, throughout the history of the EU's evolution in between two other paths.

The first can be understood as a strategy of linear enlargement through the mere inclusion of new states into the members' club (see line a). Deepening would then constitute a possible next step. The second resembles a federal community option (see line b) where deepening results in a federal *finalité* via a qualitative quantum shift—the federal constitution establishing a new base of sovereignty which only then would be opened to new members. Applying this logic in a dynamic perspective, we can explain Treaty reforms, e.g., that of Nice, along these two criteria: while a Treaty reform was necessitated by enlargement so as to set the institutional parameters before the accession of ten new member states, the negotiations were, at the same time, deliberate attempts at deepening the Union's institutional reach, e.g. by the extension of qualified majority voting (QMV) and supranational forms of governance. The underlying and more general sustained dynamism can be understood as mutually reinforcing steps of "fusion"[7]—in a process that may not always be linear, but steady. The resulting Union may not fulfill conventional criteria of the nation-state in many respects, but it is becoming more supranational and increasingly assumes state-like features and functions.

Thus, we argue that, from this perspective, the process of integration can be understood as an endogenous dynamic that is self-sustaining because it rests on opportunity structures that, if followed, establish new ones. In this vein, widening and deepening are both catalyst and product in the continuous process labelled "integration." This may help to explain what might otherwise seem an unexpected or unintended evolution of the EU system.

On a point of methodology, those two schools of thought might seem simplified, if not simplistic, perspectives. However, their underlying analytical focus proves to be helpful for yielding more scientifically valuable insights. Much in the tradition of Popper's principles of scientific discovery,[8] our arguments must be falsifiable and applicable to a wide range of phenomena in order to be valued as a significant and meaningful contribution. A further constraint must be taken into account: these developments are probably best observed, supported or falsified, in a mid-range perspective—here understood as the period since the beginning of constructing the political system now called European Union.

The EU's development since its last enlargement by ten new member states in 2004 presents a critical test case for the arguments presented above. Are we witnessing a turning point toward a downward spiral of disintegration by enlargement, or do we find a medium term trend of successive rounds of successful enlargement and constitutional deepening in an upward spiral? Thus, let us have a closer look at both sets of arguments.

Finally, whether and how this can create "overstretch" will have to be tested and assessed against empirical evidence in the light of the so-called Copenhagen criteria, as set out by the European Council of Copenhagen of June 1993. In its declaration,[9] the European Council specifies the economic, political and legal criteria to be fulfilled by each candidate country in order to gain full membership status.

Vicious vs. Virtuous Spiral

The more conventional school of thought argues that subsequent rounds of widening have not been matched by equally successful attempts at deepening the EU, here understood as reforming the constitutional and institutional framework of the EU to enhance decision making, further generate legislative output in new policy areas, and ensure compliance in all member states. The accession of more countries with different historical backgrounds, different levels of economic performance, and different visions of the EU's *finalité* increases heterogeneity, and, by way of increased contestation and less consensus, also can erode the existing *acquis communautaire* and the effectiveness and efficiency of the common institutional framework. As the scope and density of binding regulatory policies will be reduced in a process often termed "spill-back," other states could more easily join what would then be a "looser EU," more in the sense of a free trade area or a regime of cooperation, rather than a full-blown political system. In essence, this argument predicts that the last and further enlargement will cause disintegration and deconstruction of the Union we see today.[10]

The Absorption Capacity—Institutional Overstretch or Testing the "Fourth" Copenhagen Criterion?

One essential set of arguments for the vicious spiral are based on a pessimistic reading of the impact accessions have had or will have on the institutional architecture. A good starting point, hence, forms what could be labelled the "fourth" Copenhagen criterion, i.e., "the Union's capacity to absorb new members, while maintaining the momentum of European integration."[11]

One major element in this line of thinking is sheer numbers. A look at the Treaty text reveals that widening essentially adds to the number of potential veto players,[12] or, to put it differently, it increases the probability of having blocking minorities in the Council whenever the rules allow qualified majority voting. Given the current decision-making procedures, statistical calculations and the counting of possible coalitions suggest that the likelihood of effective output-oriented decision making in a largely consensus-oriented system stands to be lowered. As the probability of agreement decreases, the options for blocking minorities increase.[13]

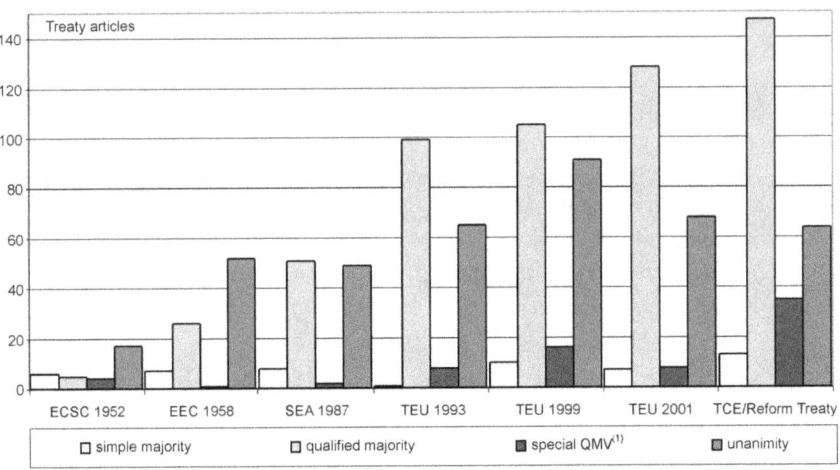

Graph 5.2: Development of QMV as mode of decision making in the Council 1952–2007

Special qualified majority includes:
- QMV with 72% of the members and 65% of the population, if decisions are not made upon proposal of the Commission of the Foreign Minister according to Art. I–25
- qualified majority decisions excluding the affected member state (QMV minus 1)
- qualified majority decisions with only a group of participating states, e.g. "enhanced cooperation" or decisions of the ?-group

Source: Wolfgang Wessels, "Keynote Article: The Constitutional Treaty – Three Readings from a Fusion Perspective," *Journal of Common Market Studies*, 43(2005), p. 23.

Concerning the rule of unanimity, more members with considerable differences may decrease the probability of securing the consensus necessary to pursue the Union's objectives and further deepen its reach into previously untouched policy areas.

These theoretical calculations, however, need not necessarily correspond to a practice of less consent—and, while we have only little experience so far from May 2004 onwards, there seems to be no indication of any such sustained trend.

In order to assess the weight of the argument on either side, we must turn to empirical evidence, i.e., to the behavior observed in the "living constitution."

Common rules, a common institutional framework, and "round-table socialization" often lead to the convergence of positions in an opportunity structure offering incentives for wider cooperation and deeper integration. In the process of bargaining and the formulation of package deals, the practice of horse-trading has proven successful—especially at the level of the European Council.

Furthermore, member states are willing and have agreed to extend the scope of application for QMV in the Council at each step of Treaty revisions[14] (see Graph 5.2).

As for the realities of the Council decision making, we observe some trends. All in all, the total amount of definitive legislative output (Graph 5.3) has moved within some margins. Importantly, no major decline or even stalling of legislative activity can so far be observed since 2004. The first year after enlargement shows a reduction in the level of total legislative output (see total in Graph 5.3).

Reasons for the drop from 2004 might be:

- "Pre-accession rush" in the first half of 2004, where total legislative output was unusually high to have the business finished before new members moved in.
- A new Commission and a new EP starting to work.
- More time needed to adopt in a larger group of twenty-five.
- New cleavages in the larger group.

As for the issue of new members as increasing problems of decision making, we find that regular voting patterns in the Council can be said to continue (see Graph 5.3).

In cases like legislative acts passing successfully, the share of "no" votes in the Council, or the contestation of votes carried out under QMV has not increased since the 2004 enlargement.[15] Also, data on the single countries' voting behavior do not show a pattern of a state or coalition being consistently outvoted where legislative acts have been adopted by QMV.[16] This indicates further, that for successfully passed legislative acts, cleavages in the Council appear to be "issue"- or "sector"-based, rather than "coalition-based."

Another indicator for the continuing efficiency of the decision-making process in the EU is shown by the real use of the co-decision procedure in successfully concluded legislative acts. The output (total acts) has not decreased and the process has been even faster (smaller numbers of conciliation).

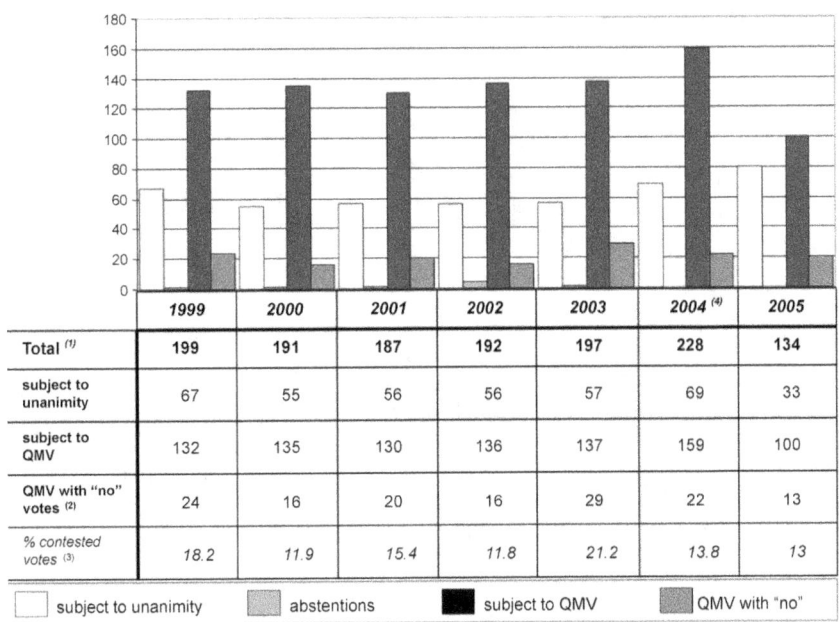

Graph 5.3: Legislative Output Adopted 1999–2005

(1) Total includes all legislative acts passed under unanimity and QMV, as well as single majority votes, not listed here.
(2) This category represents all legislative acts passed under QMV where at least one member state has voted "no". These votes are here called "contested votes". Abstentions are not considered.
(3) This represents the share (in percent) of contested votes out of all legislative acts passed under QMV.
(4) There was increased activity, a "pre-accession rush," in the months prior to enlargement.

Source: "Monthly Summary of Council Acts," available at: http://www.consilium.europa.eu/cms3_fo/showPage.asp?id=551&lang=en (last visited August 16, 2006). Compilation and calculation by Daniel Schraad, Jean Monnet Chair, Cologne. See also Fiona Hayes-Renshaw, "The Council Post Enlargement: Tables and Figures," Paper presented at the Conference "One Process of Europeanization or Several? EU Governance in a Context of Internationalisation," European University Institute, Florence, June 30, 2006.

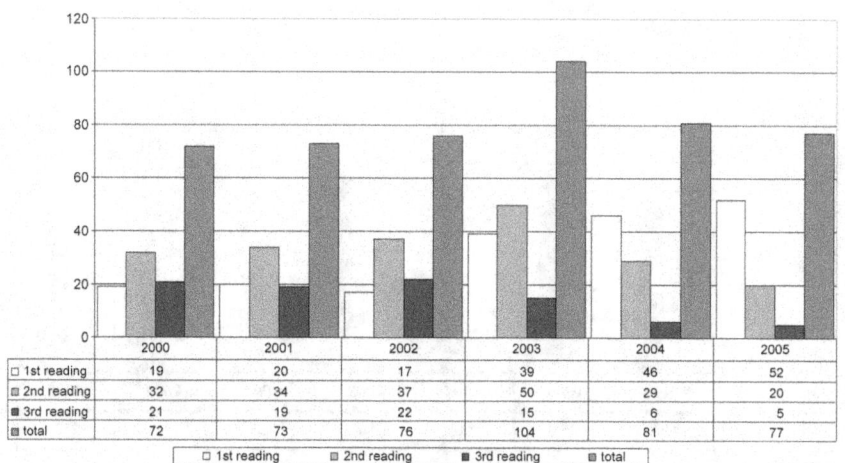

Graph 5.4: Co-decision procedures concluded 2000–2005

Source: Representation based on Fiona Hayes-Renshaw, "The Council Post Enlargement: Tables and Figures," Paper presented at the Conference "One Process of Europeanization or Several? EU Governance in a Context of Internationalization," European University Institute, Florence, June 30, 2006.

Therefore there is good reason to believe in continuity, as it appears that the necessary majorities can be gained also with a larger and more diverse European Parliament (see Graph 5.4). A slight trend of concluding legislative proposals already after the first reading may not say anything definitive about the total period of time it takes for legislation to be passed (or about legislation still in the pipeline), but it does show that the legislative process functions along the same lines as before.

The observation of any such tendencies, however, can be only supported by limited empirical evidence due to the short time span elapsed since 2004. These data may indicate no more than merely a first period of new members getting acquainted with their role in the Council. What can be said with a sufficient degree of evidence, however, is that the logic of the vicious spiral or the much feared collapse of the decision-making process has not taken place. Widening has not, as it stands, led to the disintegration of the EU's institutional architecture.

More fundamentally, most—if not all—member states understand the necessity of efficient decision-making procedures in the framework of the EC/EU as part of their national interest. States do not accede to the Union in order to pursue a negative strategy of blockade, but a positive one for securing the Union's support in issues vital to their own national preferences. This pattern of behavior indicates that the EU system offers an opportunity structure in which incentives and benefits lie in the intensive use of the given, even if inadequate, institutional architecture.

Furthermore, another argument needs to be discussed. There is no historical evidence that lends support to believing in a longer-term trend of deterioration of the EU institutional architecture. The Empty Chair Crisis in 1965 stands as a powerful reminder that, also and especially in the early Community of the founding fathers, the mere weight of vested interest by one member state can be as obstructive to the forming of consensus as is the reconciliation of a greater number of divergent interests. It is even worth arguing that the effect of diminished consensus in theory, i.e., in the treaty letters, can be offset by the opposite effect in practice: the greater the total number, the less single states or small groups of members will be inclined to oppose the pressure of a relatively larger majority.[17]

Implementing the Acquis: National Overstrain?

As the EU is a multilevel system, we have to be aware that the institutional issue does not apply only to the Brussels arena but that what we describe as "overstretch" at the Union level we might call "overstrain" at the national and regional levels. Administrative and political systems of member states are challenged to adapt to the multifaceted Brussels arena as well as to absorb and implement the technicalities of the existing *acquis communautaire*. The performance of the Union depends to a large degree on the capacity of national, regional and local administrations to deliver "on the ground."

With respect to the third Copenhagen criterion, the national transposition of the *acquis communautaire*, the vicious spiral assumes that greater differences and divergences of positions in a larger and more heterogeneous Union will lead to the weakening and reduction of the *acquis*. Such erosion can occur through the persistent failure by members to implement and abide by EC/EU legal acts, which may overstretch the Union's institutional and legal capacity to consistently monitor and secure compliance. Again, the argument of the vicious spiral assumes at this point that more and more member states, old and new, are increasingly less "fit"—institutionally and administratively—to deal with these tasks.

A look at the empirical evidence of national adaptations has clearly established that there is not only one domestic way of interacting with Brussels.[18] In the absence of any such one single way or model for member states to follow, most governments of old member states have nonetheless been able to adapt to the demands and benefits of the EU system.

However, we have only limited insight[19] into the new member states' capacity to be or become an efficient and effective multilevel player. No generic lesson can be drawn yet in view of a potential "fitness" for dealing with the *acquis*. Thus, the difficulties might be larger inside the member states than in the European arena and we might observe these effects only later in the process.

Divergence and Difference: Political, Economic, and Geopolitical Overstretch?

Beyond arguments about the impact that further widening would have on the EU architecture, i.e., potential institutional overstretch and overstrain, there has been an extended debate about the necessary or, indeed, existing degree of cultural homogeneity and/or heterogeneity within the political system. In other words, we have to discuss what a "European identity" might mean in a European would-be polity,[20] and if there are necessary and sufficient criteria to determine such a demand for a political community. We test for the different dimensions of such overstretch.

One yardstick is the first Copenhagen criterion. Taking up fundamental demands of the early federalist thinking, it stresses that "[m]embership requires that the candidate country has achieved stability of institutions guaranteeing democracy, the rule of law, human rights and respect for and protection of minorities."[21] In retrospect, this set of norms was a highly useful instrument to reform the constitutional system of many applicant states and it continues to affect national evolutions in the Balkans and in Turkey.

We should, however, stress that the wording of this threshold does not mention potential cleavages in the political or religious culture, which we will take up below.

The second Copenhagen criterion stresses the importance of a functioning market economy in all member states. The difficulties for the Union may lie in the varying capacities of national economies to adapt and transform, let alone succeed, given the diverse spectrum of national structures and performance.

The debate about the economic preconditions for entering the Single Market and Economic and Monetary Union has been fierce. On one side, while the transition economies of recent newcomers are afraid of losing the choice of some policy instruments for modernization (e.g., levels of customs), the more prosperous Western European states with a high degree of welfare standards are worried about the newly encountered competition often denounced as "social" and "environmental dumping."

Again, empirical evidence points to a number of success stories, where ever closer economic integration and full EU membership have contributed to the generation of considerable additional growth, such as in Ireland and Finland—amongst others. In fact, economic developments in Central and Eastern Europe suggest that the new members prove to be very competitive and fast at economic transformation and modernization—to the benefit of the common market, and to the detriment of some vested interests in older member states. Thus, economic overstretch appears to be less of a problem for the Union's overall economic performance, or that of its newer members, but it is most visible in those member states that display the greatest resistance to change and adaptation.

A closely related argument touches upon the different social models that exist across the Union, which can be broadly categorized into the Rhineland, Anglo-Saxon, Mediterranean and Scandinavian models, as well as an emerging model in the new member states.²² Some single market initiatives—such as the recently agreed Services Directive—reveal that in spite of significant incompatibilities underlying national understandings of a "Social Europe," we observe areas of compromise for common instruments. Also via the open method of coordination the member states have attempted to extend the reach of EU activities into areas of social welfare.

A further issue in the debate concerns geopolitical issues in the realm of the Common Foreign and Security Policy (CFSP) of the Union. A multitude of divergent foreign policy interests, so powerfully displayed over the issue of the US-led intervention in Iraq, may stand in the way of forging a common position or strategy in matters of external action. This *domaine reservé* of the nation-state has firmly resisted any pressures of supranationalization. This can be seen in the principle of unanimity as well as Treaty provisions governing CFSP or special clauses acting as "emergency brakes."²³ At the same time, we observe that the number of commonly agreed output has increased noticeably, indicating more activities of the EU as some kind of actor in the international system.²⁴ This also applies to the relatively new emergence and recent strengthening of a European Security and Defense Policy.²⁵

Empirical evidence can add to how this heterogeneity affects the workings of the Union: does it work as a brake, a catalyst or an engine for scope enlargement of the EU? One lesson seems to be that (re-)negotiations by new members have driven a continuous extension of policy areas in the Union. This trend can be explained through the logic of bargaining in the Council, where a wide spectrum of new differentiated policy areas can enter EU policy making in two ways.

First, this can be done via the standard practice of concluding package deals among member states. In the European Council, each of the heads of states and governments puts his or her preferences for EU action on the table: adding them all up leads to considerable scope enlargement and task expansion of the EU system, as witnessed over the last decades.

Secondly it can be done via "departmental cartels," where ministers can push their agendas more easily in the company of colleagues and in the absence of other rivalling or mutually exclusive interests—as would be the case in probably any national cabinet or within coalition governments.

The Debate on Fundamentals: Cultural Overstretch?

Issues of institutional efficiency and instrumental effectiveness are one part of a reflective discussion of enlargement. In view of the Copenhagen criteria; there is also the wider political debate on the less tangible fundamentals. We might call this the implicit normative, cultural, or even emotional overstretch; more provocatively, there is a hidden "fifth" Copenhagen criterion that ties into the larger question whether, and if yes to what extent, any "political community" needs a widely shared consensus on its identity and vocation.²⁶

When analyzing and testing these arguments, one should distinguish more fundamentally between objective and deeply entrenched differences and those that are constructed, cultivated, and subject to changing perceptions, self- and other-regarding. Major steps in the history and evolution of the European construction let us realise that quite a few so-called historical "untouchables" and structural divergences have been put to debate only to then be overturned by political decisions. Thus, the basic conditions such as time, history and geography do not allow us to predict future outcomes.

To approach this issue, we might look at public attitudes as revealed by surveys, e.g., Eurobarometer and the European value survey.[27] Such debates tie into what the European Court of Justice has termed the "constitutional traditions"[28] of member states. Also, the debates about the reference to a common Judeo-Christian heritage in the Constitutional Treaty's preamble, and importantly its omission, are valid examples.

While earlier debates about the Catholic/Carolingian nature and identity of the six founding members were thought to have been settled, similar debates have been reignited with the question of Turkey's accession. Full membership is discussed with reference to performance regarding the three Copenhagen criteria, to the EU's institutional ability to absorb this large country,[29] and quite often more importantly, to identity. Popular rejections, as seen in the constitutional referendums in France and the Netherlands, are taken as clear signals that this dimension is very much alive in the public debate—quite apart from the technicalities of the actual accession negotiations. This dimension is even more relevant as a Turkish accession treaty will be subject to referendums in some member countries.

Criticism of Turkey's accession often targets the country's supposed lack of a stipulated "proper Europeanness." It is argued that Turkish membership will deal the final blow to any conceivable *finalité politique* and to the common identity grounded on *fondement culturel*.

As to this set of arguments, the debates on the Constitutional Treaty have again documented that member states—old or new—are far from having established a consensus on one single vision, a *finalité politique*, an overarching *Leitbild*,[30] a "constitutional idea,"[31] or a common set of shared symbols. Across and within the different member states, we observe the coexistence of divergent political and philosophical traditions. Different experiences and opposing interpretations of history, not only of and since World War II, lead to significantly divergent expectations about what purpose the Union serves and should serve for the member states and the European citizen, or what the Union is and should be.

A classical juxtaposition of this debate focuses on a federal vision for Europe as a "United States of Europe" such as that held by Churchill,[32] Monnet,[33] or more recently Kohl[34] and Verhofstadt.[35] This is opposed to the intergovernmentalist perspective held by, for instance, General de Gaulle, who spoke of a "Europe des patries,"[36] or Tony Blair who claimed that Europe should be "a superpower but not a superstate."[37] The particular importance attached to national pride, identity, and sovereignty in some of the new member states of Central and Eastern Europe provokes opposition to what is sometimes perceived as nothing but a shift of dependency from Moscow to Brussels.

One alternative *Leitbild* or vision for the Union's *finalité* limits its purpose to the realization of mere economic integration or cooperation. According to this perspective, the EUs competences and activities should be strictly limited to those directly relevant to guaranteeing the functioning of the common market and, where necessary, be cut back. EU institutions should serve as agents of the member states to establish and uphold a single market—and not to form some kind of state. In this view, member states are the "Masters of the Treaties"[38] and the "principals"[39] in the running of the EU machinery—and not vice versa.

It is a major part of the EU's fascination that, given the lack of a single vision, any significant progress should have been made at all. The existence of different views on the *finalité* results in a complex web of pooled and shared competences across the different levels of the EU, and in several different readings of the institutional architecture.

Thus, as an example of the ambiguity of the present vision, the Constitutional Treaty might be interpreted both as a step toward a kind of federal state or, alternatively, as an instrument for reinforcing the nation state and its role in the EU architecture.[40]

Conclusion: Overstretch vs. Opportunity

Testing for overstretch along all Copenhagen criteria, real and implied, we must still be puzzled that against many odds, as enumerated by the vicious spiral, a productive dynamic should have led to a closely linked process of widening and deepening, so far at least. While the facts of a greater number of members and more heterogeneity in the Union cannot be denied, the observed consequences—so far—do not appear to follow from the explicit and implicit assumptions and predictions of the pessimistic school of thought, predicting several dimensions of overstretch. Counter to that, however, we can observe some "abnormal" effects: the ever greater numbers of and differences among member states have, in fact, led to the extension of the EU's policy scope and to repeated reforms of the institutional architecture.

Even if our set of arguments in line with a virtuous spiral is plausible, we should nonetheless be careful not to simply and indefinitely extrapolate such a trend into the future. Turkey might be a different case altogether.

But, before we are drawn to the pessimistic scenario of the vicious spiral, we should discuss in how far the case of Turkey, or even Serbia, would make a significant difference to the argument of the virtuous spiral. Based on the implicit dynamics of integration, the preparation for full membership of those countries may lead to yet another step of deepening and institutional reform. Major elements of the Constitutional Treaty, for example, could serve as a starting point for those next steps within the EU construction. This argumentation understands widening as opportunity. Thus pressures for Turkish membership might be used as a strategy for also deepening at the same time.

As in the past, it has been one of the most fascinating, if puzzling, phenomena in Europe, that distinct national entities would voluntarily converge in a process of integration—and not because of their stipulated similarities and a given shared identity, but despite their acknowledged differences. "United in [spite of] diversity"[41] remains a fundamental pattern. The limits of such a dynamic will certainly be tested.

Notes

1. Paul Kennedy, *The Rise and Fall of the Great Powers*, New York: Random House, 1987.
2. For a current debate on these objectives see, for example, the preamble and Article III -292 of the Treaty Establishing a Constitution for Europe.
3. Christopher Hill, "The Capability–Expectations Gap or Conceptualizing Europe's International Role," *Journal of Common Market Studies*, 31.3 (2003), pp. 305–28.
4. Treaty on European Union, Article 1 TEU.
5. John Peterson and Elizabeth Bomberg, *Decision Making in the European Union*, Houndmills: Palgrave, 1999, pp. 10–16.
6. Paul Pierson, "The New Politics of the Welfare State," *World Politics*, 48 (1996), pp. 143–79.
7. Wolfgang Wessels, "Keynote Article: The Constitutional Treaty—Three Readings from a Fusion Perspective," *Journal of Common Market Studies*, 43 (2005), pp. 11–36.
8. See Karl R. Popper, *The Logic of Scientific Discovery*, New York: Harper and Row, 1959.
9. European Council, *Conclusions of the Presidency*, Copenhagen, June 21–22, 1993, SN 180/93.
10. See for this debate Jens Alber and Wolfgang Merkel, "Introduction: Europas Osterweiterung: Das Ende der Vertiefung?" in: Jens Alber and Wolfgang Merkel (eds.), *Europas Osterweiterung: Das Ende der Vertiefung?* Berlin: Wissenschaftszentrum, 2006, pp. 13–31.
11. European Council, *Conclusions of the Presidency*, SN 180/1993, p. 12.
12. George Tsebelis, *Veto Players: How Political Institutions Work*, Princeton and New York: Princeton University Press, 2002.
13. For a statistical calculation of this point see: Richard Baldwin and Mika Widgrén, "Council Voting in the Constitutional Treaty: Devil in the Details," June 23, 2004, online at http://www.cepr.org/pubs/new-dps/dplist.asp?dpno=4450 (last visited August 1, 2006).
14. Wessels, "Keynote Article."
15. There is, as yet, no evidence for the total number of failed legislative acts out of those proposed.
16. For empirical evidence see Fiona Hayes-Renshaw, "The Council Post Enlargement: Tables and Figures," Paper presented at the Conference "One Process of Europeanization or Several? EU Governance in a Context of Internationalisation," European University Institute, Florence, June 30, 2006.
17. The UK position on the British rebate in the last round of negotiations on the mid-term financial perspective might be an example for this argument.

18. See Jürgen Mittag and Wolfgang Wessels, "The 'One' and the 'Fifteen'? The Member States between Procedural Adaptation and Structural Revolution," in: Jürgen Mittag, Andreas Maurer and Wolfgang Wessels (eds.), *Fifteen into One? The European Union and its Member States*, Manchester and New York: Manchester University Press, 2003, pp. 413–54; Simon Bulmer and Christian Lequesne, *The Member States of the European Union*, Oxford: Oxford University Press, 2005.
19. Barbara Lippert and Gaby Umbach, *Pressures of Europeanisation: From Post-Communist State Administrations Towards Normal Players in the EU System*, Baden-Baden: Nomos, 2005.
20. Leon N. Lindberg and Stuart A. Scheingold, *Europe's Would-Be Polity: Patterns of Change in the European Community*, Englewood Cliffs, NJ: Prentice Hall, 1970.
21. European Council, *Conclusions of the Presidency*, SN 180/1993, p. 12.
22. André Sapir, Philippe Aghion, Giuseppe Bertola, Martin Hellwig, Jean Pisani-Ferry, Dariusz Rosati, José Viñals and Helen Wallace, with Marco Buti, Mario Nova and Peter M. Smith, *An Agenda for a Growing Europe: The Sapir Report*, Oxford: Oxford University Press, 2004, pp. 65–67. The publication is based on a report of an Independent High-Level Study Group established on the initiative of European Commission President Romano Prodi.
23. See Wessels, "Keynote Article."
24. Elfriede Regelsberger, "Gemeinsame Außen- und Sicherheitspolitik," in: Werner Weidenfeld and Wolfgang Wessels (eds.), *Jahrbuch der Europäischen Integration 2005*, Baden-Baden: Nomos, 2005, pp. 241–49.
25. See Charlotte Bretherton and John Vogler *The European Union as a Global Actor*, London and New York: Routledge, 2006.
26. See, for example, David Easton, *A Systems Analysis of Political Life*, New York: Wiley, 1965.
27. For Eurobarometer see http://ec.europa.eu/public_opinion/index_en.htm (last visited August 1, 2006); for the European Values System Study Group, see http://www.europeanvalues.nl/index2.htm (last visited August 1, 2006).
28. For the establishment of Human Rights as general principles of Community law see Case 29/69 *Stauder* [1969] ECR 419; Case 11/70 *Internationale Handelsgesellschaft* [1970] ECR 1125; and Case 4/73 *Nold* [1974] ECR 491.
29. European Council, *Conclusions of the Presidency*, Brussels, June 15–16, 2006, SN 10633/1/06, p.19.
30. Heinrich Schneider, *Leitbilder der Europapolitik: 1. Der Weg zur Integration*, Bonn: Europa Union Verlag 1977.
31. Markus Jachtenfuchs, "Constitutionalizing the EU: Causes and Effects," Paper at the EUSA Ninth Biennial International Conference, Austin/Texas, 2005.
32. See Winston Churchill, "Speech to the Academic Youth," Zurich, September 19, 1946, online at http://www.europa-web.de/europa/02wwswww/202histo/churchil.htm (last visited August 1, 2006).
33. Jean Monnet, *Mémoires*, Paris: Fayard, 1975, p. 475.
34. Rede von Bundeskanzler Dr. Helmut Kohl am 3. April 1992 in Königswinter vor dem Bertelsmann-Forum zu Zielvorstellungen und Chancen für die Zukunft Europas, in: Auswärtiges Amt (ed.) *Gemeinsame Außen- und Sicherheitspolitik der Europäischen Union (GASP)—Dokumentation 10*, Bonn: Auswärtiges Amt, 1994, p. 511.
35. Guy Verhofstadt, *The United States of Europe*, London: Federal Trust, 2006.
36. Charles de Gaulle at a press conference on May 15, 1962; see Charles de Gaulle, *Discours et Messages. Tome III.: Avec le Renouveau (1958–1962)*, Paris: Edition Plon, 1970, pp. 402–9.

37. Tony Blair, Speech to the Polish Stock Exchange, Warsaw, October 6, 2000, online at http://www.busch.uni-hd.de/data/blair_warsaw.html.
38. Bundesverfassungsgericht 1993, *Brunner et al. v. The European Union Treaty* (Cases 2 BvR 2134/92 and 2159/92), Judgment of October 12, 1993.
39. See, for example, Hussein Kassim and Anand Menon, "The Principal-Agent Approach and the Study of the European Union: Promise Unfulfilled?" *Journal of European Public Policy*, 10.1 (2003), pp. 121–39.
40. Wessels, "Keynote Article."
41. See Article I-8 of the Treaty Establishing a Constitution for Europe: "The motto of the Union shall be: 'United in diversity'."

6

Learning from Failure: The Evolution of the EU's Foreign, Security and Defense Policy in the Course of the Yugoslav Crisis

Mathias Jopp and Udo Diedrichs

The evolution of the EU's Common Foreign and Security Policy (CFSP) has been analyzed intensively in the last fifteen years, particularly in the perspective of Treaty reforms and institutional adaptation.[1] What still remain promising to investigate are the driving forces and motivations that lie behind procedural and institutional dynamics of the CFSP. A key explanation for the reform of the CFSP in response to major external shocks is offered by the concept of policy learning, which has gained in prominence in recent years, particularly in the wake of discovering the merits of constructivist perspectives on the EU and its foreign policy.[2] A crucial element of learning lies in the individual and collective interpretation of events, and our assumption is that this also serves as a driving force for institutional changes suited to improve the performance of the EU as an international actor.

Taking up these ideas, we shall explore the impact of the crisis in former Yugoslavia on the process of constructing a European foreign, security and defense policy. The breakup of Yugoslavia represented a major challenge to the political order of the European continent after the end of the Cold War, and, at the same time, it put the European Community (EC)/European Union (EU) and its ambition to play a role in world politics to the hardest test ever since, marking a "baptism by fire."[3] In the early 1990s, the EC was caught by surprise, poorly prepared for handling a conflict of such dynamics and intensity: "Europe as a political entity did not exist when the crisis began, and foreign-policy coordination among EC member states in the framework of EPC had been developed to deal with external problems of secondary importance, not with high politics or questions of war and peace."[4]

The conflict in Yugoslavia threatened the identity of Europe and the European Community, Europe's "founding myth of itself,"[5] by contradicting the very substance of the foreign policy belief system developed and shared under European Political Cooperation (EPC): the primacy of peaceful coexistence and non violent conflict resolution and the growing irrelevance of borders and territorial boundaries. To the surprise of many, the relevance of borders, history and ethnic or nationalist aspirations proved to be very much alive.

The Dark Hour of Europe

The Yugoslav tragedy began with the secession of Slovenia and Croatia from the Yugoslav Federation in 1991, which had been preceded by a political and economic crisis escalating in the late 1980s. At the time it was first of all the EC that took the lead in efforts of conflict resolution since major powers such as the US or the Soviet Union showed little interest in taking care of Yugoslavia. The initial reaction of the EC member states to the crisis was oriented toward preserving the integrated federal State of Yugoslavia and not supporting its secession. A consensus existed on the grounds that the conflict should be solved by peaceful means, and nobody within the EC wished to see the Yugoslav federation break up into half a dozen new states on the European map. Also, some governments of EC member states were concerned about secessionist tendencies in the Balkans as they were confronted with separatism in their own countries.[6]

All this worked as a common denominator for diplomatic action by the Twelve until the declarations of independence by Slovenia and Croatia in June 1991. The EC reacted to this in a rather creative way with a number of political and economic measures:[7]

- The EC Troika was sent to the region in order to move the conflicting parties into negotiations for preserving the unity of the federation.
- The EC brokered the Accord of Brioni in July 1991, where Slovenia and Croatia agreed to three months' moratorium on implementing their declarations of independence, while the Yugoslav authorities promised to stop military actions, paving the way for negotiations on the future political order of Yugoslavia.
- For Slovenia, a European Community Monitoring Mission (ECMM) was set up to control the cease-fire and the implementation of the agreement, and which marked an "important step toward an active foreign policy"[8] of the EC.
- The EC convened a Peace Conference in The Hague in September 1991 to bring representatives from all Yugoslav republics to the table;
- The EC set up an Arbitration Commission (Badinter Commission) for elaborating, *inter alia*, criteria for recognition of new states.
- After the attack of the eastern Croatian city of Vukovar in November 1991 by Serbian paramilitary forces and regular Yugoslav Army troops, the EC moved toward using the instrument of recognizing the new republics emerging from ex-Yugoslavia.

- An embargo on all armaments and military equipment had been imposed upon the whole of Yugoslavia by the EC member states already in July 1991. This initiative was followed by a similar embargo by the UN on the initiative of France and Britain three months later in September that year. Furthermore, the second and third financial protocols providing for financial support of the EC to the Yugoslav Federation under the still existing cooperation agreement were suspended.
- In 1992, the WEU, in anticipation of the Maastricht Treaty, acted on behalf of the EU by starting to monitor the EU embargo with marine forces in the Adriatic and later police or customs control boats on the Danube.

However, on the whole, the EC was not very successful with its crisis management in the first phase of the conflict. The Peace Conference had largely failed, while the arms embargo had put the Serbian forces in a strategic advantage as they had inherited the bulk of the military equipment of the Yugoslav People's Army. It lasted about two years, until the embargo and the economic sanctions were only applied to Serbia and Montenegro. The recognition policy, for which the EC had developed criteria, was not conducted in a coherent fashion. Germany was highly receptive to the demands of Croatia and Slovenia, while France and the UK had traditionally good relations with Belgrade and tried to counter the perceived rising German influence in the Balkans. The German Government, under mounting pressure by the German public for doing too little about a solution of the crisis decided to move ahead and to recognize Slovenia and Croatia in December 1991. This unilateral move exercised enormous pressure on the other countries in January 1992.[9] Not only did a common approach fail in the case of Croatia and Slovenia; but also Macedonia had to stay on the waiting list for quite a long time because of Greece's refusal to accept the country's name.

But there was limited success, too; the fact that the EC institutional system had helped to prevent the fallback to classical power and alliance policies among the major Western European governments toward the Balkans was a proof of the functioning of the EU's institutional system. And, with the internationalization of the conflict that was triggered by the recognition of new states in the Balkans, the UN became more involved in the crisis and was able to send peacekeepers (UNPROFOR) to Croatia and, later, to Bosnia-Hercegovina.

The Maastricht Reform in the Shadow of the Unfolding Crisis

In the early phase of the crisis, the EC first of all had to develop instruments without formal Treaty reform in an innovative attempt to mobilise diplomatic and political resources. The Troika missions represented an important precedent.[10] Thus, the Yugoslav crisis served as a catalyst for innovation and solutions *"avant la lettre"*, before they became formally part of the CFSP toolkit.

For enhancing the visibility and consistency of the EC's position, special representatives were nominated by the member states—first Lord Carrington, then Lord Owen who were the forerunners of what would later become the EU's special representative for Southeastern Europe. The ECMM was a de facto civilian crisis management operation with the clear objective to contribute to a strengthening of discipline of the parties of the conflict to keep to their commitments. But it lacked resources and staff, and the Dutch foreign ministry even had to reactivate retired diplomats for the mission.[11] Despite its hasty creation, its poor media image and the strict limitations on its functioning, the ECMM fulfilled an important role for the EC: it showed a European presence on the ground.

The EC also made use of the close link between economic and political instruments not only through the arms embargo but also by suspending the trade and cooperation agreement with Belgrade. Although the success of this strategy was not overwhelming, and not adequate in view of the military escalation in Yugoslavia, it became a method for future contractual relations in which the EU tried to commit its external partners to standards in democracy, human rights, and respect for international law. And, finally, as uncoordinated and problematic the recognition of the EU may have been and thereby damaging the perception of the EU as a unified actor, the recognition opened the door for UN involvement and for the deployment of blue helmets to the former Yugoslavia.

Beyond these pragmatic measures, the Yugoslav crisis triggered major demands for Treaty changes, but also complicated, at the same time, the reform debate on the future EU's foreign and security policy in the framework of the intergovernmental negotiations on the Maastricht Treaty. The presidency was constantly overcharged, on the one hand, with handling a highly complex and controversial set of negotiations on institutional reform and, on the other, with trying to manage a major international crisis with limited instruments available.[12] It was particularly the Dutch presidency from July until December 1991 that came under heavy pressure due to this double stress.

It should also be noted that the items that were discussed at the Intergovernmental Conference (IGC) in connection with the creation of a CFSP and a defense policy were highly relevant for the future performance of the EC as an international actor in crisis management.[13] All questions about the shaping of the future CFSP and its transformation into European primary law were discussed between the member states against the backdrop of the Yugoslav crisis, leading to a cautious, minimalist design of the CFSP with an exclusively intergovernmental nature, unanimous decision making, and a limited set of instruments and competences. Particular ambitions like the one of Germany and Italy aiming at strengthening the ties between the EC/EPC and the UN via the two European permanent UN Security Council (UNSC) members with a view to introducing joint European positions in the UNSC also resulted from the Yugoslav experience, without, however, finding its precise wording in the final text of the Maastricht Treaty.[14] Not the least, there were clear efforts by the UK and the Dutch Presidency not to give WEU any prominent role in the management of the crisis in order to weaken successfully the arguments of those member states who favoured WEU in political practice and in treaty theory as the future defense component of the EU. Hence, the Maastricht Treaty enabled the EU only to "request" WEU to implement decisions with defense implications.

The Bosnian Tragedy

The European Union, after having recognized Bosnia-Hercegovina in April 1992, had no solution at hand for controlling the outburst of violence. The Treaty reform of Maastricht had slightly strengthened the institutional basis of the EU's foreign policy, but left the EU practically with a nonexisting security and defense dimension. Any plan for peaceful coexistence of the Croats, the Muslims, and the Bosnian Serbs (who were supported by Belgrade) failed between 1992 and 1994,[15] while ethnic cleansing became a serious case of genocide in European history.

The US administration altered its position on the Balkan tragedy and dropped the idea of Yugoslav unity, while identifying the aggressive Serbian policy as the main problem. It proposed a completely different approach by suggesting the lifting of the arms embargo against the Bosnian Muslims, and by launching air strikes against the Bosnian Serbs. These options were rejected by the Europeans at the time so that the gap between the EC and the US widened and deepened.[16] Nevertheless, the US's suggestion to enforce the no-fly ban of the UN of October 1992 over Bosnia was met with the support of the Europeans for UNSC resolution 816 in March 1993 allowing NATO to take action beyond purely monitoring breaches of the no-fly ban.

In 1994, the escalation of violence in the Balkans moved NATO even more into the center of the discussion, and, after the shelling of the marketplace in Sarajevo in February 1994, NATO threatened the Bosnian Serbs with an ultimatum, calling for a lift of the siege of Sarajevo. It was Russia's intervention that saved the Bosnian Serbs from attacks when special envoy Vitaly Churkin achieved a withdrawal of Serbian forces from the Bosnian capital. As a result of this event the big power Contact Group for Bosnia was established in spring 1994, providing for a new forum made up of the US, Russia, the UK, France, and Germany, in which the EU as an organization was not represented.

In order to respond to the ongoing ethnic cleansing, the UN had already extended in April and May 1993 the tasks of the UNPROFOR mission to also protect a number of so-called safe havens in Bosnia, *inter alia* the cities of Sarajevo, Gorazde, and Srebrenica. Two critical events—the massacre by the Serbs in the UN safe haven of Srebrenica in July 1995 and the new shelling of the marketplace in Sarajevo on August 28, 1995—triggered NATO's response. Between August 30 and September 20, 1995, operation Deliberate Force was carried out, based mainly upon US air power, supported by the UK and France, with the aim of bombing Bosnian Serbian military positions.[17]

The NATO operation prepared the ground for serious negotiations between the conflicting parties (the Bosnian Serbs being represented by Belgrade) at an airbase near Dayton, Ohio, where they accepted in the end a model for a decentralized state of Bosnia-Hercegovina, building on elements of thinking that had existed before within the EU. But it was US pressure and strength and the military threat by NATO that made the difference from previous attempts at achieving peace through negotiations. The solution to the conflict was agreed in Ohio, and the "General Framework Agreement for Peace in Bosnia and Hercegovina" was signed in Paris in December 1995.[18]

The Amsterdam Treaty Reforms and the Impact of Yugoslavia

The experience of trying to manage the Yugoslav Crisis had a tremendous impact on the debate among the EU governments in the run-up to the 1996/97 review conference of the Maastricht Treaty. Apart from the earlier problem of a fundamental split in the interests between the three larger member states, a number of systemic deficiencies of the EU's CFSP had become clear in the course of the crisis:[19]

First, there were in general no or only a little common assessment and analysis of the developing crisis. This resulted, time and again, in strongly diverging views on what to do (and how) in reaction to the conflict. Secondly, the EU lacked visibility, consistency, continuity, and coherence in its external action. The six monthly rotating presidencies and, in accordance with this, the changing Troika formations did not strengthen the image of the EU as an identifiable international actor. Thirdly, the EU's activities always came too late, lagging behind developments on the ground in former Yugoslavia. The diplomatic and economic measures taken were too weak in comparison with the escalating scale of the conflict. Stronger crisis instruments and facilitation of decision making were overdue, including the introduction of a greater flexibility allowing a group of member states to act if they wished to do so. Last but not least, the EU's policy and diplomacy were without teeth because they lacked serious military underpinning.

As far as the foreign policy of the EU is concerned, the negotiations on the Amsterdam Treaty resulted in a number of considerable improvements based on the experience made in former Yugoslavia. First, the Heads of States and Governments decided at Amsterdam in June 1997 to create the post of a High Representative for the CFSP, providing the EU with a face and a voice in foreign policy (Arts. 18 and 26 TEU/J8 and J16 Amsterdam). This decision also reflected the wish to increase coherence and consistency over a period that would cover several presidencies. It was no surprise that Javier Solana, who was to become the first incumbent of the post, spent a great deal of time in the Balkans, where he coordinated the EU's efforts, particularly in Macedonia and Bosnia. Furthermore, the possibility of sending special representatives of the EU to a crisis region, for the first time exercised in the Yugoslav case, became part of the EU treaty (Art. 18(5) TEU/J8(5)Amsterdam).

Another reform resulted in the setting up of an independent capability for information and analysis. The tasks of the Policy Planning and Early Warning Unit (PPEWU), made up of staff coming from the Council, the Commission, the member states, and WEU, included after Declaration No. 6 annexed to the Amsterdam Treaty: the monitoring and analysis of developments in relevant areas for the CFSP, the assessment of the Union's interests, the identification of areas where the CFSP should focus in the future, the "early warning of events and situations that may have significant repercussions" for the Union, and the elaboration of "policy options papers ... which may contain analyses, recommendations and strategies for the CFSP." This job description of the PPEWU, which later became Solana's policy unit, reads like a list of "gravamina" accumulated during the Yugoslav crisis.

However, flexibility did not find the way into the treaties in the area of CFSP. The experience of the Contact Group and other formations among the bigger countries stimulated resistance and scepticism on the part of medium sized and smaller states in the EU. Instead, the member states opted for a rather modest procedure of flexibility in terms of decision making with constructive abstention (Art. 23 (1) TEU/J13(1)Amsterdam). Since then the unanimity rule has been softened in so far as member states have the possibility to abstain from supporting a decision in the Council without preventing its adoption through the use of the veto right.

Consequently, the aspirations of Germany and other integration-friendly member states to introduce qualified majority voting (QMV) as a more general rule in CFSP decision making had failed already in an early phase of the Amsterdam negotiations. But the Germans were able to agree with the French on a proposal that QMV could be used on the basis of "common strategies" unanimously decided by the European Council. This proposal found its way into the Amsterdam Treaty in Art. 13 (Common Strategies ex-Art. J3) and Art. 23(2) (ex-Art. J13(2) Amsterdam) but in a rather restrictive way because of the possibility of a veto by any member state. Paradoxically, the experiences obtained in the crisis in Yugoslavia, which helped in the reforming of the CFSP, also worked as an impediment to far-reaching treaty reforms, as the tensions among the member states had nourished the fear that efficiency through QMV or flexibility might go at the cost of solidarity and that the bigger member states were constantly tempted to ignore the smaller countries.

Finally, the development of the defense dimension of European integration became an important issue at the Intergovernmental Conference. Between 1992 and 1995 WEU had undergone a considerable change and had become able to carry out low-level operations such as embargo controls or post-conflict stabilization and police missions. In June 1992, WEU had defined its Petersberg Tasks: evacuation and rescue operations, peacekeeping, and the use of combat forces in crisis management. These tasks opened the door, in principle, to a variety of crisis management activities of WEU, which strengthened its capacities step by step through a military staff, a Military Committee, and FAWEUs (Forces Answerable to WEU) earmarked by the member states for potential WEU operations.

Still, the development of WEU was a cautious and creeping process.[20] In essence WEU remained caught in the middle between NATO and the EU, notably because of the highly different interests of the British and the French.

During the Amsterdam negotiations, the French suggested together with the Germans and four other EU member states in the so-called six nations proposal of March 1997 the incorporation of Article V of the WEU Treaty, the mutual defense commitment, into the EU Treaty in the form of an opt-in protocol for those countries willing and able to do so.[21] However, due to the British and other Atlanticist member states' resistance, the maximum attainable in the negotiations was the establishment of a closer relationship between the WEU and the EU, giving the latter the possibility "to avail itself of WEU" (Art. 17(3) TEU/J7(3)Amsterdam).

Also, after lengthy discussions on the purpose of an EU defense policy alongside NATO, the Petersberg Tasks of WEU had been copied into the EU Treaty in Art. 17(2) (J7(2) Amsterdam) defining the key missions for which the EU could draw on WEU. This, in spite of British reluctance, was only possible after the neutral and nonaligned countries had made this proposal in order to bridge the gap between the British and the German/French camp and to introduce a crisis management function (instead of a collective defense role) into the Treaty.

Kosovo as a Turning Point: the EU's New Role in the Balkans

Roughly two years after the Dayton agreement had been signed, the situation in the Serbian province of Kosovo seriously deteriorated in early 1998. The EU defended the view that the situation in Kosovo would be best settled by negotiations between the government in Belgrade and the representatives of the Albanian community; a secession of Kosovo from Serbia was not regarded as a viable option. On the other hand, it was clear that something had to be done at all costs to avoid a humanitarian catastrophe.

The German government, holding the EU Presidency in the first semester of 1999, wanted to enhance its international diplomatic influence and its reputation within the Union by promoting a European contribution in conflict resolution and post-conflict stabilization. When US Ambassador Holbrooke failed to reach an agreement with Milosevic in January 1999, the Contact Group for Kosovo (which included also Italy) decided to organize an international conference at Rambouillet which began in February 1999. Germany was particularly interested in stressing the role of the EU, and initiated in parallel to Rambouillet, the concept of regular meetings of the EU foreign ministers. This was in part a reaction to complaints by some EU members concerning the "Directoire" character of the Contact Group.

After the failure of Rambouillet, the Europeans came to accept an ultimatum to the Serbian government to stop hostile actions in Kosovo, and thus were prepared to accept the use of force should the ultimatum fail. NATO, which had been planning since summer 1998 for the eventuality of taking military action, began its air strikes against Serbia in March 1999. As the bombing took time to produce the desired results, Germany used its double Presidency of the EU and of the G8 to push the process of negotiations with the Milosevic regime. In May 1999, a team consisting of the Finish President Ahtisaari, the former Russian Premier Chernomyrdin, and US Deputy Secretary of State Strobe Talbott prepared the ground for a peaceful solution. At the EU summit in Cologne in June 1999, Ahtisaari was able to announce that Milosevic had accepted a peace plan that left the status of Kosovo open, while taking it under UN administration. This was regarded as a victory for the EU and its German presidency. On the initiative of the EU, the Stability Pact for Southeast Europe was adopted in order to rebuild Kosovo, but in a broader sense also for the sake of stabilising the whole region and making it fit for eventual EU membership.[22]

The Stability Pact, in which eventually more than forty countries and organizations participated, has been heavily dominated by the EU as the main donor and economic partner of the region. The EU's policy for the western Balkans, consisting of the Stabilization and Association Process (SAP), the Stabilization and Association Agreements (SAA), the CARDS programme (Community Assistance for Reconstruction, Democracy, and Stabilization), and the perspective of future EU membership, quickly became the civilian and economic backbone of the Stability Pact, while NATO proved to be indispensable also after the end of the air campaign for the stabilization of the whole Balkan region, particularly in Kosovo, Bosnia, and in Macedonia.

The Emergence of ESDP

The Kosovo conflict had a tremendous impact on the very self-definition of the European Union. The termination of the Kosovo air campaign after three months was only possible with overwhelming US military involvement. The Europeans lacked modern military technology and equipment but also early information from the Americans in spite of the fact that it was officially a NATO operation. Deep was the depression of most Europeans due to their dependence on the US, which strengthened the wish to give the CFSP a credible military underpinning.[23]

One of the important preconditions for the development of a common defense policy of the EU was the process of a fundamental change in the British attitude, which had started already in the second half of 1998 and triggered a defense debate within the EU and WEU.[24] The most decisive step was the Franco-British Summit in Saint-Malo (December 1998), where Chirac and Blair agreed on the establishment of a European defense policy in the framework of the CFSP—even if the two countries had different views about the purpose of the whole exercise. The German Presidency, from January 1999 onwards, intensified the coordination processes within WEU and the EU. One important point was the acceptance by the United States of the development of a European defense policy—as long as it would not lead to a decoupling from NATO, to a duplication of NATO structures or to a discrimination against NATO members that do not form part of the European Union.[25] This line of argumentation was confirmed by the NATO summit communiqué in Washington on April 24, 1999.

Finally, an agreement with the neutral and nonaligned countries had been reached so that the European summit in Cologne in June of the same year could adopt a declaration on the strengthening of a common European security and defense policy that stressed that WEU would not be merged with the EU but that most of its functions would be transferred to the EU. A report of the German Presidency on ESDP outlined that appropriate intergovernmental procedures should be established within the EU for effective decision making and implementation of crisis management operations and that a permanent Political and Security Committee should be established within the EU, and also *inter alia* a Military Committee, a Military Staff, and a Situation Center.[26]

In Helsinki, in December 1999, the European Council repeated the need for the EU to make autonomous decisions on crisis management in cases in which NATO as a whole would not be involved, and agreed on a headline goal defining the objective for the EU (to be achieved by the end of 2003) to be capable of sending within sixty days up to 50,000 to 60,000 ground troops for the whole spectrum of the Petersberg Tasks for up to one year into a crisis region.[27] The succeeding Portuguese Presidency completed the ESDP in its civil crisis management dimension with a headline goal for police forces for stabilization missions amounting to 5,000 officers in total, of which 1,000 should be deployable in thirty days.[28] This was an important decision enabling the EU three years later to conduct the EU police mission (EUPM) in Bosnia-Hercegovina, which is still running today.

The ESDP in the Nice Treaty

The amendments of the EU treaty in the framework of the Nice Treaty negotiations in the second half of 2000 focused on three points: due to the absorption of the functions of WEU by the EU, any operational relationship between the EU and WEU disappeared from Article 17 TEU. Secondly, Article 25 TEU had been changed considerably in so far as the permanent Political and Security Committee (PSC/COPS) replaced the Political Committee (PC). The PSC is responsible for the whole foreign, security, and defense policy of the Union in terms of its preparation and implementation and can be mandated by the Council for managing the strategic direction and control of a running operation.

The third item concerned the question of flexibility. The general thinking on this issue was still very cautious, definitively due to the position by the UK and also the smaller member states. Hence, in contrast to the ambitions of the French and the Germans, the European security and defense policy was quickly excluded from flexibility.[29] Only within the CFSP and under rather restrictive conditions, had flexible actions been allowed, a possibility that has never been used, since in practice.

Subsequently to the Treaty amendments of Nice, the EU's defense policy became operational step by step through a number of police and military operations in Albania, Macedonia, and Bosnia-Hercegovina. And, since the finalization of the framework agreement between the EU and NATO in early 2003, the EU has two possibilities: either to rely on NATO support and assets, as was the case with the peacekeeping operation CONCORDIA in Macedonia and is the case with the operation Althea in Bosnia-Hercegovina (both operations succeeded NATO missions), or to conduct autonomous operations, as had been the case, for example, with the operation ARTEMIS in Congo in summer 1993.

Conclusions

Within only three years, and on the basis of a broad consensus among the EU governments, important institutional preconditions for an effective and efficient EU security and defense policy could be established. Since then, the EU has been clearly on the way of developing a more operational CFSP, including peacekeeping facilities, minor intervention capacities and a European Security Strategy (December 2003). Today, the EU is active in conflict prevention and post crisis management in the Balkans, Africa (Congo), and Indonesia (Aceh) and is also paying more attention to conditionality in its external relations with respect to human and civil rights, democracy, and the market economy.

In the academic debate, the record of the EU as an international actor in former Yugoslavia has been assessed in highly disparate ways. While Geoffrey Edwards identifies "limits of European Political Cooperation/Common Foreign and Security Policy ... and the central institutions of the Union in times of crisis, and the continued divergence of approaches, principles, and interests among the member states (as well as sometimes within them),"[30] Roy Ginsberg comes to the conclusion that "the EU role, political impact, and effect defy categories of either success or failure."[31] Philip Gordon arrives at the judgment that, given the poor record of the CFSP, not only in former Yugoslavia, the "interests of EU members ... do not seem likely to converge to the point where true integration of foreign and security policy becomes probable," expecting a European foreign policy that will remain "limited, fragmented and intergovernmental."[32]

There is indeed a strong point in this kind of argumentation insofar as it hints at some structural impediments to the creation of a truly common foreign and security policy. But, at the same time, it is rather fruitless to approach the CFSP ambitions from a (super-)state perspective or to claim that any single European state could do better than the EU collectively. Hence, it is more promising to analyze the CFSP/ESDP in a long term perspective and to compare the activities of the EU in the first decade of the twenty-first century with what the EU/EC was able to do ten or twenty years before in order to identify the changes on the long way toward a more collective foreign and security policy.

This does not mean that the CFSP will always work efficiently, since it is not constructed in a centralized and legally binding way. The decisive question is not so much how to avoid a break down of EU foreign policy, but what to learn from it in a longer-term perspective. The EU is an organization involved in a kind of "lifelong institutional learning," trying to incrementally improve its own set of procedures and instruments for better coping with external crises and problems. In all the Intergovernmental Conferences since Maastricht, and also in the Convention on the Future of Europe, such trends in institutional learning became visible. This should make CFSP analysts more relaxed when dealing with failures and shortfalls of EU foreign policy. There is still potential for practical progress and future institutional reforms.

Notes

1. See Elfriede Regelsberger, *Die Gemeinsame Außen- und Sicherheitspolitik der EU (GASP): Konstitutionelle Angebote im Praxistest*, Baden-Baden: Nomos, 2004.
2. See Ben Tonra, "Constructing the CFSP: the Utility of a Cognitive Approach," *Journal of Common Market Studies*, 41.4 (2001), pp. 731–56.
3. Roy Ginsberg, *The European Union in International Politics: Baptism by Fire*, Lanham: Rowman and Littlefield Publishers, 2001.
4. Mathias Jopp, *The Strategic Implications of European Integration: An Analysis of Trends in Integration Policies and their Consequences for the Transatlantic Partnership and a New European Security Order*, Adelphi paper, No. 290, London: The International Institute for Strategic Studies, 1994, p. 42.
5. Ben Tonra, *The Europeanisation of National Foreign Policy: Dutch, Danish and Irish Foreign Policy in the European Union*, Aldershot: Ashgate 2001, p. 223.
6. See Geoffrey Edwards, "The Potential and Limits of the CFSP: The Yugoslav Example," in: Elfriede Regelsberger, Philippe de Schoutheete de Tervarent and Wolfgang Wessels (eds.), *Foreign Policy of the European Union: From EPC to CFSP and Beyond*, Boulder: Lynne Rienner, 1997, p. 174.
7. See also for the following, Andreas G. Kintis, "The EU's Foreign Policy and the War in Former Yugoslavia," in: Martin Holland (ed.), *Common Foreign and Security Policy: The Record and Reforms*, London and Washington: Pinter, 1997, pp. 148–73.
8. Simon Nuttall, *European Foreign Policy*, Oxford: Oxford University Press, 2000, p. 203.
9. See Hans-Jürgen Axt, "Hat Genscher Jugoslawien entzweit? Mythen und Fakten zur Außenpolitik des vereinten Deutschlands," *Europaarchiv*, 12 (1993), pp. 351–60.
10. See Nuttall, *European Foreign Policy*, pp. 198–200.
11. See Tonra, "Constructing the CFSP," p. 229.
12. This is particularly stressed by Nuttall, *European Foreign Policy*.
13. See also for the following, Jopp, *The Strategic Implications of European Integration*, chapter I: "The Twelve and Maastricht."
14. For the modest results of theses ambitions, see Art. J 2 (3) and J 5 (4) Maastricht Treaty.
15. For a sharp French criticism of the aggressive policy of the Serbs see Nicole Gnesotto, *Lessons of Yugoslavia*, Chaillot Papers 14, Paris: Institute for Security Studies, 1994.
16. See Mathias Jopp (ed.), *The Implications of the Yugoslav Crisis for Western Europe's Foreign Relations*, Chaillot Papers 17, Paris: Institute for Security Studies, 1994, pp. 2–4.
17. The decision had already been taken in the North Atlantic Council (NAC) meetings of NATO on July 25 and August 1, 1995; see also in this connection: Richard Holbrooke, *Meine Mission: Vom Krieg zum Frieden*, Munich: Pieper Verlag, 1998, pp. 164–170.
18. See Ivo Daalder, *Getting to Dayton: The Making of America's Bosnia Policy*, Washington, D.C.: Brookings Institution Press, 2000.

19. See also for the following, Mathias Jopp, "Reformziel Stärkung der außen- und sicherheitspolitischen Handlungsfähigkeit der EU," in: Mathias Jopp and Otto Schmuck (eds.), *Die Reform der Europäischen Union. Analysen—Positionen—Dokumente zur Regierungskonferenz 1996/97*, Bonn: Europa-Union Verlag, 1996, pp. 41–58.
20. See Anne Deighton, *Western European Union, 1954–1997: Defense, Security, Integration*, Oxford and Reading: EIRU, 1997; Mathias Jopp, "Germany and the Western European Union," in: Carl Lankowski and Simon Serfaty (eds.), *Europeanizing Security? NATO and an Integrating Europe*, AICGS Research Report No. 9, Washington D.C.: American Institute for Contemporary German Studies, 1999, pp. 35–52.
21. See for the six nations proposal, Agence Europe, No. 6941, March 24–25, 1997, pp. 4–5.
22. Conclusions of the Presidency, Cologne European Council, June 3–4, 1999; the pact was finally adopted in Cologne on June 10, 1999.
23. See also for the following Mathias Jopp, *European Defense Policy: The Debate on the Institutional Aspects, IEPDOK*11/b-June/July 1999, Bonn and Berlin: Institut für Europäische Politik, 1999; Jolyon Howorth, *European Integration and Defense: The Ultimate Challenge*, Chaillot Papers 43, Paris: Institute for Security Studies, 2000.
24. Richard G. Whitmann, *Amsterdam's Unfinished Business? The Blair Government's Initiative and the Future of the Western European Union*, Occasional Papers 7, Paris: Institute for Security Studies, 1999.
25. Madeleine Albright, "The Right Balance will Secure NATO's Future," *Financial Times*, October 7, 1998, p. 22.
26. For the declaration and the report see Presidency Conclusions, Cologne European Council, June 3–4, 1999, Annex III.
27. Presidency Conclusions, Helsinki European Council, December 10–11, 1999, Annex IV.
28. Presidency Conclusions, Santa Maria da Feira European Council, June 19–20, 2000, Annex I.
29. See Claus Giering and Josef Janning, "Flexibilität als Katalysator der Finalität? Die Gestaltungskraft der 'Verstärkten Zusammenarbeit' nach Nizza," in: Mathias Jopp, Barbara Lippert and Heinrich Schneider (eds), *Das Vertragswerk von Nizza und die Zukunft der Europäischen Union*, Bonn: Europa-Union Verlag, 2001, pp. 102–11; see also in general: Udo Diedrichs and Mathias Jopp, "Flexible Modes of Governance: Making CFSP and ESDP Work," *The International Spectator*, 38.3 (2003), pp. 15–30.
30. Edwards, "The Potential and Limits of the CFSP," p. 173.
31. Ginsberg, *The European Union in International Politics*, p. 57.
32. Philip H. Gordon, "Europe's Uncommon Foreign Policy," *International Security*, 11.3 (1998), p. 89.

7
Challenges and Opportunities: Surmounting Integration Crises in Historical Context

Michael Gehler

The launch of the internal market by Jacques Delors in 1985, the Single European Act (SEA) of 1987, and the signing of the Maastricht Agreement in 1992 have fed a rich variety of new impulses into the politics of integration: in 1993 the "four freedoms" ushered in the realization of the Single Market; in 1999 twelve European states introduced the single currency (euro); 2004 saw the admission of ten new member states and the EU Constitutional Treaty was agreed by all twenty-five heads of state or government.[1]

Preliminary Conceptual and Methodological Remarks

Historians and political scientists interested in integration have had difficulty keeping up with all these developments, are indeed left panting in their wake. Never has the history of integration been more up to date or in the swim—and this at a time when the rejection of the EU Constitution in the French (May 29, 2005) and Dutch (June 1, 2005) referendums was threatening to plunge the whole EU project into one of the most acute crises it has ever experienced. There were fears that plans to extend membership to Bulgaria, Romania, Croatia and Turkey may overburden the capacities of the Union and stretch the integration process to breaking point. While some, like the former German Chancellor Helmut Schmidt and the French scholar Thierry de Montbrial, still insist on the need for European "self-assertion," others, such as the German social historian Hans-Ulrich Wehler, see the further planned enlargements as a road to self-destruction and the end of the EU.[2] But the resolution of the EU Constitutional Treaty and its ratification crisis have produced not only a "reflection period" among politicians but also a controversial debate about the future of Europe by experts, former practitioners, and scholars[3] and various constitutional debates in the different EU member states, thus creating new European public spheres.[4] All these mixed impressions and feelings are not new.

We have seen the history of integration pitch violently from one extreme to the other: first, the fervour of the 1980s and early 1990s, which saw the "second European *relance;*" then a reversion to a kind of "second Eurosclerosis" in the wake of the Amsterdam Treaty (1997, came into force in 1999) and Nice (2000, came into force 2003), neither of which did much to promote integration. Finally, the risk of nonratification of the EU Constitutional Treaty has once again underlined the value of paying close critical attention to the latest research into the history of EU Europe and its integration.[5] The ex-president of France and president of the EU Constitutional Convention, Valéry Giscard d'Estaing, put it with unimpeachable clarity when contemplating the consequences to the community of the latest round of enlargements: "That this enlargement will water down the community is not a risk but a certainty."[6]

First, I shall make some conceptual and methodological remarks. Secondly, I focus on historical constitutional attempts at reorganization in Europe. Thirdly, I present a thesis on the question of challenges and opportunities.[7] Fourthly, I shall raise the question whether Austria's 2006 EU Presidency—which serves as a case study for the structural dilemmas of short-term EU presidencies—could help to overcome the ratification crisis, and last but not least I conclude with an outlook concerning the historical time horizon of surmounting a crisis.

Conceptual and Methodological Remarks

The method that is used here is at the same time both diachronic and synchronic. First of all, various attempts at European policy will be touched upon in the historical longitudinal section, especially from the official government side with regard to content and profile, but also in their dynamics of development with respect to progress, stagnation, and retrogression. More detailed and more systematic studies are still to be carried out. What is dealt with here is merely an initial sketch of the problem. Secondly, in a contemporary history cross-section process, each of the protagonists and the motivators will then be named, along with the contemporary backgrounds and contexts as well as the immediate results and effects of their ventures. Thirdly, the closing section of the remarks then deals with a summary of the results that were presented, a division into periods, and an assessment of the attempts at the reorganization of Europe and the suggestions for a constitution, and their understanding and comprehension as a consequence of rifts, breaks, and the results of crises experiences.

Romain Kirt has spoken of Europe's history as a "history of crises,"[8] meaning crises that were political, economic, and social, but also ideological, psychological, cultural, and intellectual. We also further differentiate here between national, colonial power-specific, European, and international crises, as the discussion also has to be about intra-community crises to a greater or lesser degree: on one hand, crises of the system and of trust; on the other hand, crises of the person and of negotiation.

The term "crisis" is to be comprehended in the meaning of the original Greek "κρίσις" as a "decision" or "decisive change," that is, as a difficult situation in a dangerous time that requires a decision. In addition, "crisis" is understood here both in the "positive" effect upon unification—that is, for the course of integration in the constructive sense—and in its "negative" effect in a counterproductive manner. The term "constitution," on the other hand, is to be understood not in a sense that is strictly legal, specifically with regard to the history of law, or in terms of a written foundation for a state, but rather in a general and political sense as an attempt at order and structure of political, economic, and social situations that have been unsettled at both the European and international levels.

European History as Result of Breaks, Rifts and Crises

An initial view of the sequence of the concepts for Europe that are presented in the illustration shows that they were developed for the most part against the background of far-reaching changes that were characterized by breaks and splits.

1918. The end of the war has been viewed by Horst Möller[9] as a twofold radical change that consisted of both the internal and external revolutionizing of the world of nation-states. The collapse of the "Concert of European powers" went hand in hand with the fall of the monarchies and their transition into democratic-republican political systems and produced bigger and stronger European public spheres.

1929. "Black Friday" at the New York Stock Exchange led to the Great Depression, an economic crisis of worldwide proportions, associated with a political radicalization of international relations that did not allow any new venture in integration policy. Due to the fact of dictatorships and authoritarian regimes European public spheres became narrow and were drastically limited.

1939–41. The European war and its widening into a World War led to Europe's being deprived of power, with the consequence also of the decline of the old colonial powers.

1945. The collapse of the Nazi position of hegemony in Europe was a victory for new European public spheres but only in the Western parts of the continent, because it resulted, with the toleration and consent of the USA, in the penetration of the Red Army into Eastern and Central Europe and consequently the loss of the center of the continent and, as a further consequence of the Marshall Plan, the division of Europe—the latter one also meant the loss of the Central and East European public spheres.

1947. The Truman Doctrine was tantamount to a declaration of the Cold War on the Soviet Union, it fueled the East–West confrontation in Europe in the first decade after the war (1945–55), and it contributed to the formation and structuring of the political and economic division of the continent.

1989. The opening of the Iron Curtain and the fall of the Berlin Wall spurred on the erosion process of the post-Stalinist regimes in Central and Eastern Europe and the disintegration of the USSR, making possible the option of expanding NATO and the EU—all this created new European as well as national public spheres.

2003. The Iraq War not only represented a breach in international law, but it also gave full expression to the already-existing conflict of interests between, on the one hand, a series of EU states and, on the other hand, the USA, corresponding with a variety of new public spheres—pro- and anti-American and pro- and anti-European ones.

2004/05. What we may observe with regard to the "Eastern Enlargement" of the European Union and the failed referendums in France and the Netherlands are two parallel existing phenomena: a stronger Europeanization of politics on the one hand and also a stronger politicization of EU Europe on the other.

In the wake of these far-reaching breaks and crises, new European public spheres came into existence, which also required attempts at reorganization and triggered suggestions for a constitution:

- Richard N. Coudenhove's "Paneurope"[10] ideas of 1922–23[11] were reflexes to the triple crisis of the years from 1917 to 1919 which arose from a crisis in European political systems and a crisis in ideological orientation, in the wake of which there was also an economic crisis. The system that resulted from the Paris Peace Treaties offered only partial answers and unsatisfactory solutions to these questions and problems.
- Briand's attempts at a Europe policy in 1929–30[12] were the expression of a French crisis of supremacy in Europe: the safeguarding of the territorial status quo on the continent no longer seemed guaranteed; in view of growing German demands for revision; it also represented a crisis in the stability of the European system of states and a crisis of subduing with regard to the German potential, which was once again achieving a better position.
- Churchill's union project of 1940 was the expression of a severe crisis in the British policy on the balance of power: as a result of Czechoslovakia being crushed and Poland being divided and in view of the successful attack by the German *Wehrmacht* on France, Europe's system of states seemed to be on the brink of disintegration, which required a close British–French connection in order to be averted.

- Churchill's Council of Europe project in 1943[13] was an attempt at defense against threatening marginalization and a visible expression of the crisis of existence of Great Britain's position as a world power: with a view to the growing power of the USA and the Soviet Union, the global influence of the United Kingdom no longer appeared to be a given; indeed, there was the threat of a loss in the position of power of world policy-setting among the "Big Three."
- Churchill's Zurich Speech of 1946[14] and the activities of the Europe associations in 1947–48, with their "Europe as a third way" debate,[15] were reactions to the crisis resulting from the collapse of the anti-Hitler coalition and from Soviet-American relations that were characterized by increasing conflicts which, in view of scenarios of the Soviet communist threat, seemed to lead to a crisis of existence in the free part of the continent.
- The Marshall Plan[16] was a response to the economic disintegration crisis, the European debate about the danger of Soviet communism and thus to Western Europe's threatening political crisis of existence. Mark Gilbert does not reject the "realist" theory that integration was a clear and objective cost-benefit calculation (Joseph H.H. Weiler), but also attaches importance to the history of ideas and the long-term value debate in Europe, in which he sees something more than windy rhetoric. He sees the solution of the "German question" as a fulcrum of a successful integration and unification movement, seeking a balance between American initiatives (the ERP, the OEEC) and British proposals for closer intergovernmental cooperation, because that resolution enabled a gradual and painful, but also lasting, transformation of former belligerents into partner states.[17]
- The projects of the ECS[18] (which was also result of a debate about security and peace in Western Europe) and the European Defense Community (EDC) were the results of a crisis in France's Germany policy, that is, the problem of the management of the Germany conflict that could no longer be kept under control.
- The failure of the EDC on August 30, 1954[19] was the result of the first intra-community crisis. It once again had to do with the controversial issue of how a maximum of security toward Germany could be achieved. France no longer viewed itself as being in the position to alone and independently cover the German potential under the American protective screen. The debate about the German rearmament was a European debate and created a new public sphere.
- The "Common Market," with the successful Spaak Committee that preceded it, was a reflex to the French colonial power crisis and the additional crisis associated with that between the old and new world powers; that is, it was also a result of the failed French policy of recolonization, which had begun with Indochina (1947–54),

continued through the Suez debacle (1956), and finally concluded with the Algerian War (1958–61). The Suez crisis gave full expression to the dissent in colonial policy between the old classic colonial powers (France and Great Britain) and the new Imperial superpowers (the USSR and the USA). The results were consequences in Europe policy and integration policy.
- The Fouchet Plans[20] were harbingers of a further intra-community and institutional crisis, which was to escalate with de Gaulle's veto of the United Kingdom in 1963 and the Empty Chair policy in 1965–66.[21] This crisis was defused through the exclusion of the United Kingdom from the community and the maintaining of the dominance for the time being of France on the continent as the first among the six EEC states. It was connected with the debate about the "Europe of the Fatherlands" ("l'Europe des patries"/"Europa der Vaterländer").
- The 1970s brought fresh crises after some very positive moves toward integration in the earlier years after the Hague Summit of 1969. Helmut Schmidt and Valéry Giscard d'Estaing then brought in the European Monetary System (EMS) (1978),[22] the nucleus of the later EMU (1999). Gilbert lays great emphasis on this achievement by the EC, seeing it as something of a miracle that it should have kept together through the crisis-ridden 1970s and not relapsed into the economic nationalism and protectionism of the inter-war period. The EMS was a European response to the monetary crisis of international proportions in the 1970s as a result of the United States' disaster in Vietnam and the resource and supply problems in the energy sector (keyword: the oil shock).[23] It was also a result of an American lack of interest in European attempts at organization in connection with new outlines for world monetary policy.
- The Single European Act was a fresh departure and a springboard for more dynamic advances in integration (Single Market project),[24] which were consummated by the Maastricht compromise and the Delors Package in the wake of German reunification. The introduction of the euro in 1999 can be seen as the last exhalation of this phase, in the preparation, formation and characterization of which Jacques Delors, Helmut Kohl, and François Mitterrand played a decisive part. Thereafter, "making sense of Maastricht" became a much more difficult process.[25] Gilbert identifies four factors that in the 1990s revived and complicated the question of where the community was meant to be going: the fact that not all member states introduced the euro; the enlargement, leading to new democratic challenges in Central and Eastern Europe; the "democratic deficit" within the EU itself; and, last but not least, the changes brought about by a "unipolar" world in which the USA was the only surviving superpower. Even if the 1990s saw more progress toward a common EU foreign and

security policy than in all the preceding fifty years put together, that policy, if no longer embryonic, is certainly still in its infancy.[26]
- The Maastricht Treaty of 1991 was the result of the "long-term effect of the radical changes of 1989" (Romain Kirt);[27] above all, though, it was also the result of worries about a renewed destabilization of the European security system by an apparently less-controllable new Germany. Maastricht was therefore a response to a once again feared crisis of stability of the European system of states, with a view to the German question, which was raised again in 1989–90. The debate about the future of Germany was also a debate about the future of Europe and therefore a European debate.
- The setting up of the Convention for the Charter of Fundamental Rights[28] was an attempt at a response to the EU's growing crisis in credibility, institutions, identity, and legitimacy,[29] which is also to be viewed in connection with the resignation *en masse* of the Jacques Santer EU Commission in 1999 and which led to the measures by the EU-14 against Austria in 2000. The debate on fundamental rights also took on a current reference through the quarantine of the now unpopular Alpine republic: during the previous year, the EU had already viewed itself as the defender of human rights in Kosovo, and, during the previous period, it had, not without success, isolated Slovakia because of the latter's dubious domestic policy.
- The Constitutional Convention[30] was a reflection of the increasing crises in negotiations with government conferences and EU summits, beginning with Amsterdam in 1997, and continuing all the way to that inglorious summit in Nice in December 2000. With it, the method of government conferences seemed to have met its end. The draft of a constitutional treaty presented by the convention was then to be the victim of the Brussels Summit of December 2003. This negotiation crisis—the expression of another intra-community crisis comparable to the failure of the EDC in 1954—was accompanied by growing crises in trust between old and established members and new members as well as between "small and large."[31]
- The Iraq crisis heightened this state of tension between old and new EU members, but above all else between small and large members. In any case, this international crisis in transatlantic relations also led in a productive manner to a profiling of the convention draft with a view to foreign and security policy.
- The enlargement of the EU in 2004, which was unique in its extent and dimensions, could lead to a crisis in structuring and decision making as well as in the makeup of the leadership institutions, which would then intensify the state of tension between the small, medium, and large states in the EU. So much for crises scenarios.

The Question of Challenges and Opportunities: Thesis

In the history of Europe in the twentieth century, there were numerous and greatly differing suggestions for the structuring and reorganization of the continent from the most varied of ideological and political camps, with different intentions and messages. What was represented was a complex development with elements of progress, stagnation, and retrogression. The most progressive attempts were Coudenhove's "Paneurope" (1922–23), Churchill's British-French union plan (1940), and De Gasperi's project for a "European Political Community" (1953). Each failed in its time. The Single European Act (1987) and the Union Treaty of Maastricht (1993)—which, with regard to their integration substance, fell short of the last two suggestions cited above[32]—were the most far-reaching leaps in quality since the Treaties of Rome (1957). In the intervening period, there were also efforts at delays and attempts to water things down (such as Macmillan's project for a large free trade zone in 1956–58 for the undermining of the "Common Market" or the Fouchet Plans in 1961–62 for the further intergovernmentalization of the EEC). De Gaulle's veto victory with the Luxembourg Compromise (1966) was, after the rejection of the EDC by the Assemblée Nationale (1954), the greatest integration setback in the history from the EEC to the EU. Mark Gilbert correctly speaks of the EEC in the years from 1958 to 1969 as being "in the general's shadow."[33] Yet another sub-thesis follows this in historical perspective: every now and then, intra-community crises signified in a short term view far more potential for danger and risk for setback than did external crises.

An interplay repeatedly took place between advocates and opponents, as well as the driving and retarding forces, of integration, its being forced, and its being extended. The path toward integration over more convergence to greater cohesion did not run either in a straight line or voluntarily. There was not a clear and linear development of progress. The course ensued according to a pattern of trial and error and as the result of internal and external forces. It was a complicated zigzag path with a gradually increasing density of integration.

The term "integration process" in the sense of linearity and teleology therefore does not appear to be unproblematic, and the term "integration dynamics" in the sense of autonomous laws, becoming independent, and uncontrollability seems to be very worthy of consideration, if not more suitable. It was a procedure that was characterized, on the one hand, by a mixture consisting of intentional bargaining but also, on the other hand, by unexpected events and chance occurrences.

In the end, "third party" factors—that is, external factors that are therefore exogenous and first and foremost to be classified as external influences—had more of a supporting and stimulating effect than a slowing and obstructing one for integration dynamics.[34] Those that are worthy of mention in this context include above all else the real or fictitious potential for threat by the Soviet Union during the first Cold War (1947–53) and later during the Cuban missile crisis (1962)—the USSR had the effect of being a "negative sponsor"—but also the earlier Suez crisis (1956) and then the Vietnam War (1957–74) in connection with the collapse of the Bretton Woods international monetary system in the 1970s, the disintegration of the Soviet Union and its empire (1989–91), and finally the Iraq crisis (2002–3). It is possible that the US, at least since the new world politics of the Bush administration (2001–9), is on the best path of becoming the new negative sponsor of EU Europe. In this regard, the thesis in any case ought to be ventured that the external international, colonial, and world economic crisis scenarios had a comparatively stronger ("more positive") influence upon the cohesion of the European communities and upon the dynamics of integration as such than the internal (that is, intra-community) crises.

Integration was initially and primarily driven forward by the European nation-states (especially France, but also Belgium)—conceptualized not without self-interest and disguised as a purely economic plan, above all to save, reestablish, and consolidate after 1945 their own nation-state polity, which had been shattered by the two world wars.[35]

In addition, it was necessary to put into effect a double strategy with regard to the Germany policy, namely, firstly, to prevent a resurgence of the German nation-state and, secondly, to profitably control and make use of its economic potential. The EEC of the Treaties of Rome and the EU of the Maastricht Treaty were above all else European responses to the German question.

According to Romain Kirt, there have always been crises in Europe.[36] They are nothing new, but their effects upon the unification process and the dynamics of integration represent a new and current challenge for research in contemporary history. They are therefore to be studied even more precisely.

One thing is for sure for the time being: there is a degree of crisis of a political and economic nature that can saddle the integration with weariness and can make it possible for no new advances to be made, which then signifies the following: the extent of the crisis is so comprehensive and so paralyzing that any attempt at resuscitation fails—every new beginning remains stuck in the starting blocks and threatens to suffocate. That was the case, for example, in the 1930s. The worldwide economic crisis and the political radicalization of Europe ruined the ideas and plans of Gustav Stresemann and Aristide Briand.

Times of peace seem to be a good precondition for the prospects of success for Europe concepts. During military confrontations, suggestions for integration quickly get a reputation for superficial intentions and attempts at instrumentalization, such as Friedrich Naumann's "Mitteleuropa" (1915) or Churchill's British-French union project (1940). But peace is also not a sufficient guarantee of success for the dynamics of integration: with a view to the enlargement of the EU in 2004 and future enlargement procedures, an additional considerable if not even threatening (or actually destroying) potential for crisis is to be expected, as the belief in additional progress is in the process of decreasing, and even the frequently conjured-up irreversibility has become questionable. In this context, Sonja Puntscher-Riekmann asks us to consider that crises can also contribute to the deconstruction of that which has been achieved.[37]

In addition to concrete and real crises, feared or fictitiously imagined crises (such as the oft-cited "Eurosclerosis" in the 1970s) also play a role in a reactivated policy of integration or one that is to be revitalized. Fears of the possible consequences of an integration that is too greatly forced (for example, British "superstate" horror visions in the debate surrounding Maastricht or, again, surrounding the EU Constitutional Treaty) as well as fears of disintegration in view of the EU enlargement in 2004 can have (negative) effects. In any case, they can also turn out to be exaggerated and in the end actually promote the community's solidarity and thus the further unification process. It remains to be studied more precisely as to whether the chatter about crises in and surrounding the EU[38] had a functional and instrumental character in order to give a new boost to integration.

The economies of crises play a crucial role, which also permits, depending upon the extent, only a certain degree of controllability and management of the problem. Conflict management and the potential for surmounting the crisis must in any case still be present in a sufficient degree for a solution to be reached.

There is a definite, one might even say not insignificant need for crises, a necessity for crises, without which the dynamics of integration would not have got by, and even will also not get by in the future, which appears to be essential for advances. Romain Kirt correctly goes back to a quote by Jean Monnet, "Crises are the great unifier!"[39] The state of crisis of European integration appears to be a normal state. Without exogenous influences and external forces, a leap in the quality of integration hardly seems imaginable.

Most suggestions for and attempts at reorganization arose from emergency situations and predicaments, above all with a view to the problem area of Germany, which no longer left any way out other than taking the bull by the horns, going on the offensive, seizing the initiative (such as the Schuman Plan and the Pleven Plan), and comprehending integration as the last resort.

Aside from the dimension based upon the history of results and external effects, reference must also be made to the dimension based upon the history of treaties, institutions, and developments from the EEC to the EU and, in this regard, specifically to the intra-community crises that in the medium and long term opened up a further community-building effect.

An Example for Structural Dilemmas: The 2006 Austrian Presidency of the EU Council

Beginning on January 1, 2006, Austria took over the presidency of the Council of the European Union for the first half of the year. The preparations for the EU presidency were the main focus of Austrian foreign policy and European policy from 2003 through 2005. In the run-up to the presidency, it could already be recognized that the federal government had endeavored to de-dramatize the debate over the EU crisis. At the same time, it made its best effort to minimize the pressure from expectations with regard to the so-called EU Constitution.[40] As a country that had ratified the Constitutional Treaty on May 11, 2005, Austria endeavored to make a contribution to overcoming the ratification crisis, even though it was necessary to hear voices ranging from the critical to the disapproving not only from other EU partners, but also from its own ranks within the coalition government. The Federal Chancellery and the Foreign Ministry nevertheless made their efforts with a mixed EU strategy consisting of a combination of de-dramatization and the providing of momentum. With initiatives such as "Europe is Listening" and a "Speaker's Corner" at the Ballhausplatz,[41] the federal government did indeed attempt to gather and move opinions, capture and generate the general atmosphere, and determine the reasons for the lack of trust in the EU.

In agreement with the Commission, there was also the declared intention to hold a conference on the future of the EU on May 9, 2006, the Union's Europe Day, in order to take stock of the information that has been gathered and to agree on a road map with concrete dates at the subsequent summit meeting in June. As things stood, however, the Constitutional Treaty at first did not appear to be a top priority matter of concern for Austria, since the government itself was not able to agree about it. In contrast to the head of the government Wolfgang Schüssel, Vice Chancellor Hubert Gorbach did not consider the Constitutional Treaty in its present form to be acceptable, and he recommended new negotiations. And President Heinz Fischer also pleaded for it to be reworked. The Social Democratic Party demanded that the ratification process not go ahead, but at the same time it requested that the third part of the Constitutional Treaty in the areas of "economy" and "employment" be dramatically reworked by a new convention. As a result of the differences of opinion within the governing coalition and in view of the upcoming 2006 parliamentary elections, there was good reason for the topic to be postponed to the Finnish (second half of 2006) and German (first half of 2007) Council presidencies.[42]

It was clear that, in the brief span of time of six months, Austria would not be in the position to gain control of the exploding EU agenda and handle all of the fields of topics in an exhaustive manner.[43] A winnowing process was therefore necessary. A few days after the visit by the EU Commission members in January 2006, a follow-up to the meeting took place with the Commission president and the Austrian chancellor: sixty topics were discussed. With the agreement between José Manuel Barroso and Wolfgang Schüssel, it was emphasized that the EU presidency would proceed in two phases. Up to the spring summit in March, the topics of "employment" and "energy" would be in the forefront. The second phase up to the June summit would then be centered above all else on the debate regarding the "future of Europe."[44]

Aside from the fact that Austria would only have a limited right of involvement, it was not to be expected that Austria's EU presidency would be able to solve the entire palette of problems. What ought to be far more relevant is the smaller and medium degrees of progress that ought to be prepared and achieved in the individual specialized departments; for example, the smooth arrangement for the evaluation of Schengen, the implementation of the revised Lisbon strategy in partial areas or in the field of consumer protection, or the regulation of service guidelines. It also ought to be possible to make the EU visible for the citizens more quickly in these areas than with the lofty heights of world politics.

An open clash broke out not only between the parties in the Austrian government, but also within the strongest party at the European level, the European People's Party (EPP), as to whether the Constitutional Treaty was still alive. EPP Faction Chairman Hans-Gert Pöttering did not want to give up on this and criticized the Dutch Foreign Minister, who was from his own "party family."[45]

Among the "choices" of the Austrian EU presidency were topics that historically included the main matters of concern of Austria's foreign policy and Europe policy in the 1990s. Austria came out strongly in favor of a quick accession of the Western Balkan countries, for which it could count upon the support of the states in the "regional partnership" (Poland, Slovakia, Slovenia, the Czech Republic, and Hungary).[46] By the beginning of 2006, it was already in the offing that the Austrian EU presidency would be overshadowed by external political events and, because of this, would only be capable of acting to a restricted degree with regard to its essential matters of concern. First came the quarrel over the pricing and supply of natural gas by Russia to Ukraine, followed by the smoldering and escalating conflict surrounding Iran's atomic weapons program. The condition of Ariel Sharon, lying in a coma, and the surprisingly clear victory at the end of January by the radical Islamic Hamas movement in the elections in the Palestinian territories caused the Union to react: it was dumbfounded at first and subsequently saw its financial assistance for the autonomous Palestinian Authority called into question.[47] Added to this was the dispute, lasting weeks, surrounding the caricatures of the prophet Mohammed, with repeated rioting and protests against EU institutions and Western embassies, followed most recently in February by the avian flu, which also appeared in European countries. All of these external factors overshadowed Austria's EU presidency. Since 1945, Austria's foreign policy has contributed to the preservation of the state and its international acceptance, and it has repeatedly achieved the goals that it has set for itself (unity, freedom, independence, self-reliance, neutrality, UN membership, and EU membership).[48]

In spite of all of its efforts and its most intense endeavors, the Austrian EU presidency stood before a multitude of problems that appeared to be virtually unsolvable, of which only three will be cited here:

- The "Lisbon strategy" in light of 19 million (in reality, probably 30 million) unemployed in Europe, hesitant consumer behavior, and a modest economic situation, that is, the goal of setting sights for the EU to be the economically and competitively strongest area in the world.
- Overcoming the difficult ratification crisis of the Constitutional Treaty, which is the expression of a three-part crisis:

(a) EU states against EU states: the crisis in allocation;
(b) EU states against EU bodies and institutions: crisis in regulation and jurisdiction;
(c) EU institutions and EU citizens: crisis of legitimacy.
- Against the background of nationally organized structures and media cultures that are dominated by nationally oriented publics, positioning the European Union (and its complicated institutional structure, which is difficult to comprehend at a glance) as a reason for hope and a task for the future, and making this not only more democratic and closer to the citizen, but also more capable of making decisions and acting.

For Austria's foreign policy, the EU presidency represented an enormous challenge. It signified one of the most difficult tasks in its entire history, after the State Treaty and its own EU accession. Above all else, the country did not have ten years to deal with it as it did in 1945–55, but rather only six months, which considerably reduced or even greatly minimized the prospects for any substantial success.

Against the background of the awkward majority relationships of Austrian domestic policy (since 2005, the governing coalition has no longer had a majority in the Bundesrat), the federal government that was weakened by the split of the Freedom Party, the continuing disagreement on central issues of integration between individual members of the government, and the upcoming national parliamentary elections in the autumn of 2006, which were already casting their shadow, it had been difficult to expect the 2006 Austrian EU Presidency to play the active and powerful role of an "honest broker." Once again, the primacy of domestic policy and the policy of national interest was dominating over matters of European integration, a fundamental dilemma with which the European Union continues to be confronted as long as its Council Presidencies do not last longer than six months.

The example of the Austrian 2006 EU Presidency once again underlined the structural weakness of the semiannual EU presidency and pointed to its limits. In order to achieve decisive and far-reaching institutional reforms within the framework of the EU as well as within the context of the individual member states, they would have to have completely different means and possibilities at their disposal. The procedure of cooperation between governments has been outdated for a long time, as this "intergovernmental" method of the EU presidency continues to reign. Aside from this structural weakness, external challenges with greater and greater effects are practically always now being "exhausted" in a declamatory manner along the lines of communiqués. Either the short-term EU Council Presidencies are overshadowed and dominated by international crisis scenarios (for example, the German EU Presidency by the 1999 Kosovo crisis, the Portuguese and French Presidencies by the 2000 Austria sanctions, or the Italian Presidency by the painful aftermath of the 2003 Iraq crisis) or else they are exhibition bouts for purposes of domestic politics within the context of impending national elections (such as Italy once again in 2003 with the conflict between Prime Minister Berlusconi and then EU Commission President Prodi with the latter's ambition for the future leadership of the Italian government) which restrict their freedom of action and ability to maneuver. If negative factors of both exogenous and domestic policy origin come together, as was also symptomatic for the Austrian EU Presidency, then these may "condemn" a presidency to immobility or even paralysis.

In the 1990s, the short-term EU Presidencies were already coming up against limits. Today, in light of the tall agenda the EU is facing now, issues that have become more and more complex, and thus more difficult to solve, need more than ever a greater expenditure in energy and, above all else, more time. With all of the goodwill that Austria initially displayed in overcoming the ratification crisis of the EU Constitutional Treaty in 2005–6, it quickly came up against obstacles and limitations.

One conclusion is evident: a more strongly centralized EU governance system that is structured for a longer time frame with more continuity of leadership in terms of both personnel and policy may in the future have better prospects for success. In fact, the EU Constitutional Treaty also points in this direction, with a Council president serving for at least two and half years. Such a strengthened EU Council President would also have to be given a stronger mandate. The fundamental struggle between, on one hand, democracy and basic legitimacy and, on the other hand, efficiency and the ability to lead might therefore end up more in favor of the latter, in spite of all of the justified and necessary demands for a greater inclusion of EU citizens in the political process of decision making. In order to possibly be taken seriously in the future as a separate legal entity—that is, in order to not just be capable of representation on a global scale, but also be capable of competing on all levels—the EU will have to decide how to go about sticking by that. Whether or not that will be successful in view of communication societies in Europe that are taking on a more and more significant profile remains an exciting question. Politics still has the lead, but the gap with the people has grown larger. Can it be bridged by more leadership?

In any case, decisions are necessary and decisions require leadership.[49] The historian may argue with Walter Hallstein who explained why his book *United Europe* (1962) has the subtitle *Challenge and Opportunity*:

> The essence of politics, however, is choice. I do not want therefore, to give the impression that because the logic of economic integration is compelling and inexorable, its consequences can be put into practice without making a political choice and a number of difficult political decisions. Such choice and such decisions were needed before the process of European integration could begin. In order that it may continue, they are needed at every step of the way. And in order that an integrated Europe may make its full contribution toward solving the crucial problems that face us all, further political choice and political decisions

will have to be made, not only by the European Community, but also by its friends, allies, and partners in the free world as a whole.[50]

Conclusion: Historical Time Horizon of Surmounting a Crisis

John Gillingham asked whether the EU would be a superstate or a new form of European market economy.[51] It seems that the latter is more likely. On top of that, one cannot help but agree with the Austrian Green European Parliament Member Johannes Voggenhuber when he says that in the event that the EU constitution comes into force, the European Union will be the first supranational democracy in history without it being a pure copy of the nation-state structures.[52]

With all integration teleology, the contents of the integration remains to be checked with regard to the "truth in labeling": the project of the "home market"[53] is still unfinished, and the same holds true for the Economic and Monetary Union, which also consists of an incongruence between political union and economic and monetary union. The suggestion from the constitutional convention that has not yet entered into force stands at the provisional end of this varied, turbulent, and open development. It is the expression of a market community and a community of common values with just as unclear a territorial telos as a consciously left-open political finality. The path toward the goal of the validity of a "constitutional constitution" on the basis of a Treaty on the Constitution for Europe does not appear to be so distant. It would, however, be expected that the ratification process will be accompanied, or stimulated, by the appearance of further lively crises. What extent these will take on and whether they will then be of assistance remains to be seen.[54]

With a view to the EU and the widely varied suggestions for reorganization, there can be a discussion—on the basis of treaties, agreements, and mandates—of a historical process of the coming into existence of a constitution on the most varied of levels and in the most intense form, from sectoral to horizontal integration: from the coal and steel constitution (ECSC) through the foreign trade constitution (EEC and EC) and (home) market constitution (of the "Four Freedoms") to the monetary constitution (EMS, European Central Bank, Economic and Monetary Union, and the euro) and the constitution of values (the Charter of Fundamental Rights), that is, an intensified process as a result with a quasi-constitutional character.[55]

What chances does the EU Constitutional Treaty have after the failed referendums in France and the Netherlands? After the outbreak of this most recent and dramatic crisis in EU integration in 2005, the most that could be expected from the Austrian EU Presidency in 2006 was the design of a road map for possibly overcoming the crisis and the launch of an attempt—together with the subsequent Finnish and German EU Presidencies—to maintain and implement this road map. But much more important was the question of what could be learned from European integration crises with regard to the time horizon of surmounting them? There have been five serious crises that had to be resolved quickly or else lasted and turned out to be important:

- After the failure of the European Defense and the Political Community (in 1954), it took four years until the next attempt with the Treaties of Rome (1957–8).
- The failure of the large free trade zone of all OEEC states (in 1958) is a crisis scenario that to date has not been extensively examined. It ended up meaning a schism in Western Europe of more than ten years in trade and integration policy between EFTA and the EC (1960–72).
- The Empty Chair crisis provoked by de Gaulle (1965–6) delayed the introduction of majority decisions in substantial areas of policy within the community until the 1980s.
- It was possible to solve the crisis surrounding the implementation of the EU Treaty of Maastricht (1991) by way of "opting out" (by the United Kingdom and Denmark in 1992–3).
- Likewise, within the context of the Iraq crisis (2002–3) and the failed Brussels Summit (2003), it was possible to conclude and sign the EU Constitutional Treaty in the following year relatively quickly through the mediation of the Irish EU Council presidency.

With the first and fourth cases, leadership was a great help (from Spaak, Adenauer, and Mollet, and later Kohl, Mitterrand, and Delors). In the third case, de Gaulle was a leader, but mostly for France. The second and fifth cases were examples more of teamwork than leading personalities. If a comparison is made with regard to the time frames for overcoming these crises, then the following results emerge. The first crisis was overcome with a relatively quick technical-economic solution (EEC/EURATOM). What then followed in the 1960s, 1970s, and 1980s were conflict solutions that took more time. In the 1990s and most recently, there have been conflict solutions that once again were achieved relatively rapidly. Although more time could be afforded in the 1960s, the 1970s, and to some extent the 1980s, in face of the ratification crisis of the EU's Constitutional Treaty, which broke out in 2005, things were more pressing than ever. The pressure of expectations and the pressure for success have increased considerably as a result of the need for problem solving. It was fair to expect that any effort in surmounting the ratification crisis of the EU's Constitutional Treaty in the next few years (2008–9) would certainly have to wait until after the presidential election in France in 2007. By then, the semiannual rotating EU Council Presidency will definitively be viewed as a discontinued model, occupying its place in the history of European integration.

Notes

1. Michael Gehler, *Europa: Ideen, Institutionen, Vereinigung*, Munich: Olzog, 2005, pp. 244–53, pp. 281–314.
2. Ibid., pp. 321, pp. 343; Thierry de Montbrial, *Dialog am Ende des Jahrhunderts: Der europäische Gedanke als Selbstbehauptung eines Kontinents*, Munich and Vienna: Europaverlag, 1998; Helmut Schmidt, *Die Selbstbehauptung Europas. Perspektiven für das 21. Jahrhundert*, Stuttgart: Deutsche Verlagsanstalt, 2000.
3. See for example: Manfred Scheich, "Die Zukunft der EU—fundamentale Fragen sind zu stellen," *Unsere Sicherheit Europa. Newsletter des Österreichischen Instituts für Europäische Sicherheitspolitik*, 2 (2005), pp. 1–4; positive, with idealism and a lot of good proposals overcoming the ratification crisis of the EU's Constitutional Treaty: Ludger Kühnhardt, "Europa—quo vadis?" in: *Kirche und Gesellschaft*, No. 322, ed. Katholische Sozialwissenschaftliche Zentralstelle Mönchengladbach, Cologne: J.P. Bachem Verlag, 2005, pp. 3–16; Ludger Kühnhardt, "Wozu Europa? Auswege aus der Krise um die Europäische Verfassung," in: Ludger Kühnhardt, *Erweiterung und Vertiefung. Die Europäische Union im Neubeginn*, Baden-Baden: Nomos, 2005, pp. 151–64; with a lot of critical assumptions and a plea for more realism: Heinrich August Winkler, "Grundlagenvertrag statt Verfassung," *Frankfurter Allgemeine Zeitung*, No. 139, June 18, 2005, p. 8; Heinrich August Winkler, "Weltmacht durch Überdehnung: Ein Plädoyer für europäischen Realismus," *Merkur. Deutsche Zeitschrift für europäisches Denken*, 60.1 (2006), pp. 36–43. Others underline the need for more patience with Europe: see Rolf Gustavsson and Richard Swartz, "Die Unvollendete: Geduld mit Europa!" *Süddeutsche Zeitung*, January 12, 2006, p. 11.
4. Nina Eschke and Thomas Malick (eds.), *The European Constitution and its Ratification Crisis: Constitutional Debates in the EU Member States*, ZEI Discussion Paper C 156, Bonn: Zentrum für Europäische Integrationsforschung, 2006.
5. See Wolf D. Gruner and Wichard Woyke, *Europa-Lexikon: Länder—Politik—Institutionen*, Munich: Deutscher Taschenbuchverlag, 2004, and historians writing their articles in the *Journal of European Integration History*, Nomos: Baden-Baden.
6. Quoted after Werner Link, "Primäre und sekundäre Ziele. Die Entwicklung der Europäischen Union nach der großen Erweiterung," *Frankfurter Allgemeine Zeitung*, October 12, 2005 (from his review of Esther Brimmer and Stefan Fröhlich (eds.), *The Strategic Implications of European Union Enlargement*, Washington D.C.: Center for Transatlantic Relations, 2005).
7. In the early 1960s the first EEC Commission's President published a book in the series William L. Clayton Lectures on International Economic Affairs and Foreign Policy, which has a characteristic title: Walter Hallstein, *United Europe: Challenge and Opportunity*, Cambridge, MA: Harvard University Press, 1962.
8. Romain Kirt, "Europa in der Krise—Leidet der Alte Kontinent am 'Buddenbrook-Syndrom'?" in: Romain Kirt (ed.), *Die Europäische Union und ihre Krisen*, Baden-Baden: Nomos, 2001, pp. 17–39, also pp. 25–27. The volume contains worthy individual papers and numerous stimulating ideas but no summarizing or systematically structured analysis of a crisis typology and crisis phenomenology resulting from the numerous case studies and individual findings that were collected; now with a final analysis and reflection see: Romain Kirt, *Die Europäische Union in der Komplexitätskrise: Dysfunktionen der europäischen Integration im Zeitalter der Globalisierung*, PhD, University of Innsbruck 2006.
9. Horst Möller, *Europa zwischen den Weltkriegen*, Munich: Oldenbourg, 1998.

10. Anita Ziegerhofer, *Botschafter Europas: Richard Nikolaus Coudenhove-Kalergi und die Paneuropa-Bewegung in den zwanziger und dreißiger Jahren*, Vienna, Cologne, and Weimar: Böhlau, 2004; see also Oliver Burgard, *Das gemeinsame Europa—von der politischen Utopie zum außenpolitischen Programm: Meinungsaustausch und Zusammenarbeit pro-europäischer Verbände in Deutschland und Frankreich 1924–1933*, Frankfurt am Main: Verlag Neue Wissenschaft, 2000; Guido Müller, *Europäische Gesellschaftsbeziehungen nach dem Ersten Weltkrieg: Das Deutsch-Französische Studienkomitee und der Europäische Kulturbund*, Munich: Oldenbourg, 2005.
11. Dok. 2, "Paneuropa. Ein Vorschlag. Von R.N. Coudenhove-Kalergi," November 16, 1922, in: Michael Gehler, *Der lange Weg nach Europa: Österreich von Paneuropa bis zum EU-Beitritt. Dokumente*, Innsbruck, Vienna, and Bozen: Studienverlag, 2002, pp.22–27; Thomas Angerer, "Österreich ist Europa: Identifikationen Österreichs mit Europa seit dem 18. Jahrhundert," *Wiener Zeitschrift zur Geschichte der Neuzeit*, 1.1 (2001), pp. 55–72.
12. Wilfried Loth, *Der Weg nach Europa: Geschichte der europäischen Integration 1939–1957*, Göttingen: Vandenhoeck&Ruprecht, 1990, pp. 10–13; Peter Krüger, "Zur europäischen Dimension der Außenpolitik Gustav Stresemanns," in: Karl Heinrich Pohl, *Politiker und Bürger: Gustav Stresemann und seine Zeit*, Göttingen: Vandenhoeck & Ruprecht, 2001, pp. 194–228; Franz Knipping, *Deutschland, Frankreich und das Ende der Locarno-Ära 1928–1931: Studien zur Internationalen Politik in der Anfangsphase der Weltwirtschaftskrise*, Munich: Oldenbourg, 1987; Stephen A. Schuker (ed.), *Deutschland und Frankreich: Vom Konflikt zur Aussöhnung. Die Gestaltung der westeuropäischen Sicherheit 1914–1963*, Munich: Oldenbourg, 2000.
13. Winston S. Churchill, *Reden, Bd. 4: Vorwärts zum Sieg*, Zurich: Eugen Rentsch Verlag, 1946, pp. 67–89, here p. 74; see also Max Beloff, "Churchill and Europe," in: Robert Blake and Roger W. Louis (eds.), *Churchill*, Oxford: University Press, 1993, pp. 443–55.
14. Churchill, Winston S., "Speech to the Academic Youth," Zurich, September 19, 1946, quoted in A. Boyd and F. Boyd, *Western Union*, London: Hutchinson, 1948, pp. 141–42; online at http://www.europa-web.de/europa/02wwswww/202histo/churchill.htm (last visited August 1, 2006); Geoffrey Best, *Churchill: A Study of Greatness*, London: Hambledon & London, 2001, p. 301; John W. Young, *Britain and European Unity, 1945–1992*, London: Macmillan, 1993, p. 19.
15. Walter Lipgens (ed.), *45 Jahre Ringen um die Europäische Verfassung: Dokumente 1939–1984*, Bonn: Europa Union Verlag, 1986, pp. 191–213.
16. Günter Bischof, "Der Marshall-Plan in Europa 1947–1952," *Aus Politik und Zeitgeschichte*, B 22–23 (1997), pp. 3–16.
17. Mark Gilbert, *Surpassing Realism: The Politics of European Integration since 1945*, Landham, MD: Rowman & Littlefield, 2003, p. 10.
18. Raymond Poidevin, *Robert Schuman, homme d'État 1886–1963*, Paris: Imprimerie Nationale 1986, p. 256–63.
19. Mareike König, "Die Wiederbewaffnung der Bundesrepublik in Le Monde und Le Figaro 1950–1955," in: Matthias Schulz and Mareike König (eds.), *Die Bundesrepublik Deutschland und die europäische Einigung 1949–2000: Politische Akteure, gesellschaftliche Kräfte und internationale Erfahrungen*, Stuttgart: Franz Steiner Verlag, 2004, pp. 401–21; Wolfram Kaiser, "Une bataille est perdue, mais la guerre reste à gagner—Das Scheitern der Europäischen Verteidigungsgemeinschaft 1954 und der Durchbruch zur horizontalen Wirtschaftsintegration," in: Kirt (ed.), *Die Europäische Union und ihre Krisen*, here p. 95.
20. Wichard Woyke, "Die Ablehnung der Fouchet-Pläne oder die Krise der europäischen Verfasstheit," in: Kirt (ed.), *Die Europäische Union und ihre Krisen*, pp. 97–109.

21. Maurice Vaïsse, "La politique européenne de la France en 1965. Pourquoi 'la chaise vide'?" in: Wilfried Loth (ed.), *Crises and Compromises: The European Project 1963–1969*, Baden-Baden: Nomos, 2001, p. 193; Heiner Timmermann, "Die 'Politik des leeren Stuhls' und der Luxemburger Kompromiss," in: Kirt (ed.), *Die Europäische Union und ihre Krisen*, pp. 111–18.
22. Guido Thiemeyer, "Helmut Schmidt und die Gründung des Europäischen Währungssystems 1973–1979," in: Franz Knipping and Matthias Schönwald (eds.), *Aufbruch zum Europa der zweiten Generation: Die europäische Einigung 1969–1984*, Trier: Wissenschaftlicher Verlag, 2004, pp. 245–68.
23. Guido Müller, "Folgen der Ölkrise für den europäischen Einigungsprozess nach 1973," in: Knipping and Schönwald (eds.), *Aufbruch zum Europa der zweiten Generation*, pp. 73–93.
24. Gilles Grin, *The Battle of the Single European Market: Achievements and Economics 1945–2000*, New York: Columbia University Press, 2003, pp. 111–66.
25. Mark Gilbert, *Surpassing Realism*, pp. 203–12.
26. Ibid., p. 226.
27. Romain Kirt, *Wege aus der Legitimationskrise: Die Europäische Union auf der Suche nach einem neuen Selbstverständnis*, Esch-sur-Alzette: Le Phare, 2003, pp. 23–62.
28. Roman Herzog, *Vision Europa: Antworten auf neue Herausforderungen*, Hamburg: Hoffmann & Campe, 1996; Augustín José Menéndez, "Finalité Through Rights," in: Erik Oddvar Eriksen, John Erik Fossum and Augustín José Menéndez (eds.), *The Chartering of Europe*, Baden-Baden: Nomos, 2003, pp. 30–48, pp. 41–46; Simon Gruber, "Die Grundrechtscharta und der Grundrechtskonvent (1999–2000). Analyse und vergleichender Rückblick auf die Verfassungsentwicklung in den USA (1787–1791)," in: Michael Gehler, Günter Bischof, Ludger Kühnhardt and Rolf Steininger (eds.), *Towards a European Constitution: A Historical and Political Comparison with the United States*, Vienna, Cologne, and Weimar: Böhlau, 2005, pp. 271–302.
29. Kirt, *Wege aus der Legitimationskrise*, pp. 77–93.
30. Erhard Busek and Waldemar Hummer (eds.), *Der Europäische Konvent und sein Ergebnis: Eine Europäische Verfassung*, Vienna, Cologne, and Weimar: Böhlau, 2004.
31. Johannes Pollak and Sonja Puntscher-Riekmann, "Von Haien und Heringen oder Über die Macht von großen und kleinen Staaten in Europa," in: Michael Gehler, Anton Pelinka and Günter Bischof (eds.), *Österreich in der Europäischen Union: Bilanz seiner Mitgliedschaft/Austria in the European Union: Assessment of her Membership*, Vienna, Cologne, and Weimar: Böhlau, 2003, pp. 379–402.
32. Gilbert Scharsach, "Die Europäische Verteidigungsgemeinschaft und die Maastricht-EU. 40 Jahre Integration und kein bisschen weiter?" *Zeitgeschichte*, 24.3–4 (1997), pp. 103–30; Christof Berthold, *Die Europäische Politische Gemeinschaft (EPG) 1953 und die Europäische Union (EU) 2001: Eine rechtsvergleichende Betrachtung*, Frankfurt am Main: Peter Lang, 2003.
33. Gilbert, *Surpassing Realism*, pp. 85–117.
34. A prime example is the devastating terror attack in Madrid on March 11, 2004 with the consequence of José María Aznar being voted out of office (as a result of his questionable explanation of the attack) and the election of the EU constitution-friendly José Luis Rodríguez Zapatero as the new Spanish prime minister, which also softened Polish resistance and made the conclusion possible while Ireland still held in presidency in the first half of 2004.
35. Alan S. Milward, *The European Rescue of the Nation State*, London: Routledge, 1992.
36. Romain Kirt, "Introduction," in: Kirt (ed.), *Die Europäische Union und ihre Krisen*, pp. 11–14.

37. Sonja Puntscher-Riekmann, *Die kommissarische Neuordnung Europas*, Vienna and New York: Springer Verlag, 1998, pp. 221–29, here p. 223.
38. Johannes Christian Koecke, "Krisen und Krisengerade: Kritik eines politischen Allgemeinplatzes. Eine Antwort auf die Frage, warum es der Europäischen Union so schlecht und uns so gut geht," in: Kirt (ed.), *Die Europäische Union und ihre Krisen*, pp. 41–47.
39. As the motto for his anthology, quoted in Kirt, *Die Europäische Union und ihre Krisen*, p. 5.
40. "Die Türkei darf nicht für ihre Fußballer büßen. Österreich übernimmt 2006 den EU-Vorsitz. Ein Gespräch mit Bundeskanzler Wolfgang Schüssel über die nächste Erweiterung, die deutschen Nachbarn—und eine Europasteuer," *Die Zeit*, November 24, 2005; Eva Linsinger, "Österreich will nicht der 'Wunderheiler' Europas sein," *Der Standard*, December 12, 2005; Alexandra Föderl-Schmid, "Europa neuen Schwung verleihen," *Der Standard*, January 2, 2006; Christoph Prantner, "Die Verfassung ist nicht tot," *Der Standard*, January 10, 2006.
41. "Europa hört zu—auch wenn es unangenehm ist. Außenministerin Plassnik eröffnet den 'elektronischen Speakers' Corner' auf dem Ballhausplatz," *Die Presse*, January 9, 2006.
42. Simon Gruber, Kai-Olaf Lang and Andreas Maurer, *Aufräumarbeiten und neue Impulse für Europa*, SWP-Aktuell 2, Berlin: Stiftung Wissenschaft und Politik, Deutsches Institut für Internationale Politik und Sicherheit, 2006, p. 5.
43. Michael Gehler, "Die EU-Agenda explodiert. Trotz Lösung des EU-Finanzenstreits bleiben Österreich als 'honest broker' viele schwierige Aufgaben," *Die Presse*, January 10, 2006.
44. Transcript summary, topic: "Österreichische Ratspräsidentschaft 2006; 23. Sitzung der interministeriellen Lenkungsgruppe am 13.1.2006," BKA/BMfaA (Austrian Federal Chancellery and Austrian Foreign Ministry, BKA-405.007/0004–IV/5/2006; BMaA-3.18.45/0002–III.2/2006, Vienna, January 17, 2006, for the Chancellor: Heiss, handwritten; for the Foreign Ministry: Steinhäusl, handwritten).
45. "Heftiger Streit über Umgang mit der Verfassung. Die Spannungen in der Europäischen Union wegen des zukünftigen Kurses verschärfen sich," *Der Standard*, January 13, 2006; for a contemporary historical analysis of the European People's Party and Christian Democratic parties in Europe in the 1990s, see Steven van Hecke, "A Decade of Seized Opportunities: Christian Democracy in the European Union," in: Steven van Hecke and Emmanuel Gerard (eds.), *Christian Democratic Parties in Europe since the End of the Cold War*, Leuven: Leuven University Press, 2004, pp. 269–307.
46. Gruber, Lang and Maurer, "Aufräumarbeiten und neue Impulse für Europa," p. 6.
47. Helmut Hauschild, "EU sprachlos—Fragen und keine Antworten", in *Handelsblatt*, January 27–28, and 29, 2006; for the basics on this complex of topics, see Gunther Hauser, "Umfassende Kooperationsprozesse für den Mittelmeerraum. Der sicherheitspolitische Dialog zwischen der EU, der NATO und Israel," *David. Jüdische Kulturzeitschrift* 17:67 (2005), pp. 24–26.
48. Michael Gehler, *Österreichs Außenpolitik der Zweiten Republik: Von der alliierten Besatzung bis zum Europa des 21. Jahrhunderts* (2 vols.), Innsbruck, Vienna and Bozen: Studienverlag, 2005, pp. 995–1026.
49. Michael Gehler, "Das Dilemma der EU-Präsidentschaften," *Die Presse*, March 24, 2006.
50. Hallstein, *United Europe*, pp. 58–59.
51. John Gillingham, *European Integration 1950–2003: Superstate or New Market Economy?* Cambridge: Cambridge University Press, 2003, pp. 446–79.

52. Johannes Voggenhuber, "Der Europäische Konvent: Ausgangslage, Zusammensetzung, Arbeitsweise, Ergebnisse," lecture within the framework of the conference "Die neue Verfassung für die Europäische Union," organized by the Institut für Völkerrecht, Europarecht und Internationale Beziehungen at the University of Innsbruck, November 22–23, 2004.
53. Grin, *The Battle of the Single European Market*, pp. 111–66.
54. Michael Gehler, "From a Treaty to a Constitutional Community? The Long Path towards the 'Convention on the Future of the European Union' 1918–2003," in: Gehler, Bischof, Kühnhardt and Steininger (eds.), *Towards a European Constitution*, pp. 415–41, here pp. 430–31.
55. Ingolf Pernice, "Europäische Grundrechtscharta und Konventsverfahren. Zehn Thesen zum Prozess der europäischen Verfassung nach Nizza," *Integration* 2 (2005), pp. 194–97, here p.195.

8

Frontiers and Chances for the European Union[1]

Hans-Gert Pöttering

No other invitation in British academic life could attract me more than the opportunity to deliver the annual Adenauer Lecture at the European Studies Centre, here at St. Antony's College, Oxford. It is not just that it is a great honour to follow in the footsteps of so many distinguished predecessors, over many years. It is that—for me personally—it is especially inspiring to give a talk dedicated to the memory of Konrad Adenauer—one of the founding fathers of today's Europe, to whom my country owes so much—and one delivered here in the European Studies Centre of one of the leading universities in the world.

The former Chancellor of Oxford University, Roy Jenkins, was once asked: "What is the difference between a speech and a lecture?" He replied: "A lecture is characteristically a little longer than a speech, but not necessarily more interesting!" As a professional politician, like Lord Jenkins, I understand the perils of that distinction, and will try to keep what I say as succinct and interesting as possible, consistent with the rubric of it being a "lecture."

Adenauer and Oxford

When Konrad Adenauer was invited by Winston Churchill on his first visit to Britain as German Chancellor, in December 1951, Oxford formed part of his program. No Chancellor had been in this country since Heinrich Brüning twenty years before. Adenauer knew too well what had happened in the decades in between. He was ready to help forge a new beginning in relations between Germany and Britain, and to play a decisive part in developing what Timothy Garton Ash has since described as "a non-hegemonic order for the whole of Europe."

Adenauer looked to a Europe in which never again would any one country aspire to dominance. He had shown imagination and courage by supporting the supranational pooling of the coal and steel industries, in the ECSC created in

April that year. He was ready to accept the concept of a European army too, as indeed at one stage was Churchill.

Reflecting in his memoirs on the 1951 visit, Adenauer wrote that both countries were called upon to take common responsibility in shaping the new order of the West. He recognized and understood a certain reserve on the part of Britain in forging a common destiny with continental Europe—an instinct he must have found disappointing given Churchill's strong promotion of European unity in Opposition (from 1945 to 1951).

In his conversations with Churchill and Foreign Secretary Anthony Eden, Adenauer acknowledged that a certain dose of British restraint and political realism would always be useful. For its part, Germany would pursue the path of European integration, in a measured way, "reflected and without haste, but steady and effective," as he put it.

Adenauer's visit to Oxford left a deep impression upon him. He visited Balliol College where he saw the lists of students who had died in World Wars I and II. Among them was his own nephew, Hans Adenauer, who had been studying at the college in the late 1920s. Confronted with the horrors of history and the challenge to build a new Europe, Adenauer felt that "a community of Western, Christian culture and tradition" united our countries.

In London, Churchill asked Adenauer whether good relations might ever be possible between Germany and Poland. It is impressive, indeed moving, to note that, five decades after Adenauer's visit, Germany, Britain, and Poland are all members of the European Union—part of the free, democratic, and united Europe of today.

Achievements, Challenges, and Crises

The political achievement of unity and common interest that we have forged together in Europe since the 1950s is truly remarkable. In the West, we defined a new culture of sovereignty-sharing that has proved highly effective in allowing "unity in diversity." Then the collapse of Communism permitted the reunification of Europe, finally brought to fruition in 2004. As Milan Kundera observed, Eastern European history for most of the twentieth century was a "day with two nights," as one totalitarian regime replaced another. That nightmare is now over.

Building a peaceful, cooperative, united Europe is perhaps the most seriously underrated political achievement witnessed in recent years anywhere in the world. It gets scant recognition as such, not least (if I may be permitted to say so) in this country. Such an outcome was far from inevitable, as the contrasting experience of East Asia since 1945 testifies. It should, as a result, never be taken for granted.

In addition to this political success—and indeed in part because of it—today's Europe is also more advanced economically and socially—in terms of personal prosperity and freedom—than anything Adenauer and Churchill might have expected or hoped for when they talked in 1951. Yet the irony is that, despite dramatic progress in so many spheres, many of our fellow citizens in Europe today are increasingly consumed in pessimism and fear, and many decision makers seem overcome by inertia in the face of mounting challenges. The future seems to weigh heavily over us.

We can see the symptoms of this malaise on many fronts. Fear of globalization is one. Resistance to economic reform is another. There is a reluctance to think clearly about the challenges of our shrinking populations—whether for pensions, or health care, or public spending, or immigration, or lifelong learning. We experience a deep foreboding about climate change, matched by a strange refusal to take tough decisions on global warming. There is a pervasive sense of insecurity at home and abroad, as we confront rising domestic crime and the advent of brutal international terror. The list of concerns is written for us every day in the newspapers we read and on the news program we watch.

I often wonder how the great mid-century leaders, such as Churchill or Adenauer, or Truman or de Gaulle, would have looked at these challenges. My instinct is that they would have found our prevailing attitudes too cautious, even defeatist. They would have found today's debates too constricting and lacking in ambition. They would have been unimpressed, I think, by a political culture that too often sees limits, rather than possibilities, at every turn. I believe that they would also have seen Europe as part of the solution to the problems facing our continent, rather than part of the problem itself.

Looking at today's European Union, many see a system simply in crisis. I recognize crises, of course, but I see significant opportunities too. Ludger Kühnhardt has rightly analyzed that the European Union has been built in response to crises at many stages in its history. As Timothy Garton Ash has written, "the European project has many times moved precisely through and out of crisis."

In my own time as a Member of the European Parliament since 1979, I have witnessed the peaks and troughs of the integration process at first hand. Rarely has any major breakthrough—whether in terms of institutions or policies—not been preceded by some period of impasse, or of deep pessimism, or of obvious need for action that is unforthcoming. It would seem that often the very perception of crisis is a necessary condition, not of course a sufficient condition, to mobilize the will for change and to allow progress to happen.

In order to break free of the current crisis, it is important to think clearly about what Europe is and has the potential to be, what it can and what it should do. I would like to share some of my thoughts with you this evening. Although I was once an academic, these are the reflections of a practitioner, of someone who has spent most of his adult life in European politics, working at the coalface of practical integration on a daily basis.

The Institutional Challenge

Let me deal first with Europe's institutional challenge. I believe very deeply that none of us would be better off if there were no European Union today. Equally, all of us would be better off if the Union were more effective, democratic, transparent. And accountable. If Europe could be made to work better institutionally, this would help address more directly the problems and concerns of the citizens, and through that process, help make the European Union itself more popular and legitimate.

Institutionally, few could deny that the European Union today is facing difficulties in acting coherently and in carrying consent. The constitutional arrangements set down in the existing treaties are inadequate to meet Europe's obligations and ambitions. Yet ironically the public in some countries is reluctant to reform those institutions, for a whole diversity of reasons, only some of which have to do with Europe. Vernon Bogdanor has spoken of a "dis-connect" between the people and Europe's institutions. For too many, the latter seem to be (what he calls) an "alienated superstructure" that they do not trust.

The paradox, however, is that, with reformed institutions, the problems which our citizens face would be much easier to confront, and that, without them, they are correspondingly more difficult to solve. People rightly demand a better management of Europe's affairs in an age when so many problems have an international character—and where common European action can make a positive difference; yet many seem reluctant to use the means to precisely that end.

No program for reforming the EU's institutions and procedures has ever been as transparent or consensual as the one that led to the text of the Constitutional Treaty. Yet ironically one of many reasons why the text was rejected by majorities in France and the Netherlands was because people felt that the product was not democratic enough.

When it comes to constitutional questions, I can only speak on behalf of the EPP part of the EPP–ED Group. But I believe that the key elements of the Constitution would make Europe either more efficient or more legitimate, or both. You can see these features in the strengthened role it envisages for national parliaments, in the greater use of co-decision between the European Parliament and the Council of Ministers, and in the opening up of the Council so that it would legislate in public.

You can see the right approach in the simplification the Constitution would introduce into the structure of European legislation, in the clearer delineation it would give to the respective competences of the EU and member states, in its streamlining of the Presidency of the Council of Ministers, in its creation of a more permanent President of the European Council, as well as of an EU foreign minister, and in its provision for the first time of a form of Europe-wide popular initiative. None of these changes in Europe's institutional design is revolutionary, but they all point in the right direction. Cumulatively they add up to a better system of governance for the Union.

Of course, no institutional improvement can on its own suddenly resolve any one of the key policy challenges facing the European Union. But together they can offer the chance of putting in place a decision-making process that is on a par with the challenges we face. If you doubt that, you only need to take a look at the illogicalities and contradictions of the existing Nice Treaty, with which we are currently condemned to work.

What next for the Constitution? The text has, of course, been ratified by a majority of EU member states, whose populations constitute a majority of EU citizens, in accordance with their own constitutional practices. Others have decided to defer taking a final decision. In that sense, the document is currently in limbo, rather than dead.

The European Parliament has proposed that we look again at the Constitution during the period between 2007 and 2009, after the "period of reflection" that is now taking place. There are different views, among governments and within the European Parliament, about exactly how much of the existing text should be retained. My own hope is that, whatever the precise form, the key innovations it foresees can eventually be ratified by all member states, and the EU be given a more rational and credible foundation for action at home and in the wider world.

The Challenge of Enlargement

Let me turn next to the question of enlargement. We have rightly undertaken the historic process of enlargement, to reunite Europe as we understood it. This has been, and continues to be, a huge undertaking. The EU's status as a beacon of democracy, political stability, and relative prosperity has made membership the goal of an increasingly large number of countries to our east. As Chris Patten has long argued, enlargement has been Europe's most successful foreign policy. It has exported democracy, stability, and market-based reform to candidate countries.[1]

Enlargement, however, comes at a price. The European Union is not an international organization like the United Nations or the OECD. It involves formal sovereignty-sharing across a large range of policy areas. The larger the number of member states, the greater the diversity of interests to be brokered, the more complex the compromises to be struck. Hence in part the rationale for reforming our institutions.

Governing together depends crucially on the participants in the process believing themselves to be members of the same political community. We are now approaching—for the first time—a situation where the boundaries of the European Union might no longer correspond to what many Europeans consider to be "Europe." This is an important moment.

The prospective enlargement to Turkey, which played a part in generating the "no" votes on the European Constitution in the 2005 referendums, has brought this issue into sharp relief, at both national and European levels. The question of the Ukraine has done likewise. If Ukraine, why not Russia? A lively debate has been sparked on what it is to be a European. What are our values and identity? Do those who want to join share them? How far must they as a precondition of membership? I think that we have to be honest in facing this debate, rather than attempting to conceal it or pretending it does not exist.

This is not a static scene. The prospect of enlargement changes the very countries that aspire to it. We have started, in good faith, an enlargement negotiation with Turkey, for example, which will in itself change the very country we are dealing with. No one can tell yet whether a modernizing Turkey a decade or so from now will have progressed sufficiently far and fast to look likely to be able to take its place in the European family. In Turkey's case, the problem is compounded by the fact that, by— or soon after—the time of entry, Turkey would be the largest EU member state whilst also being one of its poorest, if not the poorest. It would have the most votes in the Council of Ministers, whilst also aspiring to be the largest net recipient of EU funds. This would be the opposite of the current situation with Germany.

Issues such as these pose the question of what in the jargon is called "the absorption capacity" of the Union—the least noticed of the famous Copenhagen criteria for enlargement. The capacity to absorb new member states was severely tested by the admission of ten new countries in 2004. My own view is that further enlargements— beyond those already imminent—will become increasingly problematic without institutional reform. And, even with reform, they will still be difficult.

Putting all these factors together, my conclusion is that we should very actively consider inventing some new intermediate option, which offers some of the de facto benefits of membership without the formal status of full membership as such. This is the so-called "privileged partnership" concept.

In a memorable passage in his new book, *Not Quite the Diplomat*, Chris Patten argues that, just as the "reconciliation of France and Germany was the necessary and admirable European accomplishment of the twentieth century," so "reconciling the West and the Islamic world, with Europe acting as a hinge between the two, is a major task for the twenty-first." He goes on to argue strongly for Turkish membership of the EU.

I think that Chris Patten's basic analysis is correct, but that the conclusion he draws is over hasty. The "hinge" of full membership of the European Union may simply not be strong enough to bear the weight of this huge role on its own. Only time will tell. In the interim, other structures and instruments must be available, if we in Europe are to carry prime responsibility for reconciling the West with our diverse neighbours, whether to our east or south.

Europe's Policy Agenda

The decisions we take on EU institutions and on enlargement will decisively affect the shape and capacity of the Union in the years ahead. If we make the right choices on those questions, we will be in a significantly stronger position to tackle the central policy challenges facing Europe today. But, in the absence of clear decisions to date, the practical policy agenda to be tackled does not go away; indeed it gets more pressing by the day.

We must continue to show that, whatever its shortcomings or ambiguities, Europe can deliver for the citizen. As Tony Blair argued in an impressive speech to the European Parliament last summer, Europe can, through its actions, build the popular support that would make it possible to reform its institutions, for example.

A critical part of the crisis the European Union is facing is one of adapting our continent to the new challenges posed in an age of globalization. The difficult birth of a new era requires change all across Europe. It requires change on the part of both the EU and the member states. At both levels, it requires leaders to find the political courage to lead the debate and citizens to recognize that opportunity involves risk and that progress cannot be built on certainty. The French and Dutch referendums were as much about these challenges as about the EU institutional structure.

Europe is, I believe, a powerful potential vehicle for confronting the challenges of globalization. A global world respects fewer and fewer national boundaries. A global world is one with big new international problems, like terror networks, migratory flows, and climate change. It is creating an open, porous, worldwide marketplace for goods, ideas, communication, and even people.

In this international marketplace, Europe's shrinking working-age population will stand in marked contrast to rising populations in the third world and even in the United States. Europe's competitiveness will depend more than ever on the skills and aptitude of its people. Interdependence will become an increasing hallmark of politics in Europe and worldwide.

The opportunity for the European Union lies in offering a framework in which to develop common answers to these questions, a framework capable of turning local, regional and national problems and fears into a bigger common solution, by working together on a continental scale. This prospect will affect every area of policy, from foreign policy and the environment to social security, health care, and pensions.

You will be relieved to hear that I will not deal with all such dimensions this evening, but I will, if I may, briefly allude to three of them: foreign policy, demographic change and economic reform. All of these policy fields have traditionally been the preserve of national governments, but the realities of today's interdependent world dictate the need for greater and greater common action.

European Foreign Policy

Let me deal first with foreign policy. Here, despite the shortcomings of weak institutional structures and often divergent perspectives among the member states to date, it is important to note that Europe's emerging foreign policy is in general nowhere near as flimsy or inadequate as some critics like to claim.

The European Union is already by far the biggest donor of development aid across the world. It is heavily engaged in bi-regional cooperation with groupings such as ASEAN, Mercosur, and increasingly the African Union. EU soft power is increasingly being put to hard use in the world's trouble spots. Take the Kimberley Process to eliminate the trade in "conflict diamonds," a multilateral and multi-organizational effort to be chaired by the European Union in 2007. Take the work in Southeastern Europe, where the EU has done much to stabilize and integrate the region.

Most importantly, take the Middle East. Both Israel and the Palestine have requested a police mission of the EU to monitor the border crossing in Rafah between the Gaza Strip and Egypt. For the first time, the EU has been recognized by both sides as a serious political factor in delivering the Road Map of the Quartet. I consider this a major breakthrough.

In the "hard power" field too, the score-card is increasingly positive. The European Security Strategy of 2003 identified at least the right issues, working in parallel with the United States, not against it. The interface between NATO and the EU is being systematically strengthened. A serious effort is being made to identify how duplication among EU national defences could be reduced and more effective burden-sharing undertaken. The new European Defense Agency has the potential to open up procurement in the EU and enhance defense capabilities.

These developments offer hope that Europe can and will play a bigger, more coherent, more responsible role in world affairs, in the context of a vibrant transatlantic partnership.

Demographic Change in Europe

Let me say a word next about demographic change. As a result of people living longer and having fewer babies, the working-age population across Europe has already begun to fall, both in absolute terms and as a proportion of the whole. The number of people aged fifteen to sixty-four in the EU will decline by 48 million between now and 2050 (a drop of some 20 percent), and the number over sixty-five will rise by 58 million. Europe will move from having four people of working age for every elderly citizen to a ratio of only two to one. The policy implications of the ageing and shrinking of populations in Europe are multifaceted and serious, and will need to be addressed.

A smaller workforce will result in lower economic growth, and possibly even deflation. There will be fewer producers in the economy and an ageing society is likely to save more and consume less. Japan's economic difficulties in recent years have already heralded the prospect of "ageing recessions." The European Commission recently predicted that such factors alone will reduce potential growth in the EU from over 2.0 percent per annum today to 1.25 percent by 2040.

Indeed, this process is already having an effect. Daniel Gros of CEPS has calculated that, over the last ten years, Germany's GDP potential growth rate has already been 1 percent lower than it would otherwise have been, because of demographic change.

Moreover, lower growth will happen just as the costs of an ageing population rise. There will be a significant increase in age-related spending on pensions, health, and long-term care. The likely increase in the burden of such items is estimated to be between 4 and 8 percent of GDP, with some member states facing even higher increases.

As a result, there are many difficult questions which policy makers have to focus on with some urgency.

- First: whether and how to encourage higher birth rates—through financial incentives, measures to make it easier for working women to raise children, enhanced day-care provision, and approaches that strengthen the legal framework and social status of families.
- Second: raising the labor-force participation rate, so increasing the percentage of the adult population engaged in employment, especially women and younger workers.
- Third: extending the length of working life, by raising retirement and pensionable ages, discouraging early retirement, and combating "ageism" in the workplace.
- Fourth: increasing the financial provision made by those in work toward their pensions, through higher contributions to funded pension schemes and/or greater personal savings.
- Fifth: whether to promote immigration, and how to ensure that immigrants admitted possess skills that add to the productive potential of the host countries.

The European Union is beginning to grapple with these difficult problems. Through the Lisbon process, it is attempting to increase the percentage of women and of both older and younger citizens who participate in the workforce. Progress so far has been positive, but modest. Pensions and social-security reform are being encouraged. A serious debate has opened up about a European migration policy, as countries realize that demography abhors a vacuum, and that inward population pressures are therefore bound to grow.

The European Union can provide a framework of mutual support and encouragement—and a forum for common commitments—as we all struggle with these challenges. The political group which I chair—the EPP–ED Group in the European Parliament—has begun an intensive discussion about the options and strategies we need to consider as we address demographic change. Our center-right think tank, the European Ideas Network, is doing excellent work in preparing the ground, with a working group chaired by David Willetts, the Conservative MP here in Britain.

Demographic change raises a crucial and fascinating nexus of issues that affect virtually every policy area of government. Addressing it will be central to the future economic and social health of our continent.

Economic Reform

This brings me to the parallel issue of economic reform. The European Union today is underperforming economically and has been doing so for some time. It is failing, in particular, to deliver jobs for its citizens. Unemployment in the industrialized countries has for two decades now been largely a European problem. We have more than 20 million people unemployed in the Union. During the past decade, the EU has enjoyed only half of the economic growth rate of the US and only one quarter of the growth rates of China and India.

The best way to create jobs in Europe is to free markets in goods, services, capital and labor—in national economies and across the EU as a whole. It offers the chance of renewal in order to safeguard and underpin our prosperity and to revitalize our societies so they can be inclusive, open, and adaptable in an era of continuous change.

Demographic change makes the case for economic reform, already strong, even more compelling. We will need to promote the greater productivity of existing workers, so that increased output offsets the deflationary effects of falling populations. We will need to encourage the greater adaptability of workers, so that we all possess skill sets that enable us to move more easily between jobs and professions during the course of working life. Education, training, and retraining will all become even more important, and will need to be funded accordingly.

Hard choices have to be made on liberalizing markets. The upcoming Services directive, to be voted on in the European Parliament, is a case in point. It offers us a chance to liberalize a key component of the European economy, complementing the progress made in opening up the single market in goods, and to a lesser extent, capital. It is important that we send a powerful signal that, notwithstanding the fear of globalization on the part of many, Europe is capable of embracing change and using for our collective prosperity.

Many countries have been pushing the right policies for some time. Here in Britain some difficult decisions were made in the 1980s that have paid off in subsequent decades. My own country is now beginning to face up to the same sort of challenges. In the race to get into the European Union, many Central and Eastern European countries locked on to the right path.

The situation in Europe is nowhere near as dire as some people like to claim. Even the conservative Heritage Foundation in Washington confirmed in its World Economic Freedom Index this month that of the world's twenty-five most dynamic economies, over half are in the European Union. But the standard we should be comparing ourselves with is the very best.

Final Reflections

Finally, let me say something about European and German politics as they have developed in 2005 and 2006.

Charles Péguy once wrote that "everything begins in mysticism and ends in politics." that tendency is not unknown in the European Union. Big-picture debates about the future of Europe have a tendency, sooner or later, to come crashing to a halt in some intense battle about financial resources or distributional politics. Many found the sight of European heads of government squabbling over the future financing of the Union over the last six months—whether in June or December 2005—a pretty unedifying spectacle. I agree.

However, I would make three observations about this budget dispute—and European politics more generally—from my experience and perspective in the European Parliament.

First, the protagonists in the budget dispute ultimately realized that they had a common interest in reaching a deal, however much that deal fell short of what might have been optimal for them individually—or for Europe as a whole. The price of failure would have been too high for the European Union, in which all member states have a huge amount invested.

I can say that Tony Blair, whatever criticisms might be leveled against the British Presidency, behaved with admirable courtesy and attentiveness toward the European Parliament throughout his six months at Europe's helm.

Secondly, as the so-called "financial perspectives" fall outside the normal budgetary procedure, the future-financing deal cannot be implemented without the approval of the European Parliament. We will now negotiate an Inter-Institutional Agreement with the Council and Commission, and intend only to agree to it if certain important changes are made to the efficiency and accountability of the way money is spent in the Union.

Thirdly, the debut of the new German Chancellor, Angela Merkel, in European politics proved to be encouragingly impressive. She played a crucial role in bringing the British and French positions closer together, a performance that bodes well for the future.

With Mrs. Merkel, we hope that the unpredictable days of the recent past are over. Her first visit after being sworn in as German Chancellor took her in quick succession to Paris, Brussels, London, and Warsaw. She visited President Bush as soon as possible, on January 11, 2006. These visits were an expression of her deeply felt desire to regain confidence for Germany's European and international policies wherever there have been doubts in past years. She demonstrated that she will exercise strong leadership on European and transatlantic matters.

In this approach, Germany is following its own legitimate interests, of course, but wants to and can do so only if the interests of all other partners, and notably the smaller ones, are also met. This was the successful philosophy of Chancellor Helmut Kohl for many years and I cannot see why Chancellor Merkel should not be less successful. Her first weeks in office have underlined the rightfulness and success of this traditional German attitude toward Europe.

I am confident that we will see more of this new style, and more importantly, the substance of a mediating, yet resolute Germany in the years ahead. I am also confident that no matter how important German-French relations are, the

European Union can only succeed if Germany, France, and Britain work together in cooperation with each other and all other EU partners. Only such a constructive spirit can generate sustainable European interests and successful European policies.

It is my sincere wish that, in this spirit of reinvigorated focus, we can all work together in the years and decades ahead. The agenda is bigger than ever. It requires commitment and realism, steadfastness and application. As part of that process, it requires the most vital possible German–British cooperation in Europe. This would serve not only the interests of both of our two countries; it would recognize our common obligation—and the common potential we can realize—to make Europe work better.

The European Union is work in progress. It is a huge and potentially invaluable undertaking. Getting it right can bring enormous benefits for our citizens. The challenges of our globalized world will make Europe more, not less, important. That is why I believe it is vital that all of us—academics, business people, civil society, even indeed politicians—work together to help Europe succeed, for our common future.

Notes

1   Adenauer Lecture 2006, St. Antony's College, Oxford, January 25, 2006.

Select Bibliography

Abernethy, David B., *The Dynamics of Global Dominance: European Overseas Empires, 1415–1980*, New Haven: Yale University Press, 2000.
Acheson, Dean, *Present at the Creation*, New York: W.W. Norton & Co., 1969.
———, *The Struggle for a Free Europe*, New York: W.W. Norton & Co., 1971.
Adenauer, Konrad, *Erinnerungen 1953–1955*, Stuttgart: Deutsche Verlags-Anstalt, 1966.
af Malmborg, Mikael, and Bo Strath (eds.), *The Meaning of Europe: Variety and Contentino Within and Among Nations*, Oxford and New York: Berg, 2002.
Agnelli, Giovanni, and Attilio Cabiati, *Federazione europea o lega delle nazioni?* Turin: Fratelli Bocca, 1918.
Albright, Madeleine, "The Right Balance will Secure NATO's Future," *Financial Times*, October 7, 1998, p. 22.
Alber, Jens, and Wolfgang Merkel (eds.), *Europas Osterweiterung: Das Ende der Vertiefung?*, Berlin: Wissenschaftszentrum, 2006.
Alphand, Hervé, *L'étonnement d'être. Journal 1939–1973*, Paris: Fayard, 1977.
Angerer, Thomas, "Österreich ist Europa: Identifikationen Österreichs mit Europa seit dem 18. Jahrhundert," *Wiener Zeitschrift zur Geschichte der Neuzeit*, 1.1 (2001), pp. 55–72.
Aron, Raymond, *L'âge des empires et l'avenir de la France*, Paris: Défense de la France, 1945.
Asmus, Ronald D., and Kenneth M. Pollack, "The New Transatlantic Project," *Policy Review*, 115 (2002), pp. 3–18.
Auswärtiges Amt (ed.), *Gemeinsame Außen- und Sicherheitspolitik der Europäischen Union (GASP)—Dokumentation 10*, Bonn: Auswärtiges Amt, 1994.
Axt, Hans-Jürgen, "Hat Genscher Jugoslawien entzweit? Mythen und Fakten zur Außenpolitik des vereinten Deutschlands," *Europaarchiv*, 12 (1993), pp. 351–360.
Baldwin, Richard, and Mika Widgrén, "Council Voting in the Constitutional Treaty: Devil in the Details," June 23, 2004, online at http://www.cepr.org/pubs/new-dps/dplist.asp?dpno=4450.
Ball, George, *The Discipline of Power*, Boston: Little, Brown, 1968.
Banchoff, Thomas, and Mitchell P. Smith (eds.), *Legitimacy and the European Union: The Contested Polity*, London/New York: Routledge, 1999.

Beck, Ulrich, and Anthony Giddens, "Nationalism has Now Become the Enemy of Europe's Nations," *The Guardian*, October 4, 2005.

Behring, Rainer, *Demokratische Außenpolitik für Deutschland. Die außenpolitischen Vorstellungen deutscher Sozialdemokraten im Exil 1933–1945*, Düsseldorf: Droste, 1999.

Beloff, Max, *The Intellectual in Politics and Other Essays*, London: Weidenfeld & Nicolson, 1970.

———, "Churchill and Europe," in: Robert Blake and Roger W. Louis (eds.), *Churchill*, Oxford: Oxford University Press, 1993, pp. 443–55.

Berggren, Niclas, and Nils Karlson, "Constitutionalism, Division of Power and Transaction Costs," *Public Choice*, 117.1/2 (2003), pp. 99–124.

Berthold, Christof, *Die Europäische Politische Gemeinschaft (EPG) 1953 und die Europäische Union (EU) 2001: Eine rechtsvergleichende Betrachtung*, Frankfurt am Main: Peter Lang, 2003.

Best, Geoffrey, *Churchill: A Study of Greatness*, London: Hambledon & London, 2001.

Bischof, Günter, "Der Marshall-Plan in Europa 1947–1952," *Aus Politik und Zeitgeschichte*, B 22–23(1997), pp. 3–16.

Blair, Tony, "Speech to the Polish Stock Exchange," Warsaw, October 6, 2000, online at http://www.busch.uni-hd.de/data/blair_warsaw.html.

Brand, Michiel, *Affirming and Refining European Constitutionalism: Towards the Establishment of the First Constitution for the European Union*, Fiesole: European University Institute, 2004.

Bretherton, Charlotte, and John Vogler, *The European Union as a Global Actor*, London and New York: Routledge, 2006.

Briand, Aristide, "Memorandum on the Organisation of a Regime of Federal Union," *International Conciliation*, Special Bulletin June (1930), pp. 327–53.

Brimmer, Esther, and Stefan Fröhlich (eds.), *The Strategic Implications of European Union Enlargement*, Washington D.C.: 2005.

Bullen, R., and M. Pelly (eds.), *Documents on British Policy Overseas*, series 2, vol. 1., London: HMSO, 1986.

Bulmer, Simon, and Christian Lequesne, *The Member States of the European Union*, Oxford: Oxford University Press, 2005.

Burgard, Oliver, *Das gemeinsame Europa—von der politischen Utopie zum außenpolitischen Programm: Meinungsaustausch und Zusammenarbeit proeuropäischer Verbände in Deutschland und Frankreich 1924–1933*, Frankfurt am Main: Verlag Neue Wissenschaft, 2000.

Busek, Erhard, and Waldemar Hummer (eds.), *Der Europäische Konvent und sein Ergebnis: Eine Europäische Verfassung*, Wien/Köln/Weimar: Böhlau, 2004.

Cederman, Lars-Erik, *Nationalism and Bounded integration: What it Would Take to Construct a European Demos*, Fiesole: European University Institute, 2000.

Charlton, Michael, *The Price of Victory*, London: British Broadcasting Corporation, 1983.

Checkel, Jeffrey T. "Social Construction and European Integration," in: Thomas Christiansen, Knut Erik Jorgensen, and Antje Wiener (eds.), *The Social Construction of Europe*, London: Sage Publications, 2001, pp. 50–64.

Churchill, Winston S., *Reden, Bd. 4: Vorwärts zum Sieg*, Zurich: Eugen Rentsch Verlag, 1946.

———, "Speech to the Academic Youth," Zurich, September 19, 1946, quoted in A. Boyd and F. Boyd, *Western Union*, London: Hutchinson, 1948, pp. 141–42; online at http://www.europa-web.de/europa/02wwswww/ 202histo/churchil.htm (last visited August 1, 2006).

Coudenhove-Kalergi, Richard N., *Pan-Europe*, New York: Alfred Knopf, 1926.

Cradock, Percy, *In Pursuit of British Interests: Reflections on Foreign Policy under Margaret Thatcher and John Major*, London: John Murray, 1997.

Daalder, Ivo, *Getting to Dayton: The Making of America's Bosnia Policy*, Washington, D.C.: Brookings Institution Press, 2000.

Dedman, Martin, *The Origins and Development of the European Union 1945–1995*, London: Routledge, 1996.

de Gaulle, Charles, *Discours et Messages*. Tome III: *Avec le Renouveau (1958–1962)*, Paris: Edition Plon, 1970.

de Grauwe, Paul, *The Economics of Monetary Union*, Oxford: Oxford University Press, 2005.

———, "On Monetary and Political Union," Catholic University of Leuven: mimeo, 2006.

———, and Marianna Grimaldi, "Exchange Rate Puzzles: A Tale of Switching Attractors," *European Economic Review*, 50 (2006), pp. 1–33.

Deighton, Anne, *Western European Union, 1954–1997: Defense, Security, Integration*, Oxford and Reading: EIRU, 1997.

de Montbrial, Thierry, *Dialog am Ende des Jahrhunderts: Der europäische Gedanke als Selbstbehauptung eines Kontinents*, Munich and Vienna: Europaverlag, 1998.

Diebold Jr, William, *The Schuman Plan: A Study in Economic Cooperation, 1950–1959*, New York: Praeger, 1959.

Diedrichs, Udo, and Mathias Jopp, "Flexible Modes of Governance: Making CFSP and ESDP Work," *The International Spectator*, 38.3 (2003), pp. 15–30.

"Die Türkei darf nicht für ihre Fußballer büßen. Österreich übernimmt 2006 den EU-Vorsitz. Ein Gespräch mit Bundeskanzler Wolfgang Schüssel über die nächste Erweiterung, die deutschen Nachbarn—und eine Europasteuer," *Die Zeit*, November 24, 2005.

Documents diplomatiques français: depuis 1954, vol. 1., Bruxelles: Peter Lang, 2005, doc. 308.

Donavan, Frank, *Mr. Roosevelt's Four Freedoms: The Story behind the UN Charter*, New York: Dodd, Mead, 1966.

Du Réau, Elisabeth, "Jean Monnet, le Comité de coordination franco-britannique et le projet d'Union franco-britannique: les moyens de vaincre le nazisme (septembre 1939—juin 1940)," in: Gérard Blossuat, and Andreas Wilkens (eds.), *Jean Monnet, l'Europe et les chemins de la Paix*, Paris: Publications de la Sorbonne, 1999, pp. 77–96.

Eade, Charles (ed.), *The War Speeches of the Rt. Hon. Winston S. Churchill*, vol. II., London: Cassell, 1952.
Easton, David A., *A Systems Analysis of Political Life*, New York: Wiley, 1965.
Edwards, Geoffrey, "The Potential and Limits of the CFSP: The Yugoslav Example," in: Elfriede Regelsberger, Philippe de Schoutheete de Tervarent, and Wolfgang Wessels (eds.), *Foreign Policy of the European Union: From EPC to CFSP and Beyond*, Boulder: Lynne Rienner, 1997, pp. 173–95.
Eichengreen, Barry, "A More Perfect Union? On the Logic of Economic Integration," Frank D. Graham Memorial Lecture, Princeton University: mimeo, 1995.
Elvert, Jürgen, *Zur gegenwärtigen Verfassung der Europäischen Union*, ZEI Discussion Paper C 148, Bonn: Zentrum für Europäische Integrationsforschung, 2005.
———, *Die Europäische Integration*, Darmstadt: Wissenschaftliche Buchgesellschaft, 2006.
Emmanoulidis, Janis A., *Overcoming the Constitutional Crisis*, München: Centrum für angewandte Politikforschung, 2005.
Erhard, Ludwig, *The Economics of Success*, London: Thames & Hudson, 1963.
Eschke, Nina, and Thomas Malick (eds.), *The European Constitution and Its Ratification Crisis: Constitutional Debates in the EU Member States*, ZEI Discussion Paper C 156, Bonn: Zentrum für Europäische Integrationsforschung, 2006.
Esposito, Frédéric, "The European Referendum: A Tool to Legitimate the European Integration Process?" in: Stuart Nagel (ed.), *Policymaking and Democracy: A Multinational Anthology*, Lanham: Lexington Books, 2003, pp. 15–37.
"Europa hört zu—auch wenn es unangenehm ist. Außenministerin Plassnik eröffnet den 'elektronischen Speakers' Corner' auf dem Ballhausplatz," *Die Presse*, January 9, 2006.
European Union, *Treaty Establishing a Constitution for Europe*, Luxembourg: Office for Official Publications of the European Communities, 2005.
Faber, Anne, and Wolfgang Wessels, "Wider Europe, Deeper Integration? A Common Theoretical and Methodological Framework for EU CONSENT," Paper for the Kick-off Meeting, November 18, 2005, Brussels, online at http://www.eu-consent.net/content.asp?contentid=740.
Featherstone, Kevin, and Claudio M. Radaelli (eds.), *The Politics of Europeanization*, Oxford: Oxford University Press, 2003.
Feldstein, Martin, "Europe's New Challenge to America," *The New York Times*, May 7, 1998.
Föderl-Schmid, Alexandra, "Europa neuen Schwung verleihen," *Der Standard*, January 2, 2006.
Fontaine, Pascal, *Le Comité d'Action pour les Etats-Unis d'Europe de Jean Monnet*, Lausanne: Center de recherche européennes, 1974.
Frankenberg, Günter, "The Return of the Contract: Problems and Pitfalls of European Constitutionalism," *European Law Journal*, 6.3 (2000), pp. 257–76.

Frattianni, Michele, and Jürgen von Hagen, "German Dominance in the EMS: the Empirical Evidence," *Open Economies Review*, 1 (1990), pp. 67–87.

Frattianni, Michele, and Jürgen von Hagen, "The European Monetary System 10 Years After," *Carnegie Rochester Conference Series on Public Policies*, 32 (1990), pp. 173–241.

Garton Ash, Timothy, *History of the Present: Sketches and Dispatches from Europe in the 1990*, London: Allen Lane, 1999.

———, *Free World: Why a Crisis of the West Reveals the Opportunity of Our Time*, London: Allen Lane, 2004.

Gasteyger, Curt, *Europa von der Spaltung bis zur Einigung. 1945–2000*, Cologne: Verlag Wissenschaft und Politik, 1990.

Gehler, Michael, *Der lange Weg nach Europa: Österreich vom Ende der Monarchie bis zur EU. Darstellung*, Innsbruck, Vienna and Bozen: Studienverlag, 2002.

———, *Der lange Weg nach Europa: Österreich von Paneuropa bis zum EU-Beitritt. Dokumente*, Innsbruck, Vienna and Bozen: Studienverlag, 2002.

———, Günter Bischof, and Anton Pelinka (eds.), *Österreich in der Europäischen Union: Bilanz seiner Mitgliedschaft/Austria in the European Union. Assessment of her Membership*, Vienna, Cologne, and Weimar: Böhlau, 2003.

———, *Europa: Ideen, Institutionen, Vereinigung*, Munich: Olzog, 2005.

———, Günter Bischof, Ludger Kühnhardt, and Steininger, Rolf (eds.), *Towards a European Constitution: A Historical and Political Comparison with the United States*, Vienna, Cologne, and Weimar: Böhlau, 2005.

———, *Österreichs Außenpolitik der Zweiten Republik: Von der alliierten Besatzung bis zum Europa des 21. Jahrhunderts*, Innsbruck, Vienna, and Bozen: Studienverlag, 2005.

———, "Die EU-Agenda explodiert. Trotz Lösung des EU-Finanzenstreits bleiben Österreich als 'honest broker' viele schwierige Aufgaben," *Die Presse*, January 10, 2006.

———, "Das Dilemma der EU-Präsidentschaften," *Die Presse*, March 24, 2006.

Gerbet, Pierre, *La Construction de l'Europe*, Paris: Notre Siecle, 1983, Paris: Imprimerie Nationale Éditions, 1999 (3rd ed.).

Gerstenberg, Oliver, "Expanding the Constitution Beyond the Court: The Case of Euro-Constitutionalism," *European Law Journal*, 8.1 (2002), pp. 172–94.

Giavazzi, Francesco, and Marco Pagano, "The Advantage of Tying One's Hand: EMS Discipline and Central Bank Credibility," *European Economic Review*, 32 (1988), pp. 1055–82.

Giering, Claus, and Josef Janning, "Flexibilität als Katalysator der Finalität? Die Gestaltungskraft der 'Verstärkten Zusammenarbeit' nach Nizza," in: Mathias Jopp, Barbara Lippert and Heinrich Schneider (eds.), *Das Vertragswerk von Nizza und die Zukunft der Europäischen Union*, Bonn: Europa-Union Verlag, 2001.

Gilbert, Mark, *Surpassing Realism: The Politics of European Integration since 1945*, Landham, MD: Rowman & Littlefield, 2003.

Gillingham, John, *European Integration 1950–2003: Superstate or New Market Economy?* Cambridge: Cambridge University Press, 2003.

Ginsberg, Roy, *The European Union in International Politics: Baptism by Fire*, Lanham: Rowman & Littlefield Publishers, 2001.

Gnesotto, Nicole, *Lessons of Yugoslavia*, Chaillot Papers 14, Paris: Institute for Security Studies, 1994.

Goodhart, Charles, and Stephen Smith, "Stabilization," *The Economics of Community Public Finance. European Economy Reports and Studies*, 5 (1993), pp. 417–56.

Gordon, Philip H., "Europe's Uncommon Foreign Policy," *International Security*, 3 (1998), pp. 74–100.

———, and Jeremy Shapiro, *Allies at War: America, Europe and the Crisis over Iraq*, New York: MacGraw-Hill, 2004.

Grant, Charles, *Transatlantic Rifts: How to Bring the Two Sides Together*, London: Centre for European Reform, 2003.

Green Cowles, Maria, Jeremy Caporaso, and Thomas Risse (eds.), *Transforming Europe: Europeanization and Domestic Change*, Ithaca and London: Cornell University Press, 2001.

Griffith, Richard T., and Frances M.B. Lynch, "L'échec de la 'Petite Europe': Le Conseil tripartite, 1944–1948," *Guerres Mondiales et conflits contemporains*, no. 152, 1988, pp. 39–62.

Grin, Gilles, *The Battle of the Single European Market: Achievements and Economics 1945–2000*, New York: Columbia University Press, 2003.

Gruber, Simon, Kai-Olaf Lang and Andreas Maurer, *Aufräumarbeiten und neue Impulse für Europa*, SWP-Aktuell 2, Berlin: Stiftung Wissenschaft und Politik, Deutsches Institut für Internationale Politik und Sicherheit, 2006.

Gruner, Wolf D., and Wichard Woyke, *Europa-Lexikon: Länder—Politik—Institutionen*, Munich: Deutscher Taschenbuchverlag, 2004.

Gustavsson, Rolf, and Richard Swartz, "Die Unvollendete: Geduld mit Europa!," *Süddeutsche Zeitung*, January 12, 2006, p. 11.

Haas, Ernst, *The Uniting of Europe: Political, Social, and Economic Forces 1950–1957*, Stanford: Stanford University Press, 1958.

Hallstein, Walter, *United Europe: Challenge and Opportunity*, Cambridge, Massachusetts: Harvard University Press, 1962.

Hantos, Elemér, "Der Europäische Zollverein," *Weltwirtschaftliches Archiv*, 23 (1926), pp. 229–38.

Hauschild, Helmut, "EU sprachlos—Fragen und keine Antworten," in: *Handelsblatt*, January 27–28, and 29, 2006.

Hauser, Gunther, "Umfassende Kooperationsprozesse für den Mittelmeerraum. Der sicherheitspolitische Dialog zwischen der EU, der NATO und Israel," *David. Jüdische Kulturzeitschrift*, 17:67 (2005), pp. 24–26.

Hayes-Renshaw, Fiona, "The Council Post Enlargement. Tables and Figures," Paper presented at the Conference "One Process of Europeanisation or Several? EU Governance in a Context of Internationalisation," European University Institute, Florence, June 30, 2006.

Herriot, Edouard, *The United States of Europe*, London: Harrop, 1930.

Herzog, Roman, *Vision Europa: Antworten auf neue Herausforderungen*, Hamburg: Hoffmann & Campe, 1996.

Hill, Christopher, "The Capability-Expectations Gap or Conceptualizing Europe's International Role," *Journal of Common Market Studies*, 31.3(2003), pp. 305–28.

Hitchcock, William I., *The Struggle for Europe: The Turbulent History of a Divided Continent, 1945–2002*, New York et al.: Doubleday, 2003.

Holbrooke, Richard, *Meine Mission: Vom Krieg zum Frieden*, München: Pieper Verlag, 1998.

Höreth, Marcus, Cordula Janowski and Ludger Kühnhardt (eds.), *Die Europäische Verfassung: Analyse und Bewertung ihrer Strukturentscheidungen*, Baden-Baden, 2005.

Howorth, Jolyon, *European Integration and Defense: The Ultimate Challenge*, Chaillot Papers 43, Paris: Institute for Security Studies, 2000.

Hug, Simon, *Voices of Europe. Citizens, Referendums and European Integration*, Lanham: Rowman & Littlefield, 2002.

Jopp, Mathias, *The Strategic Implications of European Integration: An Analysis of Trends in Integration Policies and their Consequences for the Transatlantic Partnership and a New European Security Order*, Adelphi paper, No. 290, London: The International Institute for Strategic Studies, 1994.

———, *The Implications of the Yugoslav Crisis for Western Europe's Foreign Relations*, Chaillot Papers 17, Paris: Institute for Security Studies, 1994.

———, and Otto Schmuck (eds.), *Die Reform der Europäischen Union. Analysen—Positionen—Dokumente zur Regierungskonferenz 1996/97*, Bonn: Europa-Union Verlag, 1996.

———, *European Defense Policy: The Debate on the Institutional Aspects*, IEPDOK11/b-June–July 1999, Bonn: Institut für Europäische Politik, 1999.

———, "Germany and the Western European Union," in: Carl Lankowski/Simon Serfaty, *Europeanizing Security? NATO and an Integrating Europe*, AICGS Research Report, No. 9, Washington D.C. American Institute for Contemporary German Studies, 1999, pp. 35–52.

Kassim, Hussein, and Anan Menon, "The Principal-Agent Approach and the Study of the European Union: Promise Unfulfilled?," *Journal of European Public Policy*, 10.1 (2003), pp. 121–39.

Kennan, George F., *American Diplomacy 1900–1950*, Chicago and London: The University of Chicago Press, 1951.

Kennedy, Paul, *The Rise and Fall of the Great Powers*, New York: Random House, 1987.

Kersten, Albert E., "Nederland en België in London, 1940–1944. Werken aan de na-oorlogse betrekkingen," *Colloquium over de geschiedenis van de Belgisch-Nederlandse betrekkingen tussen 1815 en 1945. Brussel 10–12/12/1980. Acta*, Ghent: Erasmus, 1982, pp. 495–520.

Kintis, Andreas G., "The EU's Foreign Policy and the War in Former Yugoslavia," in: Martin Holland(ed.), *Common Foreign and Security Policy: The Record and Reforms*, London and Washington: Pinter, 1997, pp. 148–73.

Kirt, Romain (ed.), *Die Europäische Union und ihre Krisen*, Baden-Baden: Nomos, 2001.

——, *Wege aus der Legitimationskrise: Die Europäische Union auf der Suche nach einem neuen Selbstverständnis*, Esch-sur-Alzette: Le Phare, 2003.

——, *Macroshift: Die Europäische Union in der Modernisierungskrise*, Esch-sur-Alzette: Le Phare, 2005.

——, *Die Europäische Union in der Komplexitätskrise: Dysfunktionen der europäischer Integration im Zeitalter der Globalisierung*, PhD, University of Innsbruck, 2006.

Kleßmann, Christoph (ed.), *Nicht nur Hitlers Krieg. Der Zweite Weltkrieg und die Deutschen*, Düsseldorf: Droste, 1989.

Kletzer, Ken, and Jürgen von Hagen, "Monetary Union and Fiscal Federalism," in: Charles Wyplosz (ed.), *The Impact of EMU on Europe and the Developing Countries*, Oxford: Oxford University Press, 2001, pp. 17–39.

Knipping, Franz, *Deutschland, Frankreich und das Ende der Locarno-Ära 1928–1931: Studien zur Internationalen Politik in der Anfangsphase der Weltwirtschaftskrise*, Munich: Oldenbourg, 1987.

——, and Matthias Schönwald (eds.), *Aufbruch zum Europa der zweiten Generation: Die europäische Einigung 1969–1984*, Trier: Wissenschaftlicher Verlag, 2004.

Krüger, Peter, "Zur europäischen Dimension der Außenpolitik Gustav Stresemanns," in: Karl Heinrich Pohl, *Politiker und Bürger: Gustav Stresemann und seine Zeit*, Göttingen: Vandenhoeck & Ruprecht, 2001, pp. 194–228.

——, *Das unberechenbare Europa: Epochen des Integrationsprozesses vom späten 18. Jahrhundert bis zur Europäischen Union*, Stuttgart: Kohlhammer, 2006.

Kühnhardt, Ludger, *Revolutionszeiten: Das Umbruchjahr 1989 im geschichtlichen Zusammenhang*, Munich: Olzog, 1994.

——, *Implications of Globalization on the Raison d`Etre of European Integration*, Oslo: ARENA, 2002.

——, *Erweiterung und Vertiefung: Die Europäische Union im Neubeginn*, Baden-Baden: Nomos, 2005.

——, "Europa—quo vadis?" *Kirche und Gesellschaft*, No.322, ed. Katholische Sozialwissenschaftliche Zentralstelle Mönchengladbach, Cologne: J.P. Bachem Verlag, 2005, pp. 3–16.

——, *European Union—The Second Founding: The Changing Rationale of European Integration*, Baden-Baden: Nomos, 2008.

Küsters, Hanns Jürgen, "Walter Hallstein und die Verhandlungen über die Römischen Verträge 1955–1957," in: Wilfried Loth, William Wallace and Wolfgang Wessels (eds.), *Walter Hallstein: Der vergessene Europäer?*, Bonn: Europa-Union Verlag, 1995, pp. 91–97.

Łaptos, Joséf and Mariusz Misztal, *American Debates on Central European Union 1942–1944: Documents of the American State Department*, Brussels: P.I.E. Peter Lang, 2002.

Lindberg, Leon N., and Stuart A. Scheingold, *Europe's Would-Be Polity: Patterns of Change in the European Community*, Englewood Cliffs, NJ: Prentice Hall, 1970.
Link, Werner, "Primäre und sekundäre Ziele. Die Entwicklung der Europäischen Union nach der großen Erweiterung," *Frankfurter Allgemeine Zeitung*, October 12, 2005.
Linsinger, Eva, "Österreich will nicht der 'Wunderheiler' Europas sein," *Der Standard*, December 12, 2005.
Lipgens, Walter, *Europa-Föderationspläne der Widerstandsbewegungen 1940–1945*, Munich: Oldenbourg, 1968.
———, *A History of European Integration 1945–1947: The Formation of the European Unity Movement*, Oxford: Clarendon Press, 1982.
———, (ed.), *Documents on the History of European Integration*, vol. 1.: *Continental Plans for European Union, 1939–1945*, Berlin and New York: de Gruyter, 1985.
———, (ed.), *Documents on the History of European Integration*, vol. 2.: *Plans for European Union in Great Britain and in Exile, 1939–1945*, Berlin and New York: de Gruyter, 1986.
———, (ed.), *45 Jahre Ringen um eine europäische Verfassung: Dokumente 1939–1984*, Bonn: Europa Union Verlag, 1986.
———, and Wilfried Loth (eds.), *Documents on the History of European Integration*, vol. 3.: *The Struggle for European Union by Political Parties and Pressure Groups in Western European Countries 1945–1950*, Berlin and New York: de Gruyter, 1988.
———, and Wilfried Loth (eds.), *Documents on the History of European Integration*, vol. 4.: *Transnational Organizations of Political Parties and Pressure Groups in the Struggle for European Union 1945–1950*, Berlin and New York: de Gruyter, 1990.
Lippert, Barbara, and Gaby Umbach (eds.), *Pressures of Europeanisation: From Post-Communist State Administrations Towards Normal Players in the EU System*, Baden-Baden: Nomos, 2005.
Lippmann, Walter, *The Cold War: A Study in U.S. Foreign Policy*, New York: Harper & Brothers, 1947.
Loth, Wilfried, *Sozialismus und Internationalismus: Die französischen Sozialisten und die Nachkriegsordnung Europas 1940–1950*, Stuttgart: Deutsche Verlags-Anstalt, 1977.
———, "Die europäische Integration nach dem Zweiten Weltkrieg in französischer Perspektive," in: Berding, Helmut (ed.), *Wirtschaftliche und politische Integration im 19. und 20. Jahrhundert*, Göttingen: Vandenhoeck & Ruprecht, 1984, pp. 225–46.
———, *Der Weg nach Europa: Geschichte der europäischen Integration 1939–1957*, Göttingen: Vandenhoeck & Ruprecht, 1990.
———, (ed.), *Das europäische Projekt zu Beginn des 21. Jahrhunderts*, Opladen: Westdeutscher Verlag, 2001.
———, (ed.), *Crises and Compromises: The European Project 1963–1969*, Baden-Baden: Nomos, 2001.

———, "From the 'Third Force' to the Common Market: Discussions about Europe and the Future of the Nation-State in West Germany, 1945–57," in: Dominik Geppert (ed.), *The Postwar Challenge 1945–1958*, Oxford: Oxford University Press, 2003, pp. 192–209.

Marjolin, Robert, *Architect of European Unity: Memoirs 1911–1986*, London: Weidenfeld & Nicolson, 1989.

Massigli, René, *Une comédie des erreurs, 1943–1956*, Paris: Plon, 1978.

MacDougall Report: Report of the Study Group on the Role of Public Finance in European Integration, 2 vols. Brussels: European Commission, 1977.

Menéndez, Augustín José, "Finalité Through Rights," in: Erik Oddvar Eriksen, John Erik Fossum and Augustín José Menéndez (eds.), *The Chartering of Europe*, Baden-Baden: Nomos, 2003, pp. 30–48.

Meny, Yves, "Making Sense of the EU: The Achievements of the Convention," *Journal of Democracy*, 14 (2003), pp. 57–70.

Milward, Alan S., *The European Rescue of the Nation State*, London: Routledge, 1992.

Mittag, Jürgen, Maurer, Andreas and Wessels, Wolfgang, *Fifteen into One? The European Union and its Member States*, Manchester and New York: Manchester University Press, 2003.

Mitrany, David, *A Working Peace System: An Argument for the Functional Development of International Organization*, New York: Russel & Russel, 1943.

Möller, Horst, *Europa zwischen den Weltkriegen*, Munich: Oldenbourg, 1998.

Monnet, Jean, *Les Etats-Unis d'Europe ont Commencé*, Paris: R. Laffont, 1955.

———, *Amérique-Europe: Relations de Partenaires Nécessaires à la Paix*, Lausanne: Fondation Jean Monnet, 1963.

———, *Mémoires*, Paris: Fayard, 1975; New York: Doubleday, 1978.

Moravscik, Andrew, *The Choice for Europe: Social Purpose and State Power from Messina to Maastricht*, Ithaca: Cornell University Press, 1998.

Müller, Guido, *Europäische Gesellschaftsbeziehungen nach dem Ersten Weltkrieg: Das Deutsch-Französische Studienkomitee und der Europäische Kulturbund*, Munich: Oldenbourg, 2005.

Mundell, Robert, "A Theory of Optimal Currency Areas," *American Economic Review*, 51 (1961), pp. 657–65.

Mundschenk, Susanne, and Jürgen von Hagen, "The Political Economy of Policy Coordination in Europe," *Swedish Review of Economic Policy*, 8 (2002), pp. 11–41.

Notter, Harvey A., *Postwar Foreign Policy Preparation 1939–1945*, General Foreign Policy Series 15, Washington D.C.: State Department, 1949.

Nuttall, Simon, *European Foreign Policy*, Oxford: Oxford University Press, 2000.

Patijn, D. (ed.), *Landmarks in European Unity*, Leiden: Europa Institute, 1970.

Pernice, Ingolf, "Multi-Level Constitutionalism in the European Union," *European Law Journal*, 27.1/6 (2002), pp. 511–29.

———, "Europäische Grundrechtscharta und Konventsverfahren. Zehn Thesen zum Prozess der europäischen Verfassung nach Nizza," *Integration* 2 (2005), pp. 194–97.

Peterson, John, and Elizabeth Bomberg, *Decision Making in the European Union*, Houndmills: Palgrave 1999.
Pierson, Paul, "The New Politics of the Welfare State," *World Politics*, 48 (1996), pp. 143–79.
Poidevin, Raymond, *Robert Schuman, homme d'État 1886–1963*, Paris: Imprimerie Nationale 1986.
Popper, Karl R., *The Logic of Scientific Discovery*, New York: Harper and Row, 1959.
Prantner, Christoph, "Die Verfassung ist nicht tot," *Der Standard*, January 10, 2006.
Puntscher-Riekmann, Sonja, *Die kommissarische Neuordnung Europas*, Vienna/New York: Springer, 1998.
Regelsberger, Elfriede, *Die Gemeinsame Außen- und Sicherheitspolitik der EU (GASP): Konstitutionelle Angebote im Praxistest*, Baden-Baden: Nomos, 2004.
Regelsberger, Elfriede, "Gemeinsame Außen- und Sicherheitspolitik," in: Weidenfeld, Werner, and Wolfgang Wessels (eds.), *Jahrbuch der Europäischen Integration 2005*, Baden-Baden: Nomos 2005, pp. 241–49.
Rometsch, Dietrich, and Wolfgang Wessels (eds.), *The European Union and Member States: Toward Institutional Fusion?*, Manchester: Manchester University Press, 1996.
Sainsbury, Keith, *The Turning Point: Roosevelt, Stalin, Churchill and Chiang-Kai-Shek, 1943. The Moscow, Cairo and Teheran Conferences*, Oxford: Oxford University Press, 1985.
Sapir, André, Aghion, Philippe, Bertola, Giuseppe, Hellwig, Martin, Pisani-Ferry, Jean, Rosati, Dariusz, Viñals, José and Wallace, Helen, with Buti, Marco, Nova, Mario and Smith, Peter M., *An Agenda for a Growing Europe: The Sapir Report*, Oxford: Oxford University Press, 2004.
Scharsach, Gilbert, "Die Europäische Verteidigungsgemeinschaft und die Maastricht-EU. 40 Jahre Integration und kein bisschen weiter?," *Zeitgeschichte*, 24.3–4 (1997), pp. 103–30.
Scheich, Manfred, "Die Zukunft der EU—fundamentale Fragen sind zu stellen," *Unsere Sicherheit Europa. Newsletter des Österreichischen Instituts für Europäische Sicherheitspolitik*, 2 (2005), pp. 1–4.
Schilmar, Boris, *Der Europadiskurs im deutschen Exil 1933–1945*, Munich: Oldenbourg, 2004.
Schmidt, Helmut, "Die Bürokraten ausgetrickst" and "Kampf gegen die Nationalisten," *Die Zeit*, August, 24.1990 and August, 31.1990.
———, *Die Selbstbehauptung Europas: Perspektiven für das 21. Jahrhundert*, Stuttgart: Deutsche Verlagsanstalt, 2000.
Schneer, Jonathan, "Hopes Deferred or Shattered: the British Labour Left and the Third Force Movement, 1945–49," *Journal of Modern History*, 56 (1984), pp. 197–226.
Schneider, Heinrich, *Leitbilder der Europapolitik:1. Der Weg zur Integration*, Bonn: Europa Union Verlag, 1977.
Schuker, Stephen A. (eds.), *Deutschland und Frankreich: Vom Konflikt zur Aussöhnung. Die Gestaltung der westeuropäischen Sicherheit 1914–1963*, Munich: Oldenbourg, 2000.

Schulz, Matthias, and Mareike König (eds.), *Die Bundesrepublik Deutschland und die europäische Einigung 1949–2000: Politische Akteure, gesellschaftliche Kräfte und internationale Erfahrungen*, Stuttgart: Franz Steiner Verlag, 2004.

Schuman, Robert, "Declaration of 9 May 1950," quoted in Pascal Fontaine, *Europe—A Fresh Start: The Schuman Declaration 1950–90*, Luxembourg: Commission of European Communities, 1990, pp. 44–46; English version of the Schuman Plan in *Documents on American Foreign Relations*, vol. 12, Princeton: Princeton University Press, 1951, p. 85.

Shlaim, Avi. "Prelude to Downfall: the British Offer of Union to France, June 1940," *Journal of Contemporary History*, 6 (1974), pp. 27–63.

Spaak, Paul Henri, *Memoiren eines Europäers*, Hamburg: Hoffman und Campe, 1969.

Spinelli, Altiero, and Ernesto Rossi, *The Ventotene Manifesto*, London: Altiero Spinelli Institute, 1941, pp. 385–86.

Steininger, Rolf, *Der vergessene Krieg: Korea, 1950–1953*, Munich: Olzog, 2006.

Stirk, Peter M.R., and David Weigall (eds.), *The Origins and Development of European Integration: A Reader and Commentary*, London and New York: Pinter, 1999.

Stueck, William, *Rethinking the Korean War: A New Diplomatic and Strategic History*, Princeton, NJ: Princeton University Press, 2002.

Tietmeyer, Hans, "Europäische Währungsunion und Politische Union—das Modell mehrerer Geschwindigkeiten," *Deutsche Bundesbank: Auszüge aus Presseartikeln*, 66 (1994): 1.

The Treaty of Rome Establishing the European Economic Community, 25 March 1957, London: Stevens and Sons, 1962.

Tonra, Ben, *The Europeanisation of National Foreign Policy: Dutch, Danish and Irish Foreign Policy in the European Union*, Aldershot: Ashgate, 2001.

———, "Constructing the CFSP: the Utility of a Cognitive Approach," *Journal of Common Market Studies*, 41.4 (2001), pp. 731–56.

Toynbee, Arnold Joseph, *Studies of History: Abridgement of Volumes I-VI*, New York and London: Oxford University Press, 1947.

Trotsky, Leon, "The Premises for the Proletarian Revolution," (1924), quoted in *Europe and America: Two Speeches on Imperialism*, New York: Pathfinder, 1971, p. 30.

Tsebelis, George, *Veto Players: How Political Institutions Work*, Princeton and New York: Princeton University Press, 2002.

Tsoukalis, Loukas, *The Economics and Politics of European Monetary Integration*, London: George Unwin and Allen, 1977.

Tucker, Spencer C. (ed.), *Encyclopedia of the Korean War: A Political, Social, and Military History*, 3 vols., Santa Barbara, CA: Abc-Clio, 2000.

Tyrell, Albrecht, *Großbritannien und die Deutschlandplanung der Alliierten 1941–1945*, Frankfurt am Main: Metzler, 1987.

Van Hecke, Steven, "A Decade of Seized Opportunities: Christian Democracy in the European Union," in: Steven van Hecke and Emmanuel Gerard (eds.), *Christian Democratic Parties in Europe since the End of the Cold War*, Leuven: Leuven University Press, 2004, pp. 269–307.

Verhofstadt, Guy, *The United States of Europe*, London: The Federal Trust, 2006.
Voggenhuber, Johannes, "Der Europäische Konvent: Ausgangslage, Zusammensetzung, Arbeitsweise, Ergebnisse," lecture within the framework of the conference "Die neue Verfassung für die Europäische Union," organized by the Institut für Völkerrecht, Europarecht und Internationale Beziehungen at the University of Innsbruck, November 22–23, 2004.
Voigt, Klaus (ed.), *Friedenssicherung und europäische Einigung. Ideen des deutschen Exils 1939–1945*, Frankfurt am Main: Fischer, 1988.
Von Hagen, Jürgen, and George Hammond, "Regional Insurance against Asymmetric Shock—An Empirical Study for the EC," *The Manchester School*, 66 (1998), pp. 331–53.
Wandycz, Piotr S., *Czechoslovak-Polish Confederation and the Great Powers 1940–1943*, Bloomington: Indiana University Publications, 1956.
Weigall, David, and Peter M.R. Stirk (eds.), *The Origins and Development of the European Community*, Leicester and London: Leicester University Press, 1992.
Wessels, Wolfgang, "Zur Debatte um einen europäischen Staatenbund: Sechs Thesen der Fusionstheorie," in: Roman Herzog and Stephan Hobe (eds.), *Die Europäische Union auf dem Weg zum verfassten Staatenverbund: Perspektiven der europäischen Verfassungsordnung* (Schriften des Rechtszentrums für Europäische und Internationale Zusammenarbeit RIZ Bd. 22), Munich: Verlag C.H. Beck, 2004, pp. 200–3.
———, "Keynote Article: The Constitutional Treaty—Three Readings from a Fusion Perspective," *Journal of Common Market Studies*, 43 (2005), pp. 11–36.
Whitmann, Richard G., *Amsterdam's Unfinished Business? The Blair Government's Initiative and the Future of the Western European Union*, Occasional Papers 7, Paris: Institute for Security Studies, 1999.
Winand, Pascaline, *Eisenhower, Kennedy, and the United States of Europe*, Houndmills and London: Macmillan, 1993.
Wind, Marlene, *Europe Towards a Post-Hobbesian Order? A Constructivist Theory of European Integration, or How to Explain European Integration as an Unintended Consequence of Rational State-Action*, Fiesole: European University Institute, 1996.
Winkler, Heinrich August, "Grundlagenvertrag statt Verfassung," *Frankfurter Allgemeine Zeitung*, No. 139, June 18, 2005, p. 8.
———, "Weltmacht durch Überdehnung: Ein Plädoyer für europäischen Realismus," *Merkur. Deutsche Zeitschrift für europäisches Denken*, 60.1 (2006), pp. 36–43.
Young, John W., *Britain and European Unity, 1945–1992*, London: Macmillan, 1993.
Ziegerhofer, Anita, *Botschafter Europas: Richard Nikolaus Coudenhove-Kalergi und die Paneuropa-Bewegung in den zwanziger und dreißiger Jahren*, Vienna, Cologne, and Weimar: Böhlau, 2004.
Zielonka, Jan (ed.), *Paradoxes of European Foreign Policy*, The Hague: Kluwer, 1998.
———, *Europe as Empire: The Nature of the Enlarged European Union*, Oxford: Oxford University Press, 2006.

Notes on Contributors

Dr. Udo Diedrichs is Senior Fellow in the Department of Political Science at the University of Cologne. He graduated in 1994 at the University of Bonn and received his Ph.D. in 2000 at the University of Cologne; his dissertation was about EU policy toward Mercosur. From 1995 until 2003 he served as a research fellow and project coordinator at the Jean Monnet Chair for Political Science of the University of Cologne. From September 2003 until February 2004 he was engaged as a senior researcher at the Institute for European Politics in Berlin, for coordinating a project on multinational cooperation and integration of military forces and capabilities among EU countries (funded by the German Ministry of Defense). Since February 2004, he has been working again as senior research fellow and lecturer in the Department of Political Science at the University of Cologne. His main fields of research are institutional issues of European integration, EU external policy, transatlantic relations and European foreign, security, and defense policy. Recent publications include: "Between Kosovo and Iraq: Changing Paradigms of German Foreign and Security Policy?," in: O. Croci and A.Verdun (eds.), *The Transatlantic Divide: Foreign and Security Policies in the Atlantic Alliance from Kosovo to Iraq* (2006); "The European Parliament in CFSP: More than a Marginal Player?," *The International Spectator*, 2 (2004), pp. 31–46; "Explaining the EU's Military Dimension: Theoretical and Conceptual Approaches to ESDP," in: R. Rotte and T. Sprungala (eds.), *Probleme und Perspektiven der Europäischen Sicherheits- und Verteidigungspolitik (ESVP)* (2004), pp. 34–57.

Dr. Jürgen Elvert is Professor of History of European Integration and Didactics of History at the University of Cologne. After studies of history, English philology, sociology and educational sciences in Kiel and Belfast he presented his dissertation at the University of Kiel in 1988, where he taught modern and contemporary history until 1998, receiving his Habilitation for Medieval and Modern History there in 1996. As Visiting Professor he taught at the University of Innsbruck in 1997. He has been teaching at the University of Cologne since 1999. In the same year he was made Senior Fellow of the Center for European Integration Studies (ZEI) at the University of Bonn. In 2000 he was elected

Chairman of the Ranke-Gesellschaft, Vereinigung für Geschichte im Öffentlichen Leben e.V. In 2003 he was elected as Senator in the Senate of the University of Cologne. His books include *Vom Freistaat zur Republik: Der Faktor Außenpolitik im irischen Unabhängigkeitsstreben 1921–1948* (1989); *Geschichte Irlands* (1993, 4th edn. 2003); *Nordirland in Geschichte und Gegenwart / Northern Ireland—Past and Present* (1994); *Kriegsende im Norden* (with R. Bohn) (1995); *Der Balkan: Eine europäische Krisenregion in Geschichte und Gegenwart* (1997); *Mitteleuropa: Deutsche Pläne zur europäischen Neuordnung 1918–1945* (1999); *Historische Debatten und Kontroversen im 19. und 20. Jahrhundert* (with S. Krauß) (2003); *European Union Enlargement: A Comparative History* (with W. Kaiser) (2004); *Die Europäische Integration* (2006).

Dr. **Michael Gehler** is Professor of Modern German and European History at the Stiftung Universität Hildesheim. After receiving his Ph.D. in 1987, he was Research Fellow of the Austrian Science Foundation (FWF) in Vienna 1992–96, visiting scholar at the College for New Europe in Kraków and at the University of New Orleans, an Alexander von Humboldt Fellow in 2001–2, and Guest Professor at the University of Rostock in 2004, at the University of Salzburg 2004–5 and the Catholic University of Leuven 2005. He was Professor at the Institute of Contemporary History of Leopold Franzens University Innsbruck from 1999 until 2006. He is Senior Fellow at the Center for European Integration Studies at the University of Bonn since 2000, member of the board of the Ranke-Gesellschaft, and member of the Historical Commission of the Austrian Academy of Science in Vienna. His books include *Österreichs Außenpolitik der Zweiten Republik: Von der alliierten Besatzung bis zum Europa des 21. Jahrhunderts* (2 vols.), (2005); *Europa: Ideen, Institutionen, Vereinigung* (2005); *Avrupa: Ütopya' dan Avrupa'ya, Inkilap* (2005); and *Vom Marshall-Plan zur EU: Österreich und die europäische Integration von 1945 bis zur Gegenwart* (2006).

Dr. **Manfred Görtemaker** is Professor of Modern History at the University of Potsdam. After receiving his Ph.D. in 1977, he taught political science and modern history at the Free University Berlin and in the Overseas Studies Programme of Stanford University. He was a John F. Kennedy Fellow at Harvard in 1980–1 and Krupp Foundation Senior Associate at the Institute for East-West Security Studies in New York in 1989–90. In 1992 he became Professor of Modern History at the University of Potsdam, where he also held the posts of Vice-President for Academic Affairs and Chairman of the Senate. He spent two terms as Visiting Professor at the History Department of Duke University in 1994 and at Dartmouth College in 1999. In 2002–3 he was Stifterverband Visiting Fellow at St.Antony's College, Oxford. He is Chairman of the Academic Advisory Board of the Military History Research Institute of the German

Bundeswehr. His books include *Die unheilige Allianz: Die Geschichte der Entspannungspolitik 1943–1979* (1979); *Deutschland im 19. Jahrhundert: Entwicklungslinien* (1983); *Unifying Germany, 1989–1990* (1994); *Geschichte der Bundesrepublik Deutschland: Von der Gründung bis zur Gegenwart* (1999); *Weimar in Berlin. Porträt einer Ära* (2002); *Geschichte Europas 1850–1914* (2002); *Orte der Demokratie in Berlin* (2005); *Thomas Mann und die Politik* (2005); and *Britain and Germany in the 20th Century* (2006).

Dr. Mathias Jopp is Director of the Institute for European Politics in Berlin and Visiting Professor of Political Science at the Free University of Berlin, the University of Tübingen, and the European University of Frankfurt an der Oder. After studying economics and political science at the Universities of Gießen and Frankfurt am Main, Dr. Jopp worked as Academic Assistant at the Department of Economics at the University of Gießen. In 1980 he received his Ph.D. in Political Science from the University of Frankfurt am Main. Between 1976 and 1990 he worked as a research fellow at the Peace Research Institute Frankfurt am Main, where he was Deputy Executive Director from 1986 to 1990. In 1991 he went to London and worked as senior research associate at the International Institute for Strategic Studies (IISS). From 1992 to 1995 he worked as senior research fellow at the Institute for Security Studies of the Western European Union (WEUISS) in Paris. Since 1995 he has been Director of the Institute for European Politics in Berlin. During the last ten years he has been teaching at different universities (Full Interim Chair at the Free University Berlin, Visiting Professor at the College of Europe [Bruges], Jean Monnet Professor at the University of Gießen). His recent publications include "Germany and the Western European Union," in: C. Lankowski and S. Serfaty (eds.), *Europeanizing Security? NATO and an Integrating Europe* (1999), pp. 35–52; "Flexible Modes of Governance: Making CFSP and ESDP Work," (with U. Diedrichs), *The International Spectator*, 38: 3(2003), pp. 15–30; *Die Reform der Europäischen Union: Analysen—Positionen—Dokumente zur Regierungskonferenz 1996/97* (eds. with O. Schmuck) (1996); *Das Vertragswerk von Nizza und die Zukunft der Europäischen Union* (eds. with B. Lippert and H. Schneider), (2001); *Der Vertrag über eine Verfassung für Europa: Analysen zur Konstitutionalisierung der EU*, Baden-Baden (eds. with S. Matl) (2005).

Dr. Ludger Kühnhardt is Professor of Political Science and Director at the Center for European Integration Studies (ZEI) at the University of Bonn since 1997. After studies of history, philosophy and political science at Bonn, Geneva, Tokyo and Harvard and receiving his dissertation (1983) and Habilitation (1986) at the University of Bonn, he worked as speech writer for the then German Federal President Richard von Weizsäcker between 1987 and 1989. He was Professor of Political Science at the University of Freiburg between 1991 and

1997, serving also as Dean of his faculty. He was Visiting Professor at the College of Europe, the University of Cape Town, the University of Jena, the Catholic University of Milan (since 1997), Dartmouth College, the Diplomatic Academy Vienna (since 2002), Stanford University, Seoul National University, Stifterverband Visiting Fellow at St. Antony's College, Oxford, and Visiting Professor at the Mediterranean Academy of Diplomatic Studies (MEDAC) in Malta (since 2007). He also worked as a Public Policy Fellow at the Woodrow Wilson International Center for Scholars in Washington D.C. His books include *Die Flüchtlingsfrage als Weltordnungsproblem* (1984); *Die Universalität der Menschenrechte* (1987); *Stufen der Souveränität* (1992); *Europäische Union und föderale Idee* (1993); *Revolutionszeiten: Das Umbruchjahr 1989 im geschichtlichen Zusammenhang* (1994, also in Turkish); *Von der ewigen Suche nach Frieden* (1996); *Zukunftsdenker: Bewährte Ideen des politischen Denkens für das dritte Jahrtausend* (1999); *Atlantik-Brücke: Fünfzig Jahre deutsch-amerikanische Partnerschaft* (2002); *Constituting Europe: Identity, Institution-Building and the Search for a Global Role* (2003); *Erweiterung und Vertiefung* (2005); *European Union—The Second Founding* (2008).

Dr. Wilfried Loth is Professor of Modern and Contemporary History at the University of Duisburg-Essen. After studies of German literature and language, history, philosophy and education and receiving his dissertation (1974) he worked with Walter Lipgens as assistant lecturer in Modern History at the University of Saarbrücken. After his Habilitation in Modern History in 1983 he became Professor of Political Science at the Free University of Berlin. In 1985–86 he taught Political Science at the University of Münster. Since 1986 he has been Chair in Modern and Contemporary History at the University of Essen (since 2003: Duisburg-Essen). Between 1993 and 1997 he was President of the Institute for Cultural Studies in the Wissenschaftszentrum Nordrhein-Westfalen. Since 2000 he has been Chairman of the European Union Liaison Committee of Historians. His books include *Sozialismus und Internationalismus: Die französischen Sozialisten und die Nachkriegsordnung Europas 1940–1950* (1977); *Die Teilung der Welt: Geschichte des Kalten Krieges 1941–1955* (1980, also in English and Romanian); *Katholiken im Kaiserreich: Der politische Katholizismus in der Krise des wilhelminischen Deutschlands* (1984); *Geschichte Frankreichs im 20. Jahrhundert* (1987); *Der Weg nach Europa: Geschichte der europäischen Integration 1939–1957* (1990); *Stalins ungeliebtes Kind: Warum Moskau die DDR nicht wollte* (1994, also in English and Italian); *Das Kaiserreich: Obrigkeitsstaat und politische Mobilisierung* (1996); *Helsinki, 30. August 1975. Entspannung und Abrüstung* (1998, also in English and Chinese); *Entwürfe einer europäischen Verfassung: Eine historische Bilanz* (2002).

Dr. Hans-Gert Pöttering is President of the European Parliament from 2007 to 2009. Member of the European Parliament since its first direct election in 1979.

After studies of law, political science and history in Bonn and Geneva and at Columbia University New York, he obtained his Ph.D. in political science and passed the second German state law examination. A former lecturer in political science at the University of Osnabrück, he has been Honorary Professor at this university since 1995. As a member of the German Christian Democratic Union, he was involved in the development of European foreign and security policy as Chairman of the European Parliament's Subcommittee on Security and Disarmament from 1984 until 1994. He chaired the working group on institutional reforms of the European People's Party in 1994–96 and its working group on EU enlargement in 1996–99. He is Vice-Chairman of the European People's Party and Member of the Presidency of its German Member Party CDU. From 1999 to 2007, he was Chairman of the group of the European People's Party (Christian Democrats/European Democrats) in the European Parliament. His books include: *Adenauers Sicherheitspolitik 1955–1963: Ein Beitrag zum deutsch-amerikanischen Verhältnis* (1975); *Die vergessenen Regionen: Plädoyer für eine solidarische Regionalpolitik der Europäischen Gemeinschaft* (with F. Wiehler) (1983); *Europas vereinigte Staaten* (with L. Kühnhardt) (1993); *Kontinent Europa. Kern, Übergänge, Grenzen* (with L. Kühnhardt) (1998; also in Czech); *Weltpartner Europa* (with L. Kühnhardt) (2001); *Von der Vision zur Wirklichkeit: Auf dem Weg zur Einigung Europas* (2005).

Thomas Traguth Currently Ph.D. student at the Jean Monnet Chair for Political Science at the University of Cologne. He has studied philosophy, politics and economics at the University of Oxford and politics and administrative studies at the College of Europe in Bruges. His main research focus is on theory and strategies of European integration as well as on institutional and procedural reform of the EU architecture. He has published, together with Wolfgang Wessels, on the Constitutional Treaty and has been involved in several relevant publications and papers of the Jean Monnet Chair. He is participating in a research project at the Center of Empirical Research in the Economic and Social Sciences at the University of Cologne, establishing the prime indices of European integration. He has held teaching positions on the political system of the EU at the University of Cologne, as well as at the summer school of the Gustav Stresemann Institute, Bonn, and at the Cologne Intensive Summer Programme. He assists Wolfgang Wessels in the preparation and coordination of two major lecture series on EU politics.

Dr. Jürgen von Hagen is Professor of Economics at the University of Bonn. After receiving his Ph.D. in economics at the University of Bonn in 1985, he taught economics at the Kelley School of Business, Indiana University, 1987–92 and the University of Mannheim, 1992–96. Since 1996, he is a Director at the Center for European Integration Studies (ZEI) at the University of Bonn. First winner of the Gossen Prize of the German Economics Association, he is a research fellow of the Center for Economic Policy Research (CEPR), a member of the Council of the

German Economic Association and the Academic Advisory Council of the German Federal Ministry of Economics, and a former member of the Council of the European Economic Association and the French National Economic Committee. He was elected into the Academia Leopoldina in 2002. He has been a consultant to the IMF, the European Commission, the Federal Reserve Board, the Inter-American Development Bank, the World Bank and numerous governments in and outside Europe. His publications include over sixty-five articles on monetary, international and public economics in leading international, refereed academic journals and over 100 contributions to other journals and books, and twenty published or edited monographs, including: *The European Monetary System and European Monetary Union* (with M. Frattianni) (1992); *The Maastricht Way to EMU* (with M. Frattianni and C.Waller) (1992); *EMU: Prospects and Challenges for the Euro* (with D. Begg et al.) (1998); *Stability and Growth in Europe: Towards a Better Pact* (with A. Fatas et al.) (2003).

Dr. Wolfgang Wessels is Chairman of the Jean Monnet Chair for Political Science at the University of Cologne since 1994. He holds a Master's Degree in economic and political science (1973) and a doctorate in political science from the University of Cologne (1979). He received the Venia legendi in Political Science of the University of Bonn in 1990. He is co-editor of the *Jahrbuch der Europäischen Union* and the *Europa von A-Z. Taschenbuch der europäischen Integration*. He is member of the Executive Board at the Institut für Europäische Politik (IEP, Berlin), Chairman of the Trans-European Political Studies Association (TEPSA, Brussels), founding member of the Jean Monnet Center of Excellence (North Rhine Westphalia), and Visiting Professor at the College of Europe, Bruges and Natolin. His recent publications include: *The Making of a European Constitution: Dynamics and Limits of the Convention Experience* (with S. Puntscher-Riekmann) (2006); *EU Constitutionalisation: From the Convention to the Constitutional Treaty 2002–2005. Anatomy, Analysis, Assessment* (with L. Rovná) (2006); "Keynote Article: The Constitutional Treaty: Three Readings from a Fusion Perspective," *Journal of Common Market Studies,* 43 (2005), pp. 11–36; "A 'saut constitutionnel' out of an Intergovernmental Trap? The Provisions of the Constitutional Treaty for the Common Foreign, Security and Defense Policy," in: J. Weiler and Ch. Eisgruber (eds.) *Altneuland: The EU Constitution in a Contextual Perspective,* Jean Monnet Working Paper (2004); "Theoretical Perspectives: CFSP Beyond the Supranational and Intergovernmental Dichotomy," in: D. Mahncke, A. Ambos and Ch. Reynolds (eds.), *European Foreign Policy: From Rhetoric to Reality?* (2004), pp. 61–96.

Index

acquis communautaire, 51, 58, 82
Adenauer, Hans, 132
Adenauer, Konrad, 39, 41, 124, 132, 133
African Union, 138
Ageing recessions, 138
Agnelli, Giovanni, 34
Ahtisaari, Martti, 103
Association of Southeast Asian Nations (ASEAN), 138
Atlantic civilization, 8

Ball, George, 39
Barre, Raymond, 66
Barroso, José Manuel, 119
Bech, Joseph, 41
Beck, Ludwig, 22
Beck, Ulrich, 50, 59
Beneš, Eduard, 23
Berlusconi, Silvio, 122
Berlin Wall, 4, 60
Beuve-Méry, Hubert, 28
Beyen, Jan Willem, 41
Blair, Tony, 90, 103, 136, 141
Blum, Léon, 20, 22
Bogdanor, Vernon, 134
Boggs, Hale, 37
Bourdet, Claude, 22
Brandt, Willy, 22, 65
Briand, Aristide, 34, 35
Bretherton, Russel, 43
Bretton Woods, 63, 64, 68, 117
Briand, Aristide, 112
Brüning, Heinrich, 132

Bush, George W., 141
    administration, 117
Byroade, Henry A., 38, 39

Cabiati, Attilio, 34
Carrington, Lord Peter, 97
Charlton, Michael, 45
Charter of Fundamental Rights of the European Union, 123
Chernomyrdin, Viktor, 103
Chirac, Jacques, 49, 103
Churchill, Sir Winston, 19, 20, 25, 28, 35, 36, 90, 112, 113, 116, 117, 132, 133
Cold War, 8, 53, 96, 112, 116
Common Agricultural Policy, 65
Common Foreign and Security Policy (CFSP), 13, 89, 96–107, 114
    High Representative, 100
Convention for the Charter of Fundamental Rights, 115
Copenhagen Criteria, 83–87, 89, 91, 136
Coudenhove-Kalergi, Count Richard, 25, 34, 112, 116
Council of Europe, 9, 25, 113
Couve de Murville, Maurice, 45
Crossman, Richard, 27
Cuban missile crisis, 116

da Vinci, Leonardo, 4
de Brouckère, Louis, 24
Delors, Jacques, 79, 110, 114
Delors package, 114

Democratic deficit, 114
Demographic change, 138–140
de Gasperi, Alcide, 116
de Gaulle, Charles, 20, 24, 45, 56, 57, 58, 90, 116, 124, 133
de Montbrial, Thierry, 110

Economic Cooperation Administration (ECA), 37
Eden, Anthony, 132
Edwards, Geoffrey, 105
Eichler, Willi, 22
Elvert, Jürgen, 12
Elysée Treaty, 50
Empty Chair Crisis, 12, 54, 87, 114, 123
Erhard, Ludwig, 33, 43
Etzel, Fritz, 41
Euro, 9, 109, 110, 123
Eurobarometer, 50, 59, 90
European Atomic Energy Community (EURATOM), 41, 43, 44, 124
European Central Bank (ECB), 123
European Community (EC), 96, 123
European Community of Coal and Steel (ECSC), 8, 33, 38, 40, 41, 42, 51, 52–57, 123, 131
European Commission, 50, 57, 100, 115, 119, 138, 141
European Constitutional Treaty, 3, 4, 5, 7, 10, 11–13, 91, 110, 118, 119, 120, 122, 123, 124, 134
 Constitutional Convention (Convention on the Future of Europe), 106, 110, 115
 referendum in France and in the Netherlands, 3, 5–6, 10–11, 49, 55–56, 109–110, 112, 123, 134–135
European Council, 100, 118–123
 Brussels (2003), 115
 Cologne (1999), 104
 Copenhagen (1993), 82
 The Hague (1969), 12, 55, 65
 President, 49
 rotating Presidency, 124
 qualified majority voting, 81–87, 101
European Court of Justice (ECJ), 2, 90
European Defense Agency, 138
European Defense Community (EDC), 6, 11, 33–46, 50, 54, 56–58, 113, 114, 124
European Economic and Monetary Union (EMU), 52, 55, 61–77, 88, 114, 123
European Economic Community (EEC), 4, 5, 6, 33, 42, 44, 50, 115, 117, 123
European Free Trade Association (EFTA), 45, 124
European Ideas Network, 139
European Monetary System, 55, 66–67, 114, 115, 123
European Parliament, 2, 13, 14, 50, 64, 86, 123, 133, 135, 137, 140, 141
European People's Party—European Democrats (EPP-ED), 134, 139
European Recovery Program (Marshall Plan), 4, 28, 29, 37, 111, 113
European Security and Defense Policy (ESDP), 103–105
 Military Committee, 104
 Military Staff, 104
 Political and Security Committee, 104
 Situation Center, 104
European Security Strategy, 105, 138
European Union
 accession/enlargement, 10, 12, 52–54, 58, 59, 110, 112, 115, 120, 135–136
 Council of Ministers, 134, 136
 peace keeping mission in Bosnia-Herzegovina (ALTHEA), 105

peace keeping mission in
   Macedonia (CONCORDIA),
   105
Presidency, 134
police mission in Bosnia-
   Herzegovina (EUPM), 104
European Union of Federalists, 28, 35
Europeanization, 53–56

Featherstone, Kevin, 53
Fiscal and Political Union, 72–75
finalité politique, 50, 54, 56–59,
   81–82, 90
Fischer, Joschka, 49
Fouchet, Christian, 58
Fouchet Plans, 7, 50, 111
Fulbright, J. William, 37

Garton Ash, Timothy, 8, 132, 133
Gehler, Michael, 13
General Agreement on Tariffs and
   Trade (GATT), 45
German reunification, 52
Giddens, Anthony, 50, 59
Gilbert, Mark, 116
Gillingham, John, 123
Ginsberg, Roy, 105
Giscard d'Estaing, Valery, 66, 110,
   114
Globalization, 133, 137
Gorbach, Hubert, 119
Görtemaker, Manfred, 11
Greater Middle East, 8
Gros, Daniel, 138

Hague Congress (1948), 29
Hallstein, Walter, 41, 57, 122
Hantoss, Elemér, 35
Hertenstein Conference, 35
Hitchcock, William I., 33
Hoffman, Paul G., 37
Holbrooke, Richard, 102
Hull, Cordell, 25

Immigration, 139
Iraq war/crisis, 9, 112, 115, 117, 121

Jenkins, Roy, 66, 132
Jopp, Mathias, 12
Juncker, Jean-Claude, 49

Kaiser, Jakob, 27
Kennan, George F., 36
Kennedy, Paul, 79
Kirt, Romain, 110, 115, 117
Kohl, Helmut, 90, 114, 124, 141
Kühnhardt, Ludger, 133
Kundera, Milan, 132

Labour Party, 27
League of Nations, 19, 20
Lippmann, Walter, 36
Lisbon Strategy, 120, 139
Locarno Treaty, 34
Loth, Wilfried, 11
Lothian, Lord (Philipp Kerr), 20
Löwenthal, Richard, 22
Luxembourg Compromise, 7, 116

MacDougall Report, 71, 74
Marc, Alexandre, 22
Marshall, George C., 37
Market of the South (MERCOSUR),
   138
McCloy, John J., 38, 39
Merkel, Angela, 141
Middle East Quartet,
   Road Map, 138
Milosevic, Slobodan, 102, 103
Mitterrand, François, 114
Möller, Horst, 111
Mollet, Guy, 43
Monnet, Jean, 24, 38, 39, 40, 41, 42,
   56, 57, 90, 118, 124
Munich Agreement, 20

Naumann, Friedrich, 117
North Atlantic Treaty Organization (NATO), 6, 8, 9, 40, 56, 57, 96, 100, 102, 103, 104, 105, 112, 138

Open coordination, 67–68
Opting-out clause, 5, 124
Organization for European Economic Cooperation (OEEC), 35, 37, 39, 113, 124
Organization for Economic Cooperation and Development (OECD), 135
Owen, Lord David, 98
Pan-European Union, 34
Pascal, Blaise, 4
Patten, Chris, 135, 136
Péguy, Charles, 141
Pineau, Christian, 43
Pivert, Marceau, 22
Pleven Plan, 39, 50
Pleven, René, 39
Pollak, Oskar, 22
Pompidou, Georges, 65
Popper, Karl Raimund, 82
Pöttering, Hans-Gert, 13, 120
Prodi, Romano, 122
Puntscher-Riekmann, Sonja, 117

Reform Treaty (Treaty of Lisbon), 5
relance européenne, 40–44, 57, 110
Roosevelt, Franklin D., 25, 26, 36
Rossi, Ernesto, 21

Sandys, Duncan, 29
Santer, Jacques, 115
Schuman Plan, 38, 45, 118
Schuman, Robert, 38
Schmidt, Helmut, 56, 110, 114
Schröder, Gerhard, 49
Schüssel, Wolfgang, 119
Sforza, Count Carlo, 24
Sharon, Ariel, 120
Sikorski, Władysław, 23, 24

Single European Act, 52, 55, 110, 114
Single Market,
  completion of, 67–68
Soviet Union, 6, 35, 112–113, 116, 117
  collapse, 53
Spaak, Paul-Henri, 24, 26, 40, 41, 42, 44, 57, 124
Spinelli, Aldo, 21
Stability Pact for Southeast Europe, 103
Stalin, Josef, 25, 26
Stirk, Peter, 42
Strauss, Franz Josef, 44
Streit, Clarence, 20
Stresemann, Gustav, 34
Subsidiarity,
  principle of, 55
Suez Crisis, 8, 57, 114

Talbott, Strobe, 103
Thomas, Elbert D., 37
Toynbee, Arnold Joseph, 3
Traguth, Thomas, 12
Treaties of Rome, 5, 8, 11, 57, 64, 116, 117, 124
Treaty of Amsterdam, 61, 110
Treaty of Maastricht, 7, 51, 52, 55, 59, 61, 67, 97, 98, 99, 110, 114, 115, 116, 117, 124
Treaty of Nice, 55, 61, 104–105, 135
Trotsky, Leon, 35
Truman, Harry S., 36, 133
Truman Doctrine, 36, 112
Tsoukalis, Loukas, 65
Turkey, 12, 60, 62, 76, 81, 90, 91, 110, 135–136

Ukraine, 60, 120, 136
Uri, Pierre, 42
United States, 114, 117
United States, 6, 36–38, 112–113
  dollar exchange rate, 68

engagement in the Balkans, 99
US Federal Reserve, 64

van Zeeland, Paul, 24
Verhofstadt, Guy, 90
Versailles Treaty, 19
Voggenhuber, Johannes, 123
von der Groeben, Hans, 42
von Hagen, Jürgen, 12
von Hassell, Ulrich, 22

Weigall, David, 42
Weiler, Joseph H., 113

Werner Plan, 7, 65–66
Wessels, Wolfgang, 12, 53
West European Union (WEU), 40, 97, 98, 101, 103, 104
  Petersberg Tasks, 102, 104
Willetts, David, 139
Wilson, Woodrow, 34
World War II, 5, 8, 19, 22, 35, 90, 112

Yugoslavian Wars, 13, 96–107

Zielonka, Jan, 2

www.ingramcontent.com/pod-product-compliance
Lightning Source LLC
Chambersburg PA
CBHW051436290426
44109CB00016B/1577